SCOOBY

The Glory of the Ride

Scooby: The Glory of the Ride
Copyright © 2018 by Stuart 'Scooby' Cochrane and Gary Ralston

ISBN 978-1-5272-2639-5

Typesetting by FormattingExperts.com
Cover Design by Gordon Bell
Front cover photography by David Cruickshanks

Some of the names in the book have been changed to protect the innocent and in a couple of cases, the very, very guilty!

SCOOBY

The Glory of the Ride

Stuart 'Scooby' Cochrane

with Gary Ralston

Dedications

Scooby: For Emma and Anna

Gary: For Lewis and Jennifer

Janice: For Ben and Bradin

He knows not where he's going,
For the ocean will decide,
It's not the destination,
It's the glory of the ride

Edward Monkton

FOREWORD

Cafe Mambo has rewarded me and my family with many great things in life, not least career fulfilment and lots of wonderful friendships and memories.

The person who gave it all to me was Scooby Cochrane.

If it wasn't for Scooby, I wouldn't have Mambo today – that's 100 per cent true.

In the early nineties, my wife Caroline and I were running a very successful bar in San Antonio called Bucanero. It was a pub for mostly British tourists, busy every night. However, Scooby constantly encouraged me to open a more laid back, sunset bar to resemble Cafe del Mar, which had become so popular under Jose Padilla. Scooby gave me the idea – and I was happy to follow.

We knew the fabulous sunsets we enjoy here in Ibiza would be key to any success and we came across a two-storey building that housed four holiday apartments, owned by a woman from Valencia.

Next door stood an old man's bar called Rey De Copas, which was so rundown few customers ever visited, but Scooby had a vision. "Come on," he urged. "Let's go talk to the woman." I wasn't sure, but he made me speak to her and she agreed to sell the building. I will always owe him for encouraging me to take that step because he helped us make Mambo what it is today.

Scooby is a genius. He identified music and fashion trends before anyone else, typical of a guy who was running Rainbow Rocks in Stirling

Still holding strong after all these years…Javier and Scooby.

at the age of 22 and The Tunnel, one of the best clubs in the UK, by the age of 27. He was a superstar.

We first got to know each other in 1981 when he came to Ibiza with a group of pals from Stirling and we quickly became close friends. Scooby caused mayhem that Easter when he encouraged me to drink a bottle of Jagermeister, washed down by hierbas, a local liqueur. Oh man, what a state we were in! It remains the only occasion in my life when I failed to turn up for work the following day.

Early in my career, I knew plenty about the hospitality industry and how to run bars, but understood little at that stage of popular culture, music or DJs. Scooby was my teacher. In 1987 and 1988 we would frequently go to clubs such as Amnesia and he would point out the likes of Paul Oakenfold, Pete Tong, Adamski and Frankie Knuckles.

Thanks to the success of Mambo, I can now count guys such as Pete and Paul among my friends, but I've told them it was Scooby who had to tell me who the hell they were in those early days.

Scooby knew everything and everyone and was never afraid to approach the best people in the business with his ideas and plans, but maybe he was just too nice, too open. I remember the original decline in his mental health clearly. The loss of all his family's money in the failure of the BCCI bank hit him hard and his decision to sign up with a guru in London for three days was not clever as it also affected him badly.

He has spoken openly of his problem with drugs, especially smoking too much dope. Something inside him broke – too much pressure,

2

possibly. However, whenever I think of Scooby I always smile at the memory of him standing in the sunshine of Ibiza wearing a cowboy hat and with a big Cuban cigar in his mouth, like the Spanish golfer Miguel Angel Jiminez. I'm so glad his health is holding strong and I'm so pleased he has written this book.

The Glory of the Ride? It has certainly been an adventure, my old friend.

Javier Anadon, Cafe Mambo
San Antonio, Ibiza
2018

1

In a sport not renowned for its conservative dress sense my clobber still took some beating. Even Ian Poulter would have baulked at stepping onto the first tee at Gleneagles in a get up that was more beach bum than Ballesteros.

My adidas basketball boots hung loosely around my ankles, a pair of floral print Hawaiian shorts sat easily around my skinny waist and my torso was covered in a crumpled white t-shirt. I pulled a golf ball from my pocket and casually threw it on the pristine grass in front of me as members of one of the most prestigious golf clubs in Scotland looked on incredulously.

I carefully placed my putter at my feet and stepped forward with the only other club in my possession, a dodgy pitching wedge I'd acquired from God only knows where.

I addressed the ball, looked down the fairway at miles of brilliant, green Perthshire countryside and never felt more alive as I pulled my shoulders into a backswing. It was 7am on Friday, September 3 1993 and I was fucking indestructible.

I never did make the connection. In that fraction of a second from the top of the backswing to the point of impact the starter stepped in and politely, but firmly, ushered me off the tee, back towards the clubhouse and car park where the engine on my black Toyota MR2 – registration number A14 LUV – was still warm.

The Gleneagles official invited me to leave the grounds but my mind, still jumping from two days without sleep and in an hallucinogenic buzz from countless cannabis rushes, remained alive to adventurous thrills that had made me travel the 20 miles from my home in Stirling in the first place.

Free from his security conscious glances, I skirted around the perimeter of the estate, finally picking a path to the magnificent entrance of the hotel itself where, of all people, Sir Jackie Stewart was waiting, in Harris Tweed, to welcome guests to his renowned shooting school.

I greeted him like a long lost friend and the racing legend, far too polite to snub a supporter, humoured me gently as I drew him into a conversation about my forthcoming wedding at the venue. "I'm marrying a girl from New Zealand, her name's Susan. We're inviting 400 guests. You're more than welcome to join us," I told him excitedly, the speed of my speech reaching Formula One levels (it would take me several years to learn the ever quickening sound of my voice was an early indicator of the inevitable mental crash to come).

There were only a couple of issues. Firstly, I had never been on a date with Susan – we'd met at a mind bending course in London just a month earlier and had only spoken platonically on the phone. Secondly, I was in a relationship with my beloved Jacquie – Jake – who had been my girlfriend for eight years. In addition, Gleneagles knew nothing about the wedding, not least because it had never been booked.

Minor details. I said a cheery farewell to an increasingly bemused Sir Jackie, walked into reception, and ordered them to pencil my big day in their diary. To hell with it, make it two.

One of my closest pals, Gary Neill, was also planning his marriage to fiancee Carol. I told the hotel I'd fork out for 400 guests for them as well. Suspicious, they told me the cost would run to the tens of thousands. Not an issue – and at least we would be saving on the cost of hiring DJs.

It was barely 8am, but I was already well pleased with my day's work. The previous night I'd sat in my flat and catalogued my record collection, which ran to thousands of vinyl discs, from A to Z. It wasn't enough. As the volume of the mania in my mind began to build to a peak, I catalogued them again, this time in beats per minute, from 110 to 140.

At 6am I had headed north a few miles to Dunblane to visit one of my closest pals, John Crozier, and break the news of my forthcoming nuptials. He opened the door in a state of sleepy undress to find me, energised yet agitated, desperate to tell of my new found happiness.

"John, I'm getting married," I blurted out. "When did Jake agree to that?" he asked, scratching his head, slowly coming to full consciousness. "It's not Jake, it's Susan from New Zealand," I responded eagerly. "Scoobs, mucker," he said bluntly but understandably, "it's too early in the morning for me," and calmly closed the door.

He must have suspected something was wrong mentally but, in my mind, my relationship with Susan made absolute sense. Several months previously I had begun seeking answers to questions I barely understood to ask. I was 31 years old and for much of my twenties my self-image had been happily framed like a perfectly completed 500 piece jigsaw.

However, as the 1990s approached, one or two pieces had begun to disappear from my neurological toy box while other, colourful sections had been shaken out of place or turned over to drab greys by the slings and arrows of career fate, rank bad luck, poor personal decision making and, let's be frank, outrageous substance abuse.

My drugs of choice were cannabis and, later, cocaine. In the early nineties I had a stint as a DJ at Duck Bay Marina, the nightclub on the shores of Loch Lomond. It was 23 miles door to door from my home in Stirling and I rolled seven joints for the car journey – three spliffs there, three spliffs back and a security smoke kept in the glove compartment, just in case.

My last act before going to sleep every night was to roll a joint, which I would spark to life immediately on wakening the following morning. I could easily snort a couple of grams of coke a night, and frequently did.

At £60 a gram it made for a high maintenance relationship and it was a helluva price to pay because the sharp shards of paranoia always outweighed the colourful chemical bursts in my head. The arithmetic is almost as painful. I estimate I blew the best part of a hundred grand throwing charlie up my nose or drawing good blow deep into my lungs.

I met Susan at The Forum, a self-improvement course straight from the pages of George Orwell, advertised in a magazine, the name of which I've long since forgotten. I wanted to make my life better – in what ways, I hadn't a clue – and it promised the answers over a weekend in a dingy hotel in Paddington, all for the bargain price of £600.

Susan and I bonded over paraboots, unisex French footwear and all the rage at the time. I owned a pair and quickly concluded she must be as classy as she was stylish as she had them too.

We never so much touched or even kissed, but we kept in touch by telephone a couple of times a week for the next six weeks up until my visit to Gleneagles, about which she was absolutely oblivious. I never spoke to her again.

Her friendship, however fleeting, was the only thing I took from The Forum. In reality, it was a brainwashing course, lucrative at that. At least 100 mugs like me were crammed into a basement room of that hovel hotel, all seeking self-improvement.

They bludgeoned us with messages for three days, blinded us with jargon, equations and soundbites on life, the universe and everything within it.

We weren't allowed to leave the room until the Sunday evening when the evangelical peddlers of nonsense, snake oil salesmen of the soul, had battered most of their audience into mental submission before demanding to know if we 'got it'.

The majority of the audience rose to their feet, yelling ecstatically: "We get it, we get it." One of the course organisers approached and enthusiastically asked me the same question. "I got fuck all mate," I replied bitterly, but honestly, before heading for the door, skint and all by myself and not even – for the first time that weekend – Susan on my mind.

London on a Sunday night, racked with guilt at the direction my life was taking and disgusted at being so easily conned by a cult? There was no lonelier place in the world.

At that stage, despite searching for meaning in my increasingly chaotic existence, self-analysis was not my strongest point, although I remember relating to the popular Volkswagen advert at the time. I felt like the guy who had put a million on black, only for it to come up red. I too had moved into gold, just as the clever money was moving out.

I had lost £90,000 in the collapse of the Bank of Credit and Commerce International in July 1991 which represented my life's savings and also, much worse, the £30,000 retirement fund of my father, Alex, a painter and decorator.

I'd persuaded him to lump his pension pot in with my own hard earned because the interest rate at BCCI was much more attractive than

High Street banks. A fool and his money are soon parted, they say. All good and well, but much worse when it's a fool and every penny his loving father had ever saved.

Six months later I managed to salvage £15,000 from the Bank of England compensation scheme for savers. My mind whirring, and desperate to make amends, I put £14,000 in a Co-op plastic bag and marched into Viewforth, the headquarters of Stirling Council. I emptied it onto the reception desk and said: "I want to buy my parents' house for them. Will this be enough?"

Ashamed and embarrassed, I kept my loss a secret for two years. The only numbers ruling my life until that point had been 45 rpm. Accountants and lawyers were grey men I decided had no place in my riotous life of kaleidoscopic colour. These were wonderful, fun-filled, hedonistic times but, financially, they were disastrous.

I had worked for well known Scottish restaurateur Simon Littlejohn, helping to establish his reputation in St Andrews, and he had promised me 10 per cent of the business, but it was sold from under my feet and I didn't receive a penny.

I'd been fucked out of the Plaza, which I'd helped transform into the premier rave venue in Glasgow, after being stabbed in the back by the owners and run out by gangsters who wanted the entire pie for themselves.

I had helped put Fat Sam's in Dundee on the map and co-owner Mark Goldinger held discussions about a buy out of his partners that would have given me 20 per cent of one of the best nightclubs in Scotland.

One of Mark's best pals, Ron McCulloch, persuaded me instead to run his new nightclub in Glasgow, The Tunnel. It was 1990 and Glasgow had just become the European City of Culture. I thought I was being handed the keys to a Lamborghini and it was a beautiful creation but, from a business point of view, it had the engine of a Lada.

It's little wonder my mind had reached tipping point that Friday, with the biggest task still to come – breaking the news to Jake that we were over, although not before I'd stopped off at Stirling Golf Club, after my trip to Gleneagles, to buy 100 golf balls.

My relationship with Jake's parents, Irene and Angus, had long been terse. I come from Bannockburn, a grand and historical name but really an honest to goodness village-come-housing scheme.

Jake's folks had worked and found a level of prosperity that had allowed them to fund a private education for their daughter at Dollar Academy. "How do you expect to keep Jacqueline in the style to which she has become accustomed?" I recall Angus asking me on the night my relationship with him finally broke down.

Full of piss and wind, I told him to stick it up his arse. I didn't step foot inside their family home for the next six years (Angus Kerr, God bless him, made me a meal almost every day when I was first hospitalised, brought to me by Jake).

Jake wasn't at home when I arrived at her parents' place but nothing would prevent me playing my Get Out Of Jail Free card. "I'm a heroin addict," I told Angus and Irene, lying through my teeth as it was about the only drug with which I hadn't experimented. "Tell her to forget about me."

In my increasingly agitated state, I truly believed telling such a whopper was the only way to get out of the relationship that had helped define so much of my adult life to that point. The reality – God, how far from it I was sliding – was that Jake had been the only one to see the writing on the wall.

Months before, and growing more concerned about my declining mental state, she had sought counselling services offered by her employer, a leading insurance company. She outlined my increasingly erratic patterns of behaviour and was told matter-of-factly that it sounded as if her boyfriend was having a nervous breakdown.

An hour after leaving her home there would be little doubt as I stood in the communal garden of my flat in Stirling's Riverside area, by the banks of the Forth, and emptied my new bucket of golf balls on the grass.

One by one I took a swing, each time aiming for Cambuskenneth Abbey, across the river and a distance of some 500 metres. Tiger Woods in his prime couldn't have made the shot.

One by one the balls plopped and sank in the meandering water just a few metres from my feet. In my mind, I was hitting the abbey every time. Golf is all about going under par. The game, for me, was about to become a bogey.

Maybe it was John Crozier who had sounded the alarm bell from Dunblane or perhaps it was Jake after frantic discussions with her parents but, unsurprisingly, the word was out I was having a meltdown.

They all rushed to Abbey Mill, my top floor, two bedroom rave cave with views directly to the abbey that had inspired me so much I had named one of my first pieces of music 'Cathedral Song'.

There was terrible worry for my welfare, not least from Jake and my wonderful mum, Mac. Soon the flat was packed with anxious friends and relatives, so much so I couldn't take their concern and dashed outside to hide in the bin store. I reasoned if I kept my distance they would all eventually go away.

They found me, of course, and all tried to talk me down: "It's okay Scoobs, you're all right, you'll be fine," but those words to someone who is mentally ill are like a red rag to a bull. I didn't want them to say anything, I just wanted to be left alone because in my own mind my behaviour had been, and continued to be, perfectly sane and rational.

Still, after several agonising hours the decision was made to section me. The on-call psychiatrist, a Dr Prabu, lived just over the bridge in Cambuskenneth and arrived in minutes. Jake had to convince my mum to sign the papers and she was reluctant, frightened and disbelieving all this was happening to her only child.

In the end she signed and I finally agreed to go, but only if Jake left the flat. She truly loved me and agreed immediately to depart. Canny and smart as ever, she nipped behind my back when I wasn't looking, straight into a cupboard where she then watched and listened to everything.

By now it was 8pm and I was putty in the hands of the specialist ambulance staff when they arrived to take me to the psychiatric unit at Bellsdyke Hospital, 15 miles away in Larbert. I walked downstairs without assistance and sat in the back of the ambulance, looking out through the open door at the semi-circle of concerned faces that represented all the pillars of my life.

They included Gary, whose wedding I had booked just hours earlier at Gleneagles. He came into my life in 1985 when I had just opened Rainbow Rocks nightclub in Stirling and was advertising for staff. He strolled in wearing a top hat and fur coat, a string of pearls, silk shirt, denims and cowboy boots. "Don't say a word mate," I told him. "You're hired."

Next to him was my boyhood pal, hairdresser Steven Croal, a big time raver like me. Ron Cameron, the former owner of the Meadowpark Hotel in Bridge of Allan was also a concerned face, as was my dear friend Vinny Doyle, another Rainbow Rocks stalwart, now sadly no longer with us.

John Crozier and Fraser Hotchkiss, whom I first got to know at McQ's nightclub in Bannockburn, were also worried witless and so were Mac, Jake and the Kilgannons, Billy and James. Billy was one of my dad's best friends and James was like my wee brother. I took him to raves, taught him to play the guitar and also occasionally bought him clothes, once to his disgust.

I dragged him into Marks and Spencer in Glasgow and forked out on a pair of grey flannels and a blue blazer. "If you're going to drive me about, you have to at least look like a chauffeur," I told him, deadly serious.

At the time I owned a Ford Fiesta. We must have looked ridiculous, but at least we raised a laugh.

One notable absentee was my father who, throughout all my years of illness before his death in 2006, visited me only once in hospital. I bore him absolutely no ill will. How could I? He was my dad and I loved him dearly. He was the strongest man I knew and yet he struggled with my mental illness.

His way of dealing with it was to take the dog for a walk. Its name was Doobie – sorry dad, you never did have a clue about the cannabis origins of the name I gave it, or why the kids burst out laughing every time you called it to heel in the park. It was the best exercised animal in Stirling.

In all honestly, my dad's absence didn't even register as I looked out the back door at all those faces, their expressions etched with worry, fear and love. It was a scene I found utterly unbearable as I eventually broke. "Shut the fucking door!" I screamed at the top of my voice, a Niagara of emotion beginning to finally flow, "Shut the fucking door!"

The ambulance must not have gone above 30mph on its way to Bellsdyke but in my mind it was reaching speeds of 100mph as I howled my horror, a primitive and guttural sound coming from the darkest corners of my very soul.

Once at Bellsdyke they put me, still agitated, into a room and lay me on a bed where I had what can only be described as an out of body experience. I really felt myself lift from the thin mattress beneath me, albeit momentarily, before I heard the voice of an English female doctor, which brought me back into contact with my physical self again.

11

The bright lights of the room became harrowing, burning through the back of my eyes and into the very centre of my brain but a chemical cosh of drugs, legitimately administered this time, was injected into one of the cheeks of my arse and quickly served its purpose.

It was the first of 23 psychiatric admissions I would go on to experience totalling three years, six months and two days. Within minutes on that first night the lights dimmed and faded to darkness.

It would be another 16 years before the black veil would finally lift and I could see my life with clarity again.

2

Papa got a brand new pig bag on the same night I bombed half a gram of sulph in a Bannockburn boozer and started a war in my own mind to match the ferocity of the fighting on the surrounding fields 700 years earlier.

Even local historians still bicker on the exact location in 1314 where Edward II's army was routed by Robert the Bruce. If it was the site where they later built the toilets of McQ's nightclub, then it almost marked the loss of another poor soul. This time, it was not so much independence won by a Scot as freedom from mental turmoil that was given up for a very long time.

Franny and I had known each other for years, uneasily at first. We kept a wary distance, even though we were raised just a few streets apart. The space between us was maintained by our respective secondary schoolings as he was a pupil at St Modan's in Stirling, while I attended Bannockburn High.

He was also a year older. In truth, he was a bit of a rascal in his early teens – mischievous, boyhood pranks, nothing malicious – while I was something of a goody two shoes.

I used to DJ at Bannockburn Youth Club discos as a kid, in an old Nissen hut behind the local primary school, playing records such as 'Get It On' by Marc Bolan and T Rex, David Bowie's 'Sorrow' and The Sweet's 'Ballroom Blitz'.

In hindsight, it was not a bad setlist for a 14-year-old in 1976, although I should hold my hands up and confess the first record I ever bought was Benny Hill's 'Ernie (The Fastest Milkman In The West)'. Not a secret to let slip around our style-conscious streets in the seventies.

Franny was also a regular at the discos. He was a good looking so-and-so and by my early teens I was also beginning to catch the attention of a couple of girls. Franny started dating one of my schoolgirl pals and wariness gave way to warmth as we quickly became good mates, sharing similar outlooks in music and fashion.

Our friendship was sealed for good one night in McQ's when we got absolutely blootered on Canadian high balls. Such sophistication. We were 16 and 17-years-old.

The central belt of Scotland had a thriving provincial club scene in the late seventies and early eighties that didn't just welcome punters through the doors on Friday and Saturday nights.

Toledo Junction in Paisley, for example, had a 'Funkin' Monday' that attracted a hairdressing crowd – it was their day off – under DJ Dave 'CL' Young and Jackie O's in Kirkcaldy on a Wednesday night was also a place to be seen.

Even the Rob Roy hotel in Aberfoyle pulled them in from all over on a Sunday evening. McQ's on a Thursday night was massively popular as Fraser Hotchkiss drew an audience from Ayrshire to Fife the envy of many, playing everything from jazz funk to the Sex Pistols to new romantic.

He was the first DJ I ever heard play Spandau Ballet. He had the crowd eating from his hand and Franny and I were regulars even though, for the most part, we were underage.

At the age of 16 I'd established a set at The Tamdhu, a pub/club next door to McQ's that had grown in popularity. The Tamdhu had become known as the venue of choice for Stirling's young team, including the under-18s, before they matured and moved to join their elders at McQ's.

Despite our tender years, Franny and I weren't exactly wet behind the ears when it came to pub and club etiquette. We had a foot in both camps. Already part of the furniture at The Tamdhu, the staff at McQ's were also happy to turn a blind eye to our under age attendance next door.

However, one Thursday in the spring of 1981 we decided to give McQ's a rare swerve because word was out about a gig at the Pathfoot building at Stirling University by an up-and-coming funk band, Pigbag.

14

They had recorded an instrumental 'Papa's Got A Brand New Pig Bag' that was making waves on the underground music scene (it would reach number three in the charts the following year) and we were desperate to hear what all the fuss was about.

Franny secured a couple of tickets but the night was almost over before it had begun when we popped into McQ's to see some friends, our lift to the university a few miles away previously negotiated with our pal Karen McGregor, who drove an Escort Mark II in a subtle shade of luminous canary yellow.

A night out required a degree of sartorial flamboyance and Franny and I were kitted out in suits that were, literally, to die for. The style of the time was zoot suits, narrow waisted baggy trousers, long jackets that boasted wide shoulders and lapels, pulled tight across the hips, with shirts and silk ties.

We had sourced a tailor on Glasgow's Gallowgate who sent us back to Stirling looking like honorary members of the Cab Calloway fan club. We were in truly original styling, with strong whispers the rag trade retailer had a line straight to the nearby city morgue where the homeless and destitute were stripped of clothing they no longer needed after they'd popped their spats.

The trousers came not with zips, but buttons. Franny and I went to the gents together at one point and a local, in those less enlightened times, saw us huddled shoulder to shoulder around a urinal, fumbling at the front of our trousers, and drew a hasty and regretful conclusion.

Punches were thrown, but the spirit of those gangster get ups rubbed off as we prevailed – in all honesty, it was Franny who led from the front with me cowering behind him – and Mr Offended walked off with a ringing in his red and swollen ears.

It was probably just as well he hadn't walked in half an hour earlier as he would have seen us emerge from a cubicle together, eyes wide and a world of chemical adventure about to be explored. We would soon be yapping like Yorkshire terriers at a postman's leg.

I cannot recall with crystal precision the moment I had decided to take drugs but, at the age of 18, it seemed somehow inevitable. I had been a DJ since my early teens and drugs, especially cannabis, had long been socially acceptable, especially to those in their early twenties who hung around The Tamdhu and McQ's.

Music and drugs have always gone hand in hand, from the speed tablets – known as 'blues' – of the Mod movement to the poppers and sulph of the high energy scene to the acid and ecstasy explosion around the later rave culture.

It was my turn to dive in. Tom Daley has never jumped off his springboard with greater enthusiasm.

Why amphetamine sulphate, good old speed? It was the most accessible drug at the time and, unlike cannabis, it could be ingested quickly and in (relative) public. There were two options – snorting it up the nose, or rolling it in a Rizla paper and swallowing it whole, known as bombing. Franny and I plunged in, detonated the fuse, and went dynamite.

A gram of speed cost a fiver and our hit was secured from a fellow student at Falkirk College where, for reasons unknown even to me, I had signed up for an HNC in Business Studies after leaving school. I was out of the lecture hall more often than I was in it.

An old pal, Billy Rowan, had a lucrative venture selling curtains around markets in towns and districts such as Ingliston, Bathgate and Falkirk and I was a willing accomplice. Like Rodney to his Del Boy, my pitch was straightforward as I stood at the back of his van, doors wide open to show off piles of stock, bellowing: "Curtains! Four-ninety-nine for a big 90 drop!"

To this day, I still don't know what it means, but it was obviously music to the ears of local housewives who kept us run off our feet with orders.

Billy could turn a sow's ear into a silk purse. On one occasion he bought a load of carpets, damaged beyond repair – I naively thought – in a flash flood. It was the height of summer and he laid them out in a quiet field near the North Third reservoir in Stirling. He returned two days later when they were bone dry, gave them a quick shampoo and hoover, and punted them for close to their original price.

However, it was just my luck my Aunt Mary caught me playing truant from college when she turned up at Falkirk market looking for a new piece of net curtain for her kitchen window.

Quite rightly, she turned me in to my mum and the parental influence was still strong as I returned to my college course with my tail between my legs, although my academic career didn't last much beyond a year.

At McQ's, the speed seized control quickly and efficiently as we all piled into the back of Karen's car, where we were joined by her pals Lorraine Rose and Joyce McKerchar. We met a crowd of mates who preferred to hang around the Barnton Bistro in the town centre, which was as close as Stirling ever came to a Bohemian hangout, although it still fell far short of the Bloomsbury Set.

Stuart Allan, the McChord brothers, Coco Coyne and Corky were Roxy Music freaks. "We're from the Bauhaus," they used to tell us, deadly serious. We'd laugh and reply: "We're from Braehead and Bannockburn, ya dinguls."

It was slapstick stuff because we enjoyed each other's company socially. Stirling was too small a town for any friction to develop. If you didn't know someone directly, they were always a friend of a friend. We respected each other's musical tastes and differences, even if there was occasional piss taking.

The group was completed by John Aitkenhead – Aitkey – who was quite possibly the worst Elvis impersonator I've ever heard, but maybe the richest. Later, I worked in Littlejohn's restaurant in Port Street and Aitkey had a flat upstairs and you could set your clock by his daily routine.

He'd roll out of bed at 11am and wander along to The Thistles shopping centre, guitar in hand, where he'd give passers-by two hours of 'Heartbreak Hotel' and 'Blue Suede Shoes' of dubious musical merit. He somehow always earned enough for a lunch in our place of steak pie, sticky toffee pudding and a bottle of Furstenberg. His order never changed.

He'd pop upstairs for a couple of hours' kip and be back on his busking patch for 4pm, coining it in for a slap up dinner of sirloin steak, banana split and a half carafe of wine. In the ghetto? No chance – he lived like a lord.

The Pigbag gig was terrific. Driver Karen apart, the others were on alcohol and Franny and I felt like the young pretenders, our hearts racing, emotions and senses enhanced by the sulph, a clarity of sound and vision beneath the stage lights. Initially, every experience was heightened under the influence, but… and there was a big 'but'.

Franny clicked with speed and yet, on reflection, the opening line of my admission sheet on each of my subsequent psychiatric admissions echoed everything I went through that first night on it. That included a quickened and pressurised speech pattern until, eventually, I was unable to speak at all.

It moved to a restlessness and I still recall stretching out on my bed in the wee small hours after the gig, unable to sleep, my heart pounding like the heaviest drumbeat we'd heard on stage a few hours earlier.

Excitement and bravado slowly gave way to fear as I fidgeted constantly on my mattress. My mum and dad were fast asleep through the wall and yet I didn't dare call them, scared of their likely reaction. I didn't like it.

The Friday fall out was horrendous. A grey shroud moved down from my depressed mind and draped itself uncomfortably around my weary shoulders, where it hung for just over a day. Every fibre of my body felt as if it had been burned, or at very least singed at the edges.

Without a decent night's sleep I felt dishevelled, out of sorts, out of time and out of place. It was the most unpleasant hangover I had ever experienced and this time I hadn't even touched a Canadian cocktail.

I learned long ago to rationalise my dislike of sulph and, afterwards, other stimulant hallucinogens such as ecstasy and acid. I was fortunate to DJ frequently to crowds of thousands and it was all about control. I could take the dance floor up, down or any way I wanted with my music, but if I took a stimulant hallucinogen I handed over my power to grip their emotions.

At heart, I'm a control freak and I never liked not having a firmer grasp on my own reality. I took sulph on a couple more occasions after the Pigbag gig in a fruitless attempt to find a connection with it, but it just wasn't the drug for me.

Now cannabis, that was a different story.

3

A golden thread of music weaved its way through the tapestry of my childhood and yet a black and unsettling strand dominated the foreground of my earliest memory.

The content and context of the dream I suffered from the age of four – I still can't go as far as label it a 'nightmare' – continued to perplex and trouble me for many decades afterwards. Only in recent times have I come to understand it to have been, in my strong opinion, a premonition of the psychological distresses that would blight a large chunk of my adult life.

Remember, this vision came to me – and on more than one occasion, over a period of approximately two years – when I was only a child, long before I'd rolled my first joint or taken a debut line of charlie. Nature or nurture? I'm still not sure.

Here's the dream: I was a kid, alone but untroubled, at peace, in a beautiful but unfamiliar landscape in the middle of nowhere on a gloriously warm and sunny day. I was sitting at an ornate iron table, painted white, and on the table stood a vase, displaying a vibrant red rose.

It was serene. Suddenly, however, the peace was shattered by a rumbling off to my left and into the picture came a massive rock, rolling down towards me from a nearby hill. I yelled at it to stop and, just before it arrived to flatten me and the table and shatter the vase and rose, I woke up. My emotion on awakening so suddenly was confusion, rather than concern. What did it all mean? I encountered the same dream half a dozen times, up until the age of six when it suddenly stopped, and it never made any sense to me at the time.

It does now. In time, I've come to recognise the table, the vase and the rose as my vulnerabilities and the rock as my life, rolling out of control and destroying the fragile securities on which all of existence is created. In effect, the rock belonged to the landscape as much as the sunny field in which I sat so unconcerned.

One part of me moved to destroy the contented other, a prediction of the bipolar disorder that would later claim the mental equilibrium so many of us take for granted.

Or maybe that's all over-analysis and I was just a sensitive child. After all, one of my earliest memories was being carried in tears by my parents from our church, the Bannockburn Allan, before the Christmas service had even finished. I howled at the words of 'Away in a Manger', distraught at the prospect of poor Jesus going without a bed. How could anyone be so cruel to a new born child?

It's a question I could also have asked my cousin, Jean. She came to stay for 18 months, when I was around four, while her parents, my Uncle Sam and Aunt Jean, established their new home in Canada before calling her across the Atlantic.

Jean was barely a year older than me, but soon spotted my Achilles heel. She was really more of a sister than a cousin and so, of course, frequent fights and arguments followed, much to the annoyance of my mum, Mac. She would regularly send us upstairs to our rooms after another row and Jean never failed to draw tears from me by bursting into a lusty chorus of 'Away in a Manger'.

After a while, I spotted a chink in her own emotional armour as she would bawl just as loudly at the old song by The Alexander Brothers, 'Nobody's Child'. God knows what the neighbours must have thought at such a mournful sing-off going on through the walls.

My childhood was idyllic. I was raised by Alex and Mac in a three bedroom council house on Station Road in Bannockburn and although I was an only child I had dozens of aunts, uncles and cousins around Stirling and Glasgow. Mac – her real name was Marion McDougall – came from Govan in Glasgow and first set eyes on my dad when she came to her cousin's wedding in Stirling at the age of 14.

He never stood a chance. There was a seven year age difference and he told her she was far too young. She had to wait another nine years, but eventually got her man. They tried for eight years to have a child before I was born and the family of three was our perfect unit. I was all they ever wanted.

Our upbringing, like most in our community, was poor but not impoverished. My dad, born and raised in Bannockburn, was a painter and decorator and, for a time, even had his own business but he was never particularly good at asking for money and it didn't survive.

He and mum were churchgoers and I still have a vision of my father reading his bible every night, a wee 'low flier' – usually a nip of Famous Grouse – on the table at his side. Mac committed to three jobs, all cleaning stints undertaken around my school hours. She worked in the Stirling Council headquarters at Viewforth from 5am until 8am and then returned later in the evening. In between, she cleaned the homes of a local doctor and policeman.

We were blessed. There was always food on the table and my father and mother always worked to provide for their family. They weren't wealthy enough to buy my Christmas craving one festive season, a bright yellow Chopper bicycle in their first year of production, but I got the next best thing – Taylor Stevenson's hand-me-down Raleigh 20, which lasted me for years.

Money may have been tight but I also made two visits to Canada as a child to holiday with family on both sides who had emigrated, including Jean. These were such happy times I could no longer even be bothered winding her up with songs of a blind kid in an orphanage.

What is it about my childhood that provokes such a warmth when I look back? I can't recall a single day of rain in the summers of my youth – long hot days spent thrusting lollipop sticks in the spokes of our bike wheels, running around the woods at the North Third reservoir and playing soldiers, although I've only just about forgiven Ross Drummond for shooting me with an air gun.

The dynamics of the street felt different back then. Bannockburn wasn't too big and we knew our boundaries. We were in and out of Jenny Rennie's sweet shop on a daily basis for sherbet flying saucers, sweet tatties and parma violets and our dads bought their morning papers from McCrorie's newsagent while our mums shopped for food at Sandy Gowan's the grocer.

A generation of Bannockburn kids were dressed from head to toe at Annie Neilson's clothes store and it was there I was bought my first ever football shirt, in the dazzling light blue of Man City.

The only foreboding sound in childhood came every time we played under Thunder Bridge and the trains rattled angrily on the tracks above our heads as we dipped our toes in the famous burn below.

Those were days that never seemed to end, playing football in Bannockburn Park with Smavy and the McNab brothers, Rab and Gordon, as well as Oor Dick, Harry Bruce, Fambo Lochrie, Gum Wilson, Kenny Shaw, Ian Fleming, William Gillan and Sweeney Todd.

For adventures further afield I was often packed off for a couple of days to my granny's home in Cardonald, Glasgow. Her name was Morag – we called her Morag the Toerag, but only when she wasn't around – and she lived there with her son, my Uncle Jackie.

I didn't realise it then, but Jackie had suffered a couple of mental health episodes and I've often wondered if it's hereditary (experts reckon it can be). He had been in the merchant navy and I later learned of softly whispered stories around the family about a girl who broke his heart so badly he couldn't return to work. His joy was reading, as many as 10 books a week, and he was also a great cook, not to mention a carer for Morag, whom I loved to bits.

We may have been kids, but we were not averse to earning, from paper rounds to jobs on the ice cream van. At the age of seven, I even picked up my first paid gig as a delivery boy for McNaughton's the butcher.

Our next door neighbour, Rab Laird, worked there and needed someone to help him on his rounds every Saturday. At 7am it might have been an early start, but it had its perks as no sooner had we finished loading the van than Rab would fry the very best sausages, bacon and eggs on an open fire to fortify us for our graft. All these years later and nothing in life has ever tasted quite as good.

Rab would separate the heavy packages and I would run up and down stairwells and garden paths around Stirling and the surrounding villages delivering the goods. The only time I saw a crease on his brow came late in the shift, usually in a lay-by on the outskirts of Cowie, when he would pull over in the van and take out his thick 'tick' book and spend 20 minutes calculating who owed what.

I'm not entirely sure he was allowed to offer credit, but the customers appreciated his courtesy and the books always balanced. The day would end on our return to the shop around 4pm when I would be forced to wash out the van, which by this stage stank to high heaven. I was paid the princely sum of £1.50 and felt like Rockefeller.

Music was a factor in my life from an early age and it was Rab's daughter, May, who helped me claim a part of history – and almost my first girlfriend as well, if I hadn't been so bashful. In fairness, I was only nine and May, who was 10, invited me to join her every Saturday morning at the Stirling and District Junior Gaelic Choir at the Boys' Brigade hall, next door to what would later become my home from home at Rainbow Rocks nightclub in Stirling town centre.

There were 20 of us, boys and girls, and I was useless at singing in Gaelic, a language I appreciated but didn't really understand, although I looked ever so bonny in my smart wee kilt.

We were entered for the Mod in Inverness that year, 1972, and lo and behold we won the gold medal for our class. The achievement was hardly greeted as earth shattering back in Stirling – I phoned home to break the fabulous news to my parents only to be told off for running up a fortune by reversing the charges. It mattered little as I was on cloud nine, not just on the back of our winning performance.

I also experienced my first crush on a girl and, would you believe, my feelings were reciprocated. Better still, Morven's dad was none other than Calum Kennedy, aristocracy of the Scottish traditional music scene.

I must stress the romance between Morven and I stretched no further than a few nervous conversations and we may even have sneaked some hand holding over the couple of days in Inverness. Breathlessly we parted and she later sent word, inviting me to come and watch her dad perform in concert at the Albert Halls in Stirling. Too scared and far too nervous, I never accepted her kind offer.

It was around this time I first became aware of the power of music. I have a vivid recollection of a Sunday morning at my Uncle Billy and Aunt Elsie's house in Beith, the sunshine streaming through the window and onto their brand new radiogram, sitting in the corner of the living room like a coffin waiting on the next available cadaver.

They were playing the new Simon and Garfunkel LP 'Bridge Over Troubled Water' and it was the first time I'd ever heard 'Cecilia'. I lifted the needle, with their permission, and played it time and again. I'd never heard anything as amazing and happy.

I had only recently picked up the guitar, following the example of some of the older guys who attended church. I bought my first instrument in Hayes Music Shop in Friar's Street, probably with the proceeds of my job as a butcher boy, and took the bus out to Cowie to visit my cousin Hughie McCallum, who gave lessons.

He taught me the only three chords I've ever known or needed. I played with the church band, hymns and the likes, and a couple of years later I attempted to put a band together with my schoolmates John Cooper and Brian Docherty. The only track we ever mastered was 'David Watts' by The Jam.

Unsurprisingly, the band came to nothing, although I can still play the guitar – just as badly as before. I've only written one song for the guitar in my life. Three guesses which episode inspired 'I Wave to you from the Ambulance'?

My family in Canada turned out to be fantastically generous – and not just for those wonderful holidays, the first with granny Morag to Winnipeg and then Vancouver. Two of my aunts over there, Jennie and Margaret, made the return journey on a couple of occasions and were always keen to spoil the Cochranes.

One memorable year they purchased for me, from Radio Music Stores in Bannockburn, a white Hitachi cassette player and mum and dad were also presented with a mahogany radiogram, a majestic Hungarian Rhapsody model.

My parents were huge music fans and I recall a couple of LPs from their collection. My dad had a soft spot for jazz and Ella Fitzgerald was a favourite and they also had Nana Mouskouri on vinyl, although no Beatles or Rolling Stones to boost my street cred. Remember, the first single I bought was that Benny Hill novelty disc and my first LP was one of those awful MFP releases – 'Music For Pleasure', a collection of hits of the day covered by a pile of rotten session singers.

However, the Hitachi sparked something in me and a friend of the family also presented me with an 'Ultra' amp. I managed to wire the amp to the cassette player and suddenly music in our house got a lot louder, with added bass and treble, and a lot more interesting.

I was a regular at the Boys' Brigade – I would go on to be awarded its highest honour, the Queen's Badge – and hung around the church social scene with older kids whose musical influences soon rubbed off.

Before too long I was into buying cassettes and listening to prog rock, with Rick Wakeman a huge favourite. I played his albums 'Journey to the Centre of the Earth' and 'The Myths and Legends of King Arthur and the Knights of the Round Table' to death.

I loved those big, orchestral beats and the ability of music to take listeners like me, a kid from Bannockburn, on a journey to far flung places. Around the same time, on Christmas Eve, I walked into the church manse and was awestruck at seeing Queen perform 'Bohemian Rhapsody' on television. Wow. I was blown away. With Freddie Mercury in one ear and Rick Wakeman in the other, I knew I was on an odyssey.

Outside my bedroom walls, life continued with little drama but plenty of joyful innocence. I was a slightly podgy kid, a bit bookish, and never caused my parents any great trouble. I picked up my nickname early in life – I still can't remember who gave it to me – because of my love of Scooby Doo cartoons.

I had good pals at Bannockburn Primary School and was never stuck for company on those long summer days, but best friends would not arrive in my life until later in my teenage years when guys such as Franny and Fraser Hotchkiss came along.

I coasted through life at Bannockburn High without major incident. I wasn't a top class student by any manner of means and my five 'O' Grades and two 'Highers' weren't exactly straight 'A's. Despite that, in my fifth year they made me vice captain, which came as something of a shock as I hadn't even been a prefect before then.

I was only ever belted once at secondary school and on my very first day too. My registration teacher was a battleaxe called Miss Lyons, nicknamed 'Knoxy' by the kids. I wandered into her class on my opening morning, completely lost in more ways than one, and enquired in all sincerity: "Is this Miss Knox's class?"

Bannockburn High, like most schools of its type and time, was a zoo. Believe it or not, Donald's ice cream van did a roaring trade outside the school gates at lunchtime selling 'singles', solitary cigarettes, the perfect play set for juvenile smokers.

I went on to work in the van around Bannockburn at night after becoming pally with Donald's son, Terence O'Hare, who attended St Modan's. I was full of pride, but also couldn't help smiling, when I saw Terence's superfit son Chris O'Hare run for Team GB in the 1500 metres at the Rio Olympics in 2016.

There was never any chance of this blue eyed boy being caught enjoying a sneaky cigarette behind the bike sheds and my low profile also kept me away from some of the worst excesses of teenage tribalism.

Each scheme and village had its own 'gang' at the time and at Bannockburn High that included the YST (Young St Ninan's Toll), the KKK (Krazy Kowie Krew), the PYT (Plean Young Team), the BYT (Bannockburn Young Team) and, from Hillpark, the MBT (Mental Burn Team). It was mostly older kids who were involved and, thankfully, I was never dragged into aligning with one set of initials against the other.

Music was beginning to have more of an impact in my teenage years and I attended my first concert in March 1976 at the famous Apollo in Glasgow. I was only 13 and Ann Laird, older sister of my choir pal May, took me under her wing as she was six years my senior when we went to see Status Quo in their 'Blue For You' tour.

I had borrowed Quo albums from Ann to play on that trusty Hungarian Rhapsody and was becoming something of a rocker, listening to tracks such as 'Caroline' and albums including 'Piledriver'. Ann spoiled me rotten at the Apollo, forking out on a scarf, badge and programme to keep me happy but I was already in seventh heaven in the sweat pit of that esteemed arena.

Even that tough Glaswegian audience were eating from Francis Rossi's hand that night and there was something about the assuredness and confidence of Quo's performance that struck a chord, in more ways than one. They had the power to make people happy, a gift I must have coveted at the time, even if I couldn't have consciously expressed my desire.

Rita Thompson must have recognised the yearning. She ran the Busy Bees Youth Club in Bannockburn with her husband Davie, aided by trusty 'bouncer' John Barrie who successfully managed to keep an unruly bunch of 10-16 year-olds in check for a couple of hours every Monday night.

It was a council funded enterprise, in those old Nissen huts behind Bannockburn Primary School, and with little to do at nights around the scheme – it isn't exactly located on the outskirts of Disneyworld – it was always packed.

They offered football and table tennis, with a cafe serving soft drinks and sweets. Best of all, there was a small hall that had been converted into a disco, with a picture of King Crimson's 'In the Court of the Crimson King' plastered on one wall and a mural of Pink Floyd's 'Dark Side of the Moon' on the other. Unfamiliar with both albums, the striking artistry of their covers intrigued me.

One night in 1976, not long after I'd turned 14, I arrived for my usual fun and games with pals, only to be hit by the crushing news the DJ hadn't turned up and there would be no music played. Who knows if she sensed my disappointment, but Rita simply turned to me and asked: "Fancy a go?"

The set up was simple – two turntables, two faders and a microphone, but it might as well have been the cockpit of a Boeing 747 as I glanced at my new plaything.

I was nervous, but not daunted. This was an opportunity to be embraced, not rejected. I looked down at a collection of around 50 LPs and reassured myself with the fact the audience scattered around the hall always came to listen to the music, not to dance.

Clumsily, I fingered through the pile of discs and settled on 'Gold Plated' by the Climax Blues Band. I know what people like, I told myself. I stuck the needle over the start of their biggest hit 'Couldn't Get It Right' and dropped it in the groove. A magical stereo sound filled the air, like oxygen firing a furnace.

Only after a couple of minutes did I find the courage to look up, to see dozens of heads around the room nodding contentedly in time to the beat of the song I had selected. My heart swelled with pride. Suddenly, I knew what I wanted to do with my life.

4

Kirkcaldy is affectionately known as the Lang Toun but it would still be stretching it to suggest Bentley's nightclub rivalled Milan or Paris as one of the world's leading fashion centres.

The new romantic era entered my life like a brick through a window in 1980, when I was just 17, but perhaps a provincial town on the Fife coast wasn't the most fitting location to mimic the style of the synth pop boys from bands such as Spandau Ballet, who had emerged from punk to become the media darlings of the London music scene.

Blame Martin and Gary Kemp or, equally as likely, my best pal Franny and our mutual mucker Stuart Donaldson, a dead ringer for David Sylvian from Japan. They had seen Spandau Ballet's video for their top five hit 'To Cut A Long Story Short' and decided the Islington kids had a fashion sense worth following.

Emboldened by their confidence and determined not to be left in their wake, a week later I decided to debut the look for myself on a night out east of Cowdenbeath.

Bentley's, like its neighbour and rival Jackie O's, has long since been demolished and replaced by housing and, thankfully, no pictures have survived of my get up that winter's evening when I dressed as if Les McKeown was suffering a crisis of confidence and caught between a career in the Bay City Rollers and The Three Musketeers.

A pair of tartan trews had been sourced and cut halfway up the shins, with the remaining fabric sewn into a sash and thrown nonchalantly over my left shoulder. The trousers, meanwhile, had been tucked into a pair of white football socks while, from army surplus, my old man had commandeered a pair of brown brogues, most likely Argyll and Sutherland Highlanders' issue and probably last worn at Balaclava.

The tartan sash was slanted against a frilly white women's blouse, an adventurous purchase from the local branch of Edinburgh Woollen Mill. My blonde hair was cut and styled (with a Denman brush, of course) into a perfect wedge, with a dash of black eyeliner highlighting my baby blues.

In the end, it was a local sweetheart named Sandra Linton and her two pals, Laura Caira and Marisa Valente, who came to my rescue. Laura and Marisa were of Italian stock and well connected in Kirkcaldy, so the initial growls of hostility from local lads at my outlandish dress sense thankfully gave way to a grudging acceptance of the new dandy from Stirling in their midst.

What was it about me being challenged to fights in toilets on the back of the way I dressed? Unlike McQ's a few months earlier with Franny leading from the front, this time the challenge went ignored by yours truly. I've never hit out or been struck by a blow in my life, but as I walked out the loos that night I was still subconsciously rolling my knuckles in readiness for the inevitable punches to come.

Strangely enough, I could cope with the jibes about my dress sense. I was confident in what I was all about. I didn't want to be the 'norm', whatever that 'norm' happened to be. However, Sandra and the girls stepped forward and introduced themselves when I got back into the main body of the club and the angry boys backed off. The blows never did follow, although Sandra pounded at my heart strings for a couple of months afterwards.

Bentley's was a superclub before the term had even been invented. It sat away from the town centre, in the middle of a housing scheme, and was owned by an entrepreneur named Eddie Melville, whose business Monday to Friday was car exhausts and tyres. It was a big place and although the dress sense was fairly conservative, fashion eccentrics were eventually accepted.

In later years, I would become close friends and a business partner of Colin Barr, who became a doyen of the Glasgow nightclub scene, and I first met his future wife Kelly in Bentley's when she was dolled up in top hat and tails, wearing fishnet tights and high heel shoes. By that stage

I had moved from Spandau Ballet to Haircut 100, copying lead singer Nick Heyward by donning shin boots and army jodhpurs, white shirt and yellow tie, topped with Aran knitwear. Fantastic days.

The club scene across Scotland in the early eighties was wonderfully fluid and, one or two incidents apart, it wasn't outrageously territorial. We thought nothing of driving more than an hour from Stirling across to Kirkcaldy for a night in Bentley's or Jackie O's, for example, and we often went much further afield, even to the outskirts of Aberdeen.

Stirling town centre welcomed its first late night venue in 1980 called Le Clique, on the site of a Georgian villa that was once a Masonic hall, and it boasted the latest licence in the area at 2am. Even still, we would frequently pour out of there after closing and drive 100 miles north to Stonehaven to catch the last hour of the legendary jazz-funk all nighters hosted by the Commodore Hotel.

The events were the brainchild of Tony Cochrane, one of the best and shrewdest of all Scottish promoters. He was way ahead of his time and his club at the Commodore pre-dated the arrival of the all nighter raves by at least a decade.

Tony's cousin, Bernie, worked for Scottish Television and was director of a programme from the late seventies called 'The Best Disco In Town', a forerunner of Pete Waterman's 'Hitman and Her', which drew such large audiences for ITV in the small hours of Sunday mornings throughout the eighties and nineties.

The format was simplicity itself during an era in which disco was riding high as the music of choice in Scottish clubland. Tony and STV toured a string of regional nightclubs – including our own McQ's – and invited the best dancers to showcase their moves in a grand final in front of an audience at the STV studios at Cowcaddens in Glasgow.

Tony was, in short, the programme's talent spotter and the role gave him a position of influence with club owners and local politicians, which he used to good effect in the north east.

All-night licences were so rare as to be non-existent and yet Tony still managed to convince local councillors of the benefits to the area's social and economic well being by allowing clubbers from all over Scotland to party between 10pm-7am one Saturday a month. Well, perhaps not.

It was a little mischievous, but Tony actually applied to the council under the name of 'The Scottish Soul Society' and the politicians were taken in by the gravitas of the title, believing it to be a sober and august organisation formed to further the minority interest of a musical niche.

They were spot on as party we did, with crowds drawn from Aberdeen, Dundee, Glasgow, Bathgate, Edinburgh and Stirling by a fusion of jazz and funk spun by a skilfully selected line up of established DJs as well as up-and-coming young hopefuls.

The nights were legendary, as was the intake of amphetamine sulphate and 'blues'. Chemist shops in the towns and villages dotted up and down the A90 were regularly broken into on the eve of events at the Commodore, with speed tablets the booty of choice.

The atmosphere was never less than harmonious, despite the geographical spread of punters. Human pyramids were constructed on the dance floor and soul trains and dance-offs pulled regularly throughout the night. Underpinning it all was Tony's reputation in the industry, which was solid.

He and I would team up in later years to run magnificent raves at the Plaza ballroom in Glasgow. One of my biggest regrets, to this day, remains dumping Tony out of my business life. It was a mistake I should never have made.

I first fell in love at a club in Bo'ness called McTavish's which, previously, had been trading as the slightly more exotically sounding La Fabrique. There was no Auld Alliance on show the Sunday night I turned up with my cousin Dick and his mate Zokko. I locked eyes with Liz Cameron on the dance floor while they set about fending off stares from irate locals around the bar.

We stayed long enough for Liz and I to declare our passions and swap numbers before Dick and Zokko dragged me to the door and back towards our car. We pulled away with a squeal of wheels just as a half slab of concrete crashed through the rear window, although nothing was ringing in my ears but the sound of birdsong.

Liz came from Whitburn and before I secured my driver's licence that meant a 5.30pm bus from Bannockburn on the first stage of a journey that also included changeovers at Falkirk and Bathgate before Cupid's arrow delivered me to her doorstep at 8pm.

The only issue? The return journey began with a bus from Whitburn at 8.20pm but those 20 minutes, 1200 glorious seconds, were worth it all. A few months later Liz moved to Italy to become a nanny. She asked me to follow her out there, but that was a bus trip too far even for lovestruck me.

Maybe it was all the travelling on public transport that inspired me to learn to drive and pretty soon I was in possession of my first car, a 1275 GT Mini. It had been listed for sale by an old woman in Cumbernauld at a reasonable £700 and my pal Ronnie Hutton, who reckoned he knew a thing or two about engines, gave it the once over.

He emerged from under the bonnet to tell her a zuber screw was missing and the gangle pin was faulty. It would cost a few quid to get it fixed. He suggested £500 was a much fairer price and the seller, noting the concerned look on his face, quickly agreed to the knockdown deal as I pulled a pile of £20 notes from my pocket.

We were two miles from Stirling in the new car before I dared ask: "Ronnie, what's a zuber screw and a gangle pin?" He just looked at me and laughed: "Scooby, how the fuck would I know?"

These days were young and carefree, exactly as they should have been. Girls came and went, with exclusivity in teenage relationships never demanded and rarely offered. I moved into my first flat, in Bayne Street in Stirling, with my pal Paul Chisholm and it should probably have come fitted with a revolving door.

On the first weekend in my new place my mum, Mac, thought it would be a good idea to nip over on the Sunday morning and cook her boy breakfast in bed as a special treat. She let herself in with the spare key and gently pushed open my bedroom door, only to see two sets of feet sticking out the bottom of the duvet. She quickly concluded I was thriving in my new environment and the sacrifice of the usual home comforts was something I was willing to make.

Sandra also came through to Stirling from Kirkcaldy with Laura and Marisa every now and again for a change of scene, although a strain was put on our relationship when I broke the news I was off to Majorca on a holiday with the boys and, I sheepishly confessed, a couple of local girls as well.

A hairdresser, Sandra kindly offered to style my hair perfectly for my week in the sun, then promptly left me with a barnet later modelled by Lloyd Christmas in 'Dumb and Dumber'. Her plan worked a treat as I didn't get so much as a sniff of perfume over seven days at Banana's and Alexander's Disco in Magaluf and her canny tactic still makes me laugh out loud in fondness of the fun times we enjoyed together.

Girls apart, my life revolved around music and fashion. Five or six nights a week were spent in clubs across the central belt, engaging with new DJs and listening to live music.

Davie Walters ran a soul-funk night at Club de France which, no-one will be surprised to learn, was in Coatbridge and not the Cote D'Azur. His music was amazing, but the major attraction was the dance troupe contracted to the venue called Parisienne Flesh. If they had ever visited the Left Bank it must have been the name of a pub in Renfrewshire as they all came from Paisley.

They were a stunning group of girls and, better still for us testosterone-fuelled teens, didn't wear much at all. They were dancing the night a young American saxophonist performed on stage, although Ronnie and I were distinctly underwhelmed by his style of easy listening jazz. Few who were present that night could ever have imagined Kenny G would go on to such worldwide acclaim.

Another favourite destination was Valentino's in Edinburgh's Lothian Road, which had emerged in 1980 as a venue for groundbreaking new artists such as The Cure, New Order, Teardrop Explodes and Adam and the Ants. I had already seen Echo and the Bunnymen there in October but there was little buzz about a band out promoting their new album on Burns' Night, January 25, 1981.

It was a Sunday and even with local band The Fire Engines as support, only around 30 people had paid the £2 entrance fee for a show that also promised a 'late bar, disco and video'. True enough, we sat around watching a large screen to the side of the stage which was, inexplicably, showing Bugs Bunny cartoons.

The band were announced on stage and stepped up from the audience, promptly succeeding where Elmer Fudd had failed by blowing us all away.

Even now, that gig by U2 remains the best I've attended. The energy of a youthful Bono was something to behold and it was impossible to conclude anything but we were in the presence of greatness, even then.

Their album 'Boy' had just been released and pretty soon it was never off my turntable. The track 'Out of Control' might still be the best record

I've ever heard. The gig was life changing. I had missed out on the punk era – just – but heard in U2 a raw edge that had its roots in the revolutionary sound from just five years earlier.

I didn't have to examine myself too hard to conclude part of me related to the brash, confident demeanour of Bono, who gripped that crowd of 30 as easily as he would later control audiences of 300,000.

Fraser Hotchkiss, my friend and DJ mentor, revealed recently his first memory of me was leading a conga of revellers from The Tamdhu next door into McQ's, where he was on the decks, before heading straight out the door again and back onto our original dance floor.

I was cocksure, arrogant even. I didn't have any brothers or sisters and always felt I was ahead of the rest, especially in terms of music. I was breaking records such as Magazine's 'The Light Pours Out of Me'. I was one of the first to play 'Vienna' by Ultravox, aided by the former Hearts and Celtic footballer John Colquhoun, who grew up in Stirling. John is a keen and knowledgeable music fan and thrust the record into my hand one night and urged me to give it a chance.

My supreme confidence was reflected in my dress sense, which was shaped by my job in Stirling's leading clothes store, Avanti. I was 17 and walked in off the street and asked for a sales assistant's post to supplement my primary income as an up-and-coming DJ at The Tamdhu.

Avanti's owner, Tony Tortolano, wasn't daft. He offered staff a 40 per cent discount on the clothes they bought and every penny I earned went straight back into his till. In the meantime, I was a walking advert around town for fashions that make us roll our eyes now, but which were very much statements of their time.

Franny and I, for example, bought matching Italian flying suits by the designer Bobo. His was yellow, mine red and they were all-in-one numbers of zips and thin fabric. I boasted a wardrobe of Mitchell Walker suits, single breasted linen cuts in pink, lilac and every other hue of the rainbow.

I also wore Inega stretch denims, which were a breeze to squeeze into compared to the Gentle Folk brand of satine jeans popular with girls. Perhaps the pinnacle of my haute couture was a bespoke white leather suit, with lilac shirt and shoes, commissioned from Glasgow tailor Gordon Traynor for my 18th birthday party. I was so enchanted I immediately ordered another two, in dashing pink and a more sober brown.

At that stage, money wasn't an issue. I was earning well and working hard and expensive habits, fashion costs aside, did not impact on my lifestyle. An occasional joint was passed around McQ's and I took a puff every now and again, but the drug of choice was predominantly alcohol and I didn't care much for that. I didn't abstain but the taste really was not for me and, as a DJ, it was vital I was in control of my environment as anything less would have led to messy and unprofessional sets which would have been a crushing blow to my ego and growing reputation.

On a much more pragmatic level, as a DJ you were always last out the door on a Friday or Saturday night and therefore your chances of being caught by police drink-driving on quieter roads were greatly increased. Alcohol, I decided from a very young age, would form no great part in my life.

Those early, heady nights spent playing records at the Busy Bees youth club had continued throughout my teenage years, boosted by my promotion to vice captain of Bannockburn High as it opened another avenue to learn what would quickly become my fledgling trade. I was tasked with organising Christmas and end of term dances for every year group and soon I was a whizz on the school's mobile disco unit.

In the meantime, I was paying more attention to the structure and playlists of Radio One in particular, especially DJs such as Kid Jensen and Noel Edmonds who made it sound easy, nothing was ever too forced.

By the age of 16 I had started going to pubs with my pals, particularly Muirhead's in Bannockburn, which later became the Newmarket Inn. The music was predominantly disco, but within every session there would be a 20 minute break and DJ Jimmy Masterson would emerge and play a short set of Northern Soul.

Don't ask where the Northern Soul crew came from, but come they did, and I stood transfixed at their vigour, style and energy on the dance floor. They scattered talcum powder under their feet then built up an elegant sweat before slipping off into the night as quickly as they had arrived.

My school days passed by unremarkably and my fourth and fifth years at Bannockburn High were as memorable as elevator muzak. My old man pushed for me to go to university or at least find a trade but my Uncle Billy managed something I could never have achieved by hitting the nail on the head.

He reminded dad that his boy was pretty handless and so a trade was out of the question. He added: "He should stick in at music, he's good at that. Our Stuart could become the new Terry Wogan." Mum was easy about plans for my future, focused only on the happiness of her son.

A major turning point in my life had arrived at the age of 16 when I was offered the job as glass collector at The Tamdhu by the owner himself, Tam Coll. Unsurprisingly, everyone simply referred to him as Tam Dhu and he was a Marmite character, loved and loathed in equal measure.

Tam took a shine to me, even forgiving me a mishap early in my new employment when we catered a wedding reception and I spilled a bowl of tomato soup down the dress of the bride. Understandably, the good lady went mental, her face soon matching the new colour of her designer outfit.

Tam was also a qualified social worker and used all his counselling skills to smooth over the situation, placating the poor woman while I was pushed behind the scenes and onto the dishes, where I could do less harm.

Life can very often turn on a single moment and my opportunity arose one quiet Sunday evening when The Tamdhu's regular DJs, Brian Cooper and Brian Fairlie, failed to trap for their regular weekly gig. Brian, a former striker with Hibs, owned a mobile disco unit he stored at the pub and Tam, knowing I'd DJ experience around the village, asked if I fancied coming off the subs' bench.

I put down a couple of empty pint glasses and stepped into my new office, behind a battery of brilliant lights, and lost myself in music for a couple of hours.

Honestly, hardly anyone came through the doors that night but I was pleased with my makeshift set, believing I'd laid down a marker for the future. Tam was a socialist Labour man, a local councillor to boot, and didn't suffer fools. The other side of his curmudgeonly character was that when he did connect, you potentially had an ally for life. He was also a fine operator with a keen eye for business and he saw potential in me, as well as the pub.

The relationship between The Tamdhu and McQ's was complex. They lived cheek by jowl, two pubs and nightclubs who didn't particularly like each other, even if they both catered to different markets.

It was like Rangers and Celtic in the football world. They eyed each other with wary suspicion, but understood they relied on each other as, collectively, they formed part of an important entertainment hub for the people of Stirling and central Scotland.

They had similar capacities of around 300 and there was an unwritten agreement not to plant tanks on each other's lawns. Each of the places had a vibrant pub and lounge trade seven days a week which remained constant.

The Tamdhu's biggest club nights were a Monday and Friday, with a bit of a Saturday trade also boosting turnover. McQ's also operated on a Monday night, especially when Tony Cochrane and STV were scouting for 'The Best Disco In Town', but Thursdays were the most important nights of the week and Saturdays came a close second.

Licensing laws were such that in order to stay open until 1am, both venues also had to offer food. A night out at McQ's and The Tamdhu came with a ticket that guaranteed The Bee Gees over the loudspeakers and scampi in a basket through the kitchen's serving hatch.

Crucially for me, The Tamdhu attracted a younger audience and Tam spotted the chance to extend its influence by building the business around my growing talent as a DJ. The two Brians were told their services were no longer required and as that left us a mobile disco unit down, Tam had no option but to invest.

I felt like a Premier League striker being sold the dream of a new club as Tam laid out his plans on which, being a man of honour, he quickly delivered. Stirling musician Ted Christopher owned Roadshow Music in Bridge of Allan and Tam forked out a fortune on lights, decks, amps and speakers for his new signing.

He smothered me with equipment and even opened an account at one of the local record stores so I would never be short of vinyl. He put his money where his mouth was – and I was determined to deliver.

Slowly but surely The Tamdhu grew more and more popular until, at the risk of sounding trite, it became a movement for kids. The atmosphere was akin to that of a gang hut. Teenagers came for the love of the music and it was a safe environment. If pushed, I could recall a couple of scraps, but nothing major.

We were all under the watchful eye of bouncer Bandy Cairney, who viewed us all with paternal compassion. He was a huge fan of Roxy Music and David Bowie and always looked out for this skinny runt in particular as I was occasionally on the receiving end of a barbed comment on the elegance or otherwise of my new pink jeans or lemon linen trousers. A nightly fix of Bryan Ferry or a track from 'Scary Monsters' kept him sweet.

In partnership with Ted Christopher, Tam also promoted the ATOM club on a Monday night, which was an acronym for Any Type Of Music. The format was simple – a live band, followed by a disco hosted on several occasions by yours truly. Ted had a range of music industry contacts and one night we turned the corner to find a gleaming, silver Winnebago parked outside the pub.

It was on hire to Australian psychedelic rock band The Church, whose single 'Under the Milky Way' would later feature in the movie 'Donnie Darko'. I was in awe of the band. In later years they would release their second album, 'The Blurred Crusade'.

I would inevitably drive home to Stirling from Choice nightclub in Glasgow at 4am, stoned. Under the Castlecary arches, the railway viaduct near Cumbernauld, I would turn off my car headlights, hit the play button on that cassette in my stereo player, and coast home the last 10 miles on the motorway guided by nothing stronger than moonlight.

Ted's ATOM nights were fabulous, anything goes events that featured a new romantic band one week, punk the next, followed by funk and even heavy metal. They were a joy to DJ, although the latex mob were always a challenge as there was only so much Whitesnake one man could stand.

Ted also championed local bands. Those French Girls, pretty boy new romantics, even secured an album deal. I also rated The Curious Rain, influenced as they were by Echo and The Bunnymen, as well as 22 Beaches. They were electro pop princes – and one princess – from Raploch and Cultenhove, two of Stirling's more notorious housing schemes. In those days of mend-and-make-do Jackie Sharkie played her synth on stage balanced precariously on top of her mum's ironing board.

All the time I was soaking up experiences, accumulating musical knowledge and DJ know-how that would stand me in good stead for years to come. Tam was a passionate music fan and would haul me through to the fabled Bungalow Bar in Paisley on midweek nights to catch bands and artists, many of them unsigned. The Bungalow was a musical mecca and hosted everyone from The Clash and The Jam to The Skids. I saw Glasgow band H2O play there, as well as Gourock bluesman Henry Gorman. Good times.

Early on in my DJ career I recognised it was easy to play it safe and, naturally, at the Busy Bees and school discos that's exactly what I did, relying heavily on hits from the Radio One playlist based around the charts at the time.

As I matured, it was no longer as satisfying. I developed a wider range of musical tastes and influences and was keen to share my enthusiasm and new found knowledge with audiences at The Tamdhu. I was just too young for punk, but still counted on The Skids and The Stranglers as turntable staples.

I adored Magazine, born from The Buzzcocks, and new romantic vibes from bands such as Ultravox and Orchestral Manoeuvres in the Dark sounded fresh and exciting. I played 'Messages' by OMD for six weeks solid before the crowd eventually got it. In the early days I would play requests, if I could. Later on it became more about the mixing of music and less about direct engagement with the crowd via microphone.

Good DJs dare to be different and I learned from the best in Fraser Hotchkiss. He was a huge influence and I would occasionally sneak into McQ's and watch enviously at how skilfully he worked his audience on the dance floor.

Fraser adored music and even went to Miami in 1980 and returned with boxes of new records to play to a Scottish crowd. He was the first DJ I heard turn to 'Rapper's Delight' by the Sugarhill Gang, the song credited with sparking the hip hop revolution in the States.

We raved about new sounds such as 'Whip It' by Devo. Occasionally we would be taken by surprise. Shalamar's 'Right In The Socket' was a song that did little for me in its seven inch format, but the 12 inch cut? It was staggeringly good. It was the era of Cheryl Lynn's 'Got To Be Real', 'You Got The Floor' by Arthur Adams, Jackie Moore's 'This

Time Baby', and even all seven and a half minutes of 'Lovin' Is Really My Game', by Brainstorm.

Following Fraser's lead, I would take a chance with a new record and if the floor emptied I knew how to bring them back again. Occasionally, like 'Messages' by OMD, the record was a grower. Other times, it hit the spot first time.

If it didn't, we could make a withdrawal from the bank of Bowie, Roxy Music and Tamla Motown and the floor would quickly fill again. Freda Payne may have lamented being left a solitary band of gold by her man, but what a gift her record was to any DJ who had temporarily misjudged the mood of his crowd.

It was exhilarating to lift and carry the audience on a wave of musical euphoria and that should have been intoxicating enough, but sadly it wasn't always. I detest the current trend of describing any event in life as a 'journey' but that's exactly the phrase for a night in the DJ booth.

The records you played at the start of your set were as vital as those in the middle and the end. It's easy to play to a room packed with revellers, but playing to a crowd of 30 and enticing half of them up to dance and keeping them there? That's a craft.

Tam put no boundaries on what I played and it became clear we were mining a rich vein of public appreciation, especially as we entered the eighties and disco slowly gave way to more edgy, industrial sounds.

One Sunday night a pal, Bannockburn bouncer Danny McPhail, invited me to Aberfoyle where DJ Dave 'CL' Young had built a sizeable audience at the Rob Roy hotel on the back of a setlist of funk, jazz and disco, featuring artists such as The Commodores and Shalamar.

Danny introduced me as a young guy from Stirling learning his trade and politely asked Dave to give me five minutes at the decks. Dave readily obliged and five minutes turned into half an hour as I ran through a setlist that included Gary Numan, U2, Teardrop Explodes and OMD.

In music, as in all areas of life, you have to adapt or die. I could sense in Dave a recognition, which he embraced, that time and trends were moving on.

Sadly, so was I. The absolute highlight came the Saturday night when I hosted my 18th birthday party wearing that white leather suit and all the older boys from McQ's came next door for an hour to see just what the fuss around The Tamdhu was all about.

Reputations were sealed that night for me – and Tam Coll's business. I had taken it from a crowd of 12 on a Sunday night until now, a couple of years later, they were queueing around the block to get in. It had become more than a disco, it had become a go-to venue with credibility and Tam was keen to take it to the next stage.

In the early eighties, that meant turning to video and he was one of the first in Scotland to commission state-of-the-art televisions around his place that would lock it into an increasingly multi-media age.

Again, he put his money where his mouth was and invested in industry standard equipment such as a Matamp Supernova mixer desk and Technics SL-1200 turntables, still hugely valued names in the business today. The sound was boosted by Big Daddy amps, top of the range kit. Tam did it all for me and yet a week before the club re-opened our relationship was in the gutter.

Sadly, we had a massive argument about an issue I can no longer even remember and I told him to stuff his job. Similar arrogance would also cost me my post in Avanti, when the manager dared ask me to move a box of clothing from one corner of the stockroom to the other.

I was too full of my own self-importance to apologise and Tam, rightly, was too proud and long in the tooth to go cap in hand to an 18-year-old in a bid to resolve a situation that was probably not even of his making.

Two stubborn individuals refused to yield an inch on their belief they had been wronged in an argument now lost in the mists of time and there would be no reconciliation.

I sat at home and stewed for a week before Fraser called with an offer out the blue from McQ's. There was an opening and they wanted to know if I fancied the gig. I may not have had a conga line behind me this time, but I was ever so happy to dance through their doors as a resident DJ.

5

In hindsight, we should have seen the allegations of child abduction coming long before the flashing blue lights from six police cars greeted us ominously at the Craig's roundabout in Stirling town centre.

They forced the double decker bus into a side street then led us in a convoy of vehicles, sirens wailing, towards the main cop shop a half mile up the road at Randolphfield.

As the only sober person on board it quickly fell to me to recover all hash, coke, uppers, downers, poppers, pills and sulph and drop them from an upstairs window, on the blindside of the cop cars, while we raced up the dual carriageway at 50 miles an hour.

Talk about a confetti of chemicals.

The smell of hash hung heavy in the air, but thankfully the whiff of diesel was stronger. Little wonder. Eight hours earlier we'd carted an industrial generator onto the bus, powering a mobile disco unit we'd set up at the back of the ground floor to belt out everything from Boston to James Brown.

The emergency exit off to the side of the DJ booth had been forced open in a vain bid to circulate fresh air, the door jammed in place by the sanitary machine we'd stolen off the wall of the ladies' loo in a pub in Tillicoultry.

Ronnie's Bar didn't serve half measures when it came to organising a day out at the seaside.

In fairness the kid, a boy of around 12, looked distraught his adventure was coming to an end as we were guided into the car park at the police station. Who could blame him? Dot and Leslie, the best bar-maids in the business, had taken turns at clasping him close to their ample bosoms. Their maternal concern had been shining through ever since we'd picked him up half an hour previously, six miles along the road in the village of Throsk.

The details, like the fug of hash on the bus, are hazy. Our bus had slowed on entering the village anyway, although the riotous party on board remained in full swing. The driver, who had been well weighed in financially, was turning more blind eyes than Quincy Magoo and threw another Nelson's when we ordered him to stop all together at the sight of the youngster hitching a lift by the side of the A905.

The kid quickly explained he'd fallen out with his mum after an argument and wouldn't mind a lift into the centre of Stirling, the very direction we were heading. His mum had screeched the family car to a halt and told him to get out, presumably in a fit of frustration she very quickly regretted. However, in the couple of minutes she'd turfed him out and then U-turned to buckle him back into the passenger's seat he'd disappeared. Every parent's worst nightmare, admittedly.

A couple of villagers were on hand to tell of a kid jumping onto a double decker bus, its emergency exit wide open, music blaring and disco lights whirring and with a youthful group of passengers who didn't exactly look as if they had climbed on board to head for the weekly supermarket shop.

All's well that ends well. The cops may have been suspicious about our chemically altered state of minds, but not our intentions. The kid was reunited with his relieved mum while Ronnie Hunter, the owner of the eponymously titled bar, used every ounce of his silver tongue to talk us out of nothing more serious than a flea in the ear.

Ronnie's Bar, on Viewfield Place in Stirling, wasn't so much a pub as a way of life. It was opened in 1982 by the aforementioned Ronnie Hunter, a printer from Cumbernauld, and Alan Queen, a coach builder from Polmont. They were two mates who spotted a gap in the market, took a chance and for two, glorious years the spirit of their pub burned brightly before it collapsed and was left trashed against a backdrop of financial losses and relationship breakdowns.

Stirling in the early eighties was something of a desert for decent pre-club destinations – McQ's, Le Clique and The Tamdhu were primarily nightclub venues, which left only Ronnie's and the recently opened Beanstalk.

I was wily enough to poke my head around the door of both establishments regularly but, opinionated as ever, I remember my opening gambit to Beanstalk owner Chris Morris on the night he first turned the key of his new venture. "This will never work mate," I told him. What the hell did I know? Chris Morris went on to own Behind The Wall in Falkirk, one of the best and most successful bars in Scotland.

It would be something of a caricature to describe the Beanstalk as a poseur's palace, all squeaky clean, the latest fashions and pina coladas reflected against floor to ceiling mirrors, but a caricature is just a truth, stretched.

Ronnie's Bar was a more interesting proposition for me at that stage in my life as its regulars matched the owners in their devil-may-care attitude. It had a curious, mixed bag of a clientele, who took drugs and regularly attended concerts.

Its punters included young punks, lads from the rougher housing schemes such as Cultenhove and Raploch and, for some reason, a lot of oil rig workers, cash rich older guys who gave me my first taste of coke and regularly sparked up joints on the street and in their cars outside. My drugs education had begun.

It was a window to the world, literally, as Ronnie and Alan had positioned the bar against the huge, double glazed frame which allowed us to gaze out at the street beyond when we weren't distracted by the wondrous figures of Dot and Leslie, more often than not in mini skirts.

In those less PC times the owners knew the buttons to press to attract lusty young males. The regulars included Gordon 'Del Boy' Dobbie, who drank with his pet parrot on his shoulder. No-one cared. One day it flew out the door and rested on the phone cables across the road. Gordon was worth a few quid and called the fire brigade, begging: "I'll pay for your time, just send someone to get my parrot down."

His pleas fell on deaf ears, although his bird later returned to its trusty perch. My pal Sean Gentleman was given a job behind the bar and turned up on his first day dressed as Adolf Hitler. Why? Why not?

There was a function suite downstairs, which later became a fine restaurant, The East India Company, but which in our day was known as Hanky Panky's. I'm not sure Ronnie and Alan ever went to the trouble of securing a license, but it hosted a few wild events, on a couple of occasions with yours truly as DJ.

There were stripper nights for example, male and female. The girls ripped the shirt and trousers off the buffed young guy who turned up for their entertainment and my lasting memory is of him bolting for the emergency exit, clothes in his hands and only socks on his feet while I cowered behind the DJ booth, fearing I was next for the attention of their blood red talons.

Lock-ins were another regular occurrence. My 21st birthday party was held in McQ's – I received 20 bottles of Lagerfeld cologne, my signature sniff, from a variety of friends. My cousin Alan McDowall, who was married to Annie, a backing singer from The Rezillos, played with their band So You Think You're A Cowboy. We headed to Ronnie's after hours and stayed there until 8am and, suffice to say, it got messy.

However, we always considered doing things with a touch of class. We lifted two leather couches from the bar to the sidelines of Ladywell Park in Bannockburn one afternoon so Dot, Leslie and their pals would have a comfortable seat to watch us take on the Beanstalk in a football challenge match.

Ronnie's Bar was crammed with interesting characters. I probably visited it most days, not always at night because it wasn't an exclusively evening operation. It was not unusual to walk in at 1pm and find it packed, including a few more lively patrons trying to tempt punters with hooky t-shirts and other items of knock-off clothing.

Our big day out to the beach at Aberdour, on the Fife coast, highlighted the eccentricities of it all, including that crazy allegation of kidnapping. Admittedly, taking the sanitary machine from the walls of a Tillicoultry boozer when we stopped for a quick drink was bang out of order, we crossed the line. We used it as a caber for the Aberdour Olympics on the beach later that day and it also doubled as a rugby ball being thrown across the sands.

We had a sack race with a difference. We lined up in teams of two, boy and a girl, and the sacks were pulled over our heads rather than above our ankles.

The day had started ingloriously for me as I had slept in, but the double decker squeezed around Station Road in Bannockburn – I was back staying with my folks – and I staggered on still half asleep to be handed my packed lunch, which consisted of a stubby bottle of Special Vat cider, a sandwich and a packet of crisps.

As much as Margaret Thatcher was detested, with good reason, by many of the electorate in Stirling, particularly from the mining communities, Ronnie's Bar embraced her philosophy of free market capitalism with a vengeance.

It was liberal in all senses, especially in its attitude to sex, drugs and rock 'n' roll. It was easy to get involved and I found myself sliding comfortably into a drugs scene I didn't actively seek but was happy to entertain. No-one forced me and, in the days before ecstasy and acid and with the use of cocaine not widespread, cannabis was a popular alternative to alcohol.

Until then, hash or marijuana had been labelled for stoner use alone, guys with long hair who played heavy metal, but the reality was changing, especially as it was within the price range of most at £16 for a quarter ounce.

As a teenager and young adult, I was quite hyper. I didn't want to miss anything. Call it youthful curiosity. On nights I wasn't working at McQ's I could easily hit five bars and two nightclubs in a single eight hour stretch.

The pattern of a night out would be as follows: Ronnie's Bar at 8pm then up to the Beanstalk for a nosey before heading across Stirling to the Birds and Bees. After that I'd jump in the car again and drive to Glasgow, visit another bar or two before making my way to Panama Jax nightclub, rounding it all off with a visit to The Warehouse.

Cannabis mellowed me, took the edge of the frantic to-ing and fro-ing and sat much more comfortably with me than sulph ever did. I was dabbling, but serving an apprenticeship for what was to come. A couple of joints a night couldn't do much harm, could it?

My part-time work as a DJ was going quite well, with my move to McQ's seamless after the upheaval with The Tamdhu. I shared a Thursday night with my close pal Fraser Hotchkiss and he put some good work my way, such as engagement parties and birthday celebrations.

It was easy, nothing challenging from a DJ point of view. It was a sounding board for new records and lessons in how to work a crowd and I was also paid £30 for each function. It was pretty loose with Fraser on a Thursday night when McQ's busied. If he noticed I was struggling he'd come into the box and take over.

Music was transitioning from disco to new romantic and more industrial sounds such as New Order, but there was still a balance to be struck. In general, girls loved disco while the guys increasingly preferred an edgier vibe. It wasn't always easy to move from Booker Newberry III singing 'Love Town' to 'Blue Monday' but Fraser pulled it off and also helped me bridge the musical differences.

Life was good and my social scene continued to burgeon. I may have given up my flat on Bayne Street – Paul Chisholm and I were too much like Oscar and Felix, The Odd Couple, though it was fun while it lasted – but Club De Crozier, the apartment of my close pal John, had opened around the corner on Cowane Street. Goodness knows what the neighbours must have made of it all.

John and our pal Ronnie Hutton arrived home one night with a couple of stunners, but there was a problem. Ronnie appeared to have forgotten all about his long term relationship with his girlfriend, Ellen. After a while, they all disappeared to two bedrooms as I sat in the lounge strumming on my guitar.

There was a hammering on the front door. John jokingly stage whispered along the hall: "Bet you that's Ellen." Lo and behold, he was bang on the money. "Let me in," she hollered. "I know he's in there."

Ronnie jumped out of bed to hide and pleaded with me to kick off my shoes and dive under the covers with his new found squeeze. The door opened and Ellen entered in a fury. "Where is he?" she demanded, looking under beds and behind curtains. We pleaded ignorance and innocence and the fury ebbed from her face, the realisation slowly dawning that perhaps her man hadn't been cheating after all.

However, John took it a step too far: "I can't believe you, Ellen. You've looked everywhere in this house. About the only place you haven't searched is that cupboard over there."

He pointed to the corner and she made for it immediately, the door half hidden by a pile of clothes. She threw the door open and there was her errant man, cowering naked. Never one to take prisoners, she worked her hand into a fist, a sovereign ring glistening from the middle finger, and smacked him so hard in the face it split his nose wide open.

It wasn't the only violence we witnessed. Following the success of the Pigbag gig at Stirling University, New Order were also booked to play the Pathfoot building, but it was volatile. As something of a Dalai

Lama when it came to dust ups, I stayed up the back and watched all the scrapping down the front, next to the stage. New Order were quoted in NME the following week: "We'll take the high road and we'll take the low road, but we'll never be back in Scotland after that gig." Thankfully, it was a promise they didn't keep.

Live music continued to enchant me and another memorable gig was Eartha Kitt at Fire Island on Edinburgh's Princes Street. I was a huge fan of the new sound of high energy and she was its ultimate priestess. I wore the same white leather suit I'd had bespoke tailored for my 18th birthday but didn't realise Fire Island was a gay club. Eartha Kitt was fabulous, but I found the atmosphere too predatory. I stood all night with my back literally against the wall, never quite managing to relax.

In addition to music, we all continued to be inspired by fashion. Kenny Ritchie was an older pal who had access to the most highly sought after corner of McQ's, a VIP section without ropes, next to the bar. He told me he first set eyes on me when I walked into the place wearing a powder blue suit with a girl on my arm. Everyone turned and asked: "Who the fuck is he?" Who indeed?

Call it arrogance or maybe, with retrospect, a cloak to hide our own insecurities, but trips to London every couple of months to keep abreast of the latest fashions became essential for Sean, Fraser and me.

We bought outlandish shoes from R Soles on the King's Road. Oh, how they laughed when I turned up with a pair of steel-toed cowboy boots – a decade before George Michael wore them in the video for 'Faith'. We'd shop in Johnson's, also on the King's Road, for La Rocka suits, long jackets and shirts, styled from the fifties. We also loved Rude Boy suits from closer to home, the Lesley G boutique behind Central Station in Glasgow city centre.

Bowie released 'Let's Dance' and I aped his style from the video by forking out for a green bolero jacket with matching baggy, pleated trousers. Keen to show off, I wore it to McQ's for the first time that Thursday night – and six other guys in the club were turned out in the exact same suit.

Admittedly, my style wasn't to everyone's taste. I bought a pair of banana yellow loafers from Lesley G then swung them in a bag around to Boots' Corner, the famous Glasgow meeting point for young lovers. I was to rendezvous with my latest squeeze, a girl named Donna from Clydebank.

She asked if we could head in her car to see her grandmother, who lived in the rough and tumble housing scheme of Drumchapel. We hadn't been in her home 10 minutes before a neighbour knocked at the door and explained Donna's car had been broken into and its back window smashed.

Clearly the Lesley G bag, which I'd stupidly left in full view, was the attraction. I raced downstairs and saw granules of shattered glass all over the back seat – along with my banana yellow loafers. The thieves had looked inside the bag and decided the shoes weren't worth stealing after all.

For all the fun and frivolity, my attitude to music was becoming increasingly serious. Weekly visits to The Warehouse in Glasgow became pilgrimages to listen at the feet of a DJ named Segun, who hosted live broadcasts for Radio Clyde.

He set stunning standards. He cracked the mould for the Scottish club scene at the time because he was sourcing and breaking records – something I would strive to achieve, but not until later – and he was mixing vinyl, rather than just playing it.

More than that, he was blending records together to create a sound so smooth you could barely hear the join. An example of his craft from the time would be to take a number such as the 12 inch version of 'Use It Up And Wear It Out' by Odyssey, which came in at 126 beats per minute, and segue it seamlessly with 'In The Forest' by Baby 'O, which played at 128 bpm. On a Technics set-up you could adjust the bpm, which would allow Baby 'O to run effortlessly into Odyssey, if you were a good DJ.

However, it needed the truly exceptional to understand the tonality of the music they were mixing, the compatibility between bass and treble that would allow two distinct pieces of music to merge as one.

Think of a football striker who has to work hard to score goals against one born with the knack of being in the right place in the penalty box at the right time. Segun was Premier League class – and I wanted to be on that level.

In the years following, I grafted to hone my natural but undeveloped gift. I noted the beats per minute of every record in my collection, using a clicker and a stopwatch. After a minute I knew the bpm and I would write it on the upper right hand side of the record sleeve.

I infuriated fellow DJs – and my audience – by covering the labels of my records with white stickers. Why should I spend eight quid on an import I'd worked hard to source, only to give it away to a rival DJ or club goer when he leaned into the booth to read the label after I had set it to one side? Protective? Yes. Selfish? No way.

A sobering experience early in my career taught me a valuable lesson in humility and also reminded me I still had a road to travel if I was to ever be considered anything other than a competent nightclub DJ.

As much as I had enjoyed The Tamdhu and was finding my feet at McQ's, I was envious of the Night Magic club in Dunfermline, which attracted sell out crowds every weekend. I wanted a slice and approached them for a job, only to be referred onto a London-based agency called Bacchus, who contracted DJs for nightclubs worldwide.

They must have admired my bottle, or youthful naivety, because they called me to their studios in London to audition. I embarrassed myself by playing records when it became very clear they were headhunters who only employed serious, mixing DJs. I was garbage, rubbish, a fact all but acknowledged when my interviewer bluntly told me: "Thanks for coming kid, but you're miles off it."

As if to highlight the point he reached into his collection and picked up two copies of 'Maneater' by Hall and Oates and started to quarter cut them. In layman's terms, he let the first record go for four beats and then dropped the second one in, so it sounded like an echo. It blew me away.

He followed it up with a story about a gig he had played a few months previously at the top of Toronto's CN Tower. He had a record in his collection, 'Dancer' by Gino Soccio, which is widely recognised as the first trance record ever recorded – 20 years before trance was even recognised as a musical genre.

He was happy in the vibe the record was creating in the room when he was approached at the DJ booth. "My name is Gino Soccio," the guy told him. "You're playing my record two beats a minute too slow." This was the big boys' league. At that stage, I was Sunday amateur.

At the age of 22, I reached a crossroads in my life. In 1982 I was employed as a wages clerk by the NHS and, by cruel irony, the office in which I was based was at Bellsdyke, where I first ended up in psychiatric care in 1993. It was a good job, steady and unexciting, and I did quite well, even winning a couple of promotions.

However, it was only ever 'just a job'. I guess I was trying to fulfil my father's ambition for his son to find steady, stable employment. I drove to work every day with my colleague, Chrissie Meikle, through huge open gates behind which 800 people were being treated in psychiatric wards.

I didn't get it. Why didn't they just walk out, down the wide open drive? In later years I would come to realise the blunt truth: they had become institutionalised. They had a farm with animals, a snooker hall, pitch and putt and bowling green, as well as a laundry and joinery workshop, three meals a day and a comfortable bed. What more could you need?

I didn't dwell too much on it because I was on the move again after 12 months, to finance company AVCO. I very quickly became an assistant manager, overseeing loans and mortgages. The company sponsored West Ham and I even played at Upton Park, Scotland against England, although I could barely kick a ball.

A career path stretched out in front of me, but was it a highway to hell? In the spring of 1984 the regional manager approached one Thursday afternoon and explained a new branch of the company was opening in Newcastle. He paid me a series of glowing compliments and then asked me outright: "Do you fancy becoming its manager?"

The perks included a decent salary, two per cent mortgage, credit card expense account and a company car. The only things he failed to throw in were a wife, puppy dog and 2.2 kids. I asked for the weekend to think about it and spoke to my beloved granny, Morag. Her sage advice? "Do what's in your heart, son." Those were the wisest words I'd ever heard. I walked into the manager's office on the Monday morning and resigned on the spot.

By the end of the week I was standing in the arrivals hall at Ibiza Airport, a big box of records at my feet. Life was about to get even more interesting.

6

Club Tropicana, drinks are free. Not at all. They cost a fortune, which is why Javier Anadon and I usually headed over to Pikes Hotel, where they filmed the Wham video, at 7am for nothing stronger than a cup of coffee.

Occasionally, our budgets would stretch to a couple of ensaimadas, Ibicencan pastries as light as they are tasty. Delicately dipped into a steaming hot cup of java, they yielded beautifully, their soft brown skin matching the colour of my own fast suntanning features. As daylight slowly rose and warmed the pool in which George Michael had once cavorted, I didn't have a care in the world.

If not exactly a home-from-home then Ibiza was certainly familiar to a group of us from Stirling in the early eighties. Before I pitched up for good in the spring of 1984 with my box of records, my career in the financial services industry lying in the grubber, I had visited six times on holiday in the previous four years.

The scene in Ibiza didn't really explode until the summer of 1987 and it gradually became, sadly, what it is today – Blackpool on ecstasy. We were in on the more unspoilt, relaxed ground floor at that time and it was thanks to Fraser Hotchkiss or, more specifically, his relationship with Caroline Wilson and her partner, Javier.

Caroline and Fraser were old pals – he called her Wilson, a term of endearment that stuck. In the early seventies, Wilson worked as a young woman in Viewforth, the headquarters of Stirling Council, in a clerical position that left her unfulfilled as she sought wider horizons.

She worked alongside my Auntie Jeannie – not a blood relative but, in the good old Scottish tradition, so tight with my mum and dad she was addressed as such. Jeannie advised Wilson to go and see her daughter, my cousin Irene, who worked in Benidorm with her boyfriend Roddy, a bouncer in the Istanbul nightclub.

Wilson was a regular at their home for dinner – apparently, Irene had a ready supply of HP sauce – and took to Spanish life like a duck to water. Admittedly, her induction to a new country was helped when she met Javier, a handsome Basque, in the Manilla Club, where he was a waiter.

Wilson and Javier moved to Ibiza in 1978 and have made a spectacular success of their lives and careers. More of that later, but in the early eighties they were happily hosting the Stirling tourists several times a year.

In 1981, nine of us travelled to Ibiza and stayed at the Ali Bey Apartments in San Antonio. My Magaluf experience apart, this was the first time I'd holidayed on the Med and we created memories and mayhem in equal, joyous measure. We partied hard, particularly at Es Paradis and the Star Club, San Antonio's main venues.

The principal club was Ku, now Privilege, between the old town and San Antonio, but this was in the days before mass tourism and superstar DJs. Es Paradis, especially, won our affections and still ranks as the most beautiful club I've ever visited. It was built around an amphitheatre, with beanbags in the middle of the floor. At the end of the night they were removed to reveal a swimming pool floor and it would slowly fill from fountains around the side as the DJ played out to John Miles' 'Music Was My First Love'. It's a tradition that continues today.

The first night we attended was a toga theme party and we borrowed the bedsheets in the apartment to pay homage to Julius Caesar. Sean Gentleman was gassed and, most probably, stoned as well. I'll always love Sean, but he was a drama queen and ran to us at one point and declared in some panic he'd been jabbed by a heroin needle. He'd actually fallen in a rose bush.

We experimented with drugs in Ibiza, low level stuff, although not without consequences. I was given a crumb of cannabis resin – two joints worth, max – and decided to take it home to Scotland. However, fearful of being caught at customs I sewed it into the back patch of my jeans, all the time scenarios of Billy Hayes in 'Midnight Express' running through my active imagination.

I walked through the scanner at the airport and the buzzer went off as sweat bubbles the size of teardrops formed on my forehead. I was about to throw myself on the full mercy of Spanish justice when Franny, who had been strolling behind me, was given a pull instead.

He had bought two toy guns for his nephews and put them in his hand luggage and they'd flashed red on the X-ray scanner. I have never been so relieved in my life to see my pal almost lifted.

On another occasion, Javier was working in a bar at the bottom of San Antonio's west end called Nito's (he had a lucrative sideline selling cigarettes at a mark up). He called and told me he'd laid a line of cocaine on the bar for me alone.

I quickly rolled a 200 peseta note, failing miserably to be discreet in a bar packed with 300 revellers. I snorted it in one go. Salt! It nearly blew my nose off. Javier collapsed in a fit of laughter and called me Tony Montana after Al Pacino's character from 'Scarface', a nickname that has stuck.

Wilson and Javier were, of course, our 'in'. We hung out during the day with Wilson, who was shifting at The Highlander Bar, selling the ubiquitous all day breakfasts, and Javier always made sure we were covered for drinks at night at Nito's.

We also spent time at a bar called Flash, not least because we grew exceptionally fond of a PR/barman there called Spike. He was larger than life, great fun and – like most of the workers on the island – always with an eye for an earner when the boss's back was turned.

In his case it was dead easy. He bought a box of the bar's t-shirts and cut the sleeves off them, following the trend at the time favoured by bands such as Wham. He knocked them out for a few hundred pesetas more than they were selling behind the bar and made a fortune, all for two minutes' work with a pair of scissors.

At that stage in their lives, Wilson and Javier barely had two pennies to rub together but their warmth and generosity were overwhelming. Javier was a genuine people person, Wilson too, and they really looked after us, although we always tried to give as good as we got.

We travelled to Ibiza laden with the usual Scottish dietary supplements – Irn Bru, square sausage and Ayrshire bacon among them – and we always packed extra toiletries which, for some reason, were expensive on the island. One Easter I pitched up with Fraser and his wife Kate and Wilson and Javier put us up, even though they'd just had their first child, Christian.

On a particularly riotous evening we got wasted on hierbas, an Ibicencan liqueur, and Javier staggered off to start work in Nito's at 11pm. For the first and, probably, the last time in his life they sent him home for being incapable.

There was a cosmopolitan feel to Ibiza in the early eighties and Wilson and Javier taught me a valuable life lesson, that you didn't need a lot of money to have class. The education was unconscious but stuck as a philosophy along the lines of 'the poor can't afford to buy cheap'.

They weren't exactly on the breadline nor, at that stage, were they living high on the hog. It was the simple things. When we sat down to eat at their apartment there was always a nice ham or sausage on the table, maybe a slice of exceptional cheese.

There were a hundred ice cream parlours in San Antonio, but when we went out for dessert they always took us to Linares, a cafe that wasn't the cheapest but had the reputation for using the best ingredients.

They expanded my horizons to infinity on an island that's only 27 miles wide, a distance I travelled several times a week from my home in Bannockburn for a night out in Glasgow. A love of quality dining remains with me today.

The hectic pace of life in Scotland was not mirrored on the White Isle and slowly, as we grew more familiar with Ibiza, it began to reveal more of its charms. We had some wild nights and lazy days, hanging with Wilson or at the fabled Cafe del Mar (they did the best club sandwich in the world) with Italians, Germans, Spaniards and Swedes.

The vibe was cool, laid back. Even today you can put me in a room anywhere, play '(Don't Go Back to) Rockville' by REM and I'm there, sitting outside in the sun at Cafe del Mar with my headphones against my ears.

Musically, I had found heaven. Even in the early days, I was drawn to Ibiza by the fact its clubs refused to be stereotyped. In the UK, for example, only gay clubs played high energy and if you wanted to hear new romantic music, you had to visit a new romantic club. In Ibiza, everything went.

The leading club Ku, for instance, attracted performers as diverse as James Brown, Spandau Ballet and Imagination. It was still about the music at this stage and not the DJs, who remained relatively unknown although guys such as Carlos at Es Paradis, Pippi at Pacha and Alfredo at Amnesia were beginning to attract an audience.

They mashed it up in the sun until it reached a boiling point that whetted my appetite to discover even more. Alfredo was the Godfather of the music scene at the time and I would later dedicate my dance version of Rozalla's 'Everybody's Free (To Feel Good)' to him.

A journalist from Argentina, he arrived in Ibiza in the mid-seventies and didn't bother going home. Alfredo played everything from reggae to rock and soul, even experimenting with classical music. There was no snobbery at all – he turned frequently to pop music and I even recall him, in later years, playing Jimmy Nail's 'Ain't No Doubt'.

He bravely dropped in classics that, in usual circumstances, no DJ would have dared meddle with, including Marvin Gaye's 'What's Going On?' – performed by Cyndi Lauper.

He broke the rules, left, right and centre, mixing house music from Chicago with German techno. At the end of the night, with dawn breaking over Amnesia (it was still open air – all nightclubs in Ibiza were forced to put on roofs in the nineties to restrict the noise) he frequently finished his set with The Beloved's 'The Sun Rising'.

It was inspirational, utterly mind-blowing, especially on ecstasy. On other occasions, he thought nothing of bowing out to Marilyn Monroe. He went out on a limb, refusing to conform. He played to rules established by no-one but himself. Every single DJ who saw him in action bowed to his pioneering presence.

To some extent, the Balearic sound also owed its roots to the absence of record stores on the island. Alfredo once recalled taking in a set by a DJ on the island, Danny Tenaglia, that was put together with only two CDs. It was something of a challenge when most clubs were open for at least seven hours a night, between 10pm-5am.

Back home, clubs generally closed a few hours earlier and vinyl was freely available, so it wasn't an issue for a DJ to have boxes and boxes of records, most of which didn't extend much beyond four minutes.

In Ibiza, DJs needed records twice that length to cover the lack of inventory and the pressure of so much time, which is why the likes of Dire Straits and Pink Floyd were particularly popular. Necessity has long been the mother of invention, so when vinyl didn't reach the required length, it was mixed and mashed with other records to take it to eight or nine minutes long.

I quickly realised it was a market with demand and I soon began to pack my bags for Ibiza with cold Irn Bru for Wilson and hot vinyl for a new contact, Kiki. He was the owner of Kelson Records in the square in San Antonio and I was turning such a profit it soon paid for my holiday.

I also sold some vinyl to Carlos in Es Paradis, but I was taking as much as I was giving and my ears were wide open to everything being played in the clubs and bars, while I picked hungrily through the few records on sale in Kelson. I was a scavenger. They may not have had much, but they might still have had something new to me.

For example, I bought an electro disco version of Lou Reed's 'Walk on the Wild Side'. It's a record I would struggle to have played in Stirling because it was too slow, but the version I bought sounded credible for my audience.

As a result, when I pitched up for the start of the tourist season in 1984 I wasn't wet behind the ears about the ways of the island, although I still had burning issues to address. Where would I stay? Where would I work? How could I translate my love of music into a job that paid?

I had a couple of hundred quid in pesetas tucked inside my wallet, but it was for the basics and emergency back up only. That AVCO credit card and expense account may have sounded appealing to others but, I was pleased to say, I didn't give the rejection of that job in Newcastle a second thought. I knew I'd made the right decision.

The first stop, naturally, was Wilson and Javier's place. It was a house near the square in San Antonio, directly across the street from what would later become the renowned pre-club venue The Milk Bar, run by iconic DJ Nicky Holloway.

Javier's hard work over the previous six years was paying off and his stock was rising as he'd just opened his first bar, a pirate-themed venture called Bucanero. It was a risk. The bulk of business in San Antonio at the time was in the west end, but his place was a short distance away, in the less popular bay area.

He was already sorted for a sounds man and bar staff, but they were kind to me, allowing me to stay with them for the first few weeks before

I found my own apartment, even though they had a toddler running around and a new business to build.

Call it serendipity, but happy coincidence would take me on a walk along from Bucanero one evening where I stumbled on a place, Maxim's, opening for the season. It was a small venture, with a wooden bar inside and a white painted terrace outside in front of a busy street.

Nothing much to look at, maybe, and the tale I was told didn't fill me with much confidence. It had been opened only 12 months earlier by two Ibicencan waiters, who had previously worked the local hotels, but it hadn't been profitable, unfortunately.

It was now being run by another local, Tony. He had the most amazing grin, stunning white teeth framing a benign, suntanned face of kindly features. In an attitude I recognised from Wilson and Javier's approach to life, he also carried himself with an understated sophistication.

Simple and uncluttered, he dressed in light blue jeans and an immaculate Lacoste polo shirt. He was one of the most stylish men I'd ever met and his nickname summed him up perfectly – 'Sonrisas', which roughly translates as 'the boy with the beautiful smile'. I also quickly learned the reason he grinned so widely was because he was frequently and elegantly wasted, with cocaine his recreational drug of choice.

Nothing ventured, nothing gained. We chatted, I asked for a job, he took a shine to me and offered me a position. My record collection may have had something to do with it.

That box of records I'd packed from Stirling included some memorable vinyl. It was 1984, the year of 'Purple Rain' and 'Pride (In The Name Of Love)', Frankie Goes to Hollywood and Everything But The Girl, Billy Ocean (it was 'European Queen' then, not 'Caribbean Queen'), Matt Bianco and Lloyd Cole and the Commotions.

It was an eclectic mix from an amazing year of music. I had sold a few bits and pieces of vinyl at Kelson on arrival, but kept the majority of stock for the opportunity I hoped would come to play it on my own.

It went down a storm. In between serving drinks, I would play my music, many of the records 12 inch versions, and Tony quickly put the word out among the beautiful young Spanish kids who were residents in Ibiza that Maxim's, with this new guy playing fine sounds, was the place to be.

They clearly agreed and every night up to 20 stunning girls and cool young guys would start the night at our bar and even Carlos popped his head around the door several times a week en route to his set at Es Paradis.

Other tourists followed and pretty soon we had won our reputation. We worked it passionately. Occasionally, I would turn the music off all together and lead the crowd in a sing-song on my guitar.

It was rocking so hard we quickly added Spike to the staff from his gig at the Flash bar, even though it meant dropping his crafty t-shirt trade. We took the equivalent of a tenner a head from punters and hosted beach parties during the day, providing food, cigarettes and drink with a soundtrack from a ghetto blaster and my guitar.

Naively, we were having so much fun we ran the beach parties at break even, but I soon became wise to many of the tricks of the trade. Some bars, but not ours, would empty their slops into a bucket at the end of the night and freshen them up the following morning with ice, lemonade and chunks of fresh fruit. Most tourists were happy to accept the offer of a free glass of 'sangria' of questionable quality as they strolled past before being encouraged to step inside for a real drink.

Cigarettes, as Javier would testify, were bought in bulk from supermarkets and other suppliers and sold at decent mark ups in pubs and clubs to unknowing drinkers.

If you looked closely at most bar gantries, one side displayed drinks by prominent companies such as Smirnoff, Bacardi and Larios. They were sold earlier in the evening, when full flight had yet to be taken from sobriety.

As the night progressed and customers became more and more drunk, bar staff veered over to the other side of the bar, where the labels were similar but the drinks were by Smornoff, Bacaly and Lirios – copycat brands and pale imitations.

At Maxim's, if customers had spent handsomely over the course of the evening they were rewarded with a 'chupito', a complimentary shot of peach schnapps as a thank you from the bar. We drank with the customers, but poured our chupitos from a different bottle, filled with water. I couldn't handle drink at the best of times. Downing a couple of dozen shots over the course of a single night? It would have been a recipe for disaster.

Bucanero was also thriving but, as the season progressed, Javier hired a familiar face to keep an eye on the competition along the street. I was sitting in the square in San Antonio one afternoon, minding my own business, when a vision in a powder blue suit and trilby hat came out of nowhere. "How are you Scoobs?" Sean Gentleman enquired, fresh off the plane from Scotland and looking for a summer of adventure.

I agreed to put him up in the flat I was sharing at the top of the town with a female travel agent from Paisley – for once, it was platonic – and we arranged to rendezvous at Maxim's later that night. We kicked it on, and on, and on, until we tumbled out of Es Paradis at 5am and headed straight for the beach at Cala Salada.

Still in his swimming shorts, Sean promptly fell fast asleep on the sand and we left him to it as we went about our business for the day. We returned at 1pm when he woke up, scarlet from head to toe. "What am I going to do?" he pleaded, concerned about the effects of the sun.

We advised him simply to lie on his stomach so the tan would radiate all over. He did – and woke up again at 4pm in agony. We ate an hour later at a local fish restaurant, where the owner took such pity on him he laid him out on a slab usually reserved for his stock and hosed him down with ice cold water, much to the bemusement of passing tourists and locals.

It took Sean a few days to recover from the sunstroke and, in the meantime, he made himself at home in the apartment I was renting even though he didn't have a key. Lynn, the travel agent, and I were out one morning when he awoke late and decided to buy a drink from the supermarket around the corner.

He couldn't open the door, so climbed down the balcony on the outside of the building and made off to load up on his supplies. Unfortunately, on the return trip back up the drainpipe he was collared by the police, who had him marked as a housebreaker.

He had no Spanish and they had no English, but Sean knew I'd be at my usual haunt, where I could explain it had all been a huge misunderstanding. "Cafe del Mar, Cafe del Mar," he frantically told the police, who put him in the back of their patrol car and headed for the seafront.

All the foreign workers who plied their trade in the local bars hung out down there in the daytime, playing backgammon or, bizarrely that year, knitting in leather. In the days before free movement of workers within the European Union we all officially needed 'permissions' to work, a form of permit, but few bothered.

Sean emerged from the back of the police car outside Cafe del Mar shouting: "Scooby! Scooby!" As the police stood behind him the crowd scattered in 10 seconds flat, panicking in case the officers started asking questions about their visa status. It was quite a way for Sean to make an entrance with those who would soon become his fellow workers.

Ibiza was full of many interesting characters that summer including, it must be admitted, a team of striking miners from the UK on the blag. Clearly, money was tight at home but they had credit card fraud down to a fine art and would rack up huge bills in the fashion stores of Ibiza old town, before selling the stock on.

I couldn't resist, buying some of the dodgy gear they'd sourced from one high class store in particular. Jogging material with patches? Very cool and so trendy that summer. I was also seeing a girl from London, Jackie. She was really hot, with beautiful blue eyes and was pally with another girl, Lisa. They had come out to Ibiza for the summer and lived on their credit cards alone. Theirs was not an unfamiliar story. I had to agree, sunshine every day beat the dull uniformity of life in the UK.

We also hung out in places such as the Project Bar, a stylish haunt in the west end, run by Martin, Kenny and Jamie, three guys from Glasgow who worked in the city's Henry Afrika's nightclub. The Project Bar was owned by London DJ Trevor Fung, with whom I had a good rapport, and his partner Ian St Paul.

On a legendary evening in 1987 Trevor took Danny Rampling, Johnny Walker, Nicky Holloway and Paul Oakenfold to Amnesia and, with chemical assistance, they saw the light. I had a cameo role too as they dropped into the Star Club, where I had a residency, earlier in the evening.

The following year they were responsible for starting the acid house craze in London at clubs such as Shoom, Spectrum, Trip and Land of Oz. (As an aside, promoter Tony Cochrane organised an all nighter at Arbroath in 1990 with Trevor top of the bill. I went along to catch up with him only to find it wasn't my pal from Ibiza headlining at all but a kid who, admittedly, was his spitting image. No-one, including Tony, knew any better – it was Rudy, Trevor's little brother.)

Maxim's continued to go from strength to strength and I didn't even miss home as every other week a plane seemed to unload another group of pals from Stirling for a fortnight's holiday. I learned a valuable lesson early on, however.

New friendships were formed in the party atmosphere of Maxim's and phone numbers were always swapped, particularly with pretty girls. It was one thing chatting them up in the sunshine of Ibiza, but quite another to visit them in drab local pubs in towns such as Irvine in the dead of winter.

The novelty quickly wore off. Numbers continued to be exchanged, but in subsequent years the friendships remained rooted only in the time and place of Maxim's and contact was never re-established on my return to Scotland.

At Maxim's I worked seven days a week for the 20 weeks of the summer season and it fell to me, Tony and Spike to ensure every night was a Saturday night because kids didn't come on holiday to follow the same familiar patterns of back home.

We caned it every single day and night of the week. We opened at 7pm and closed the doors eight hours later. After that we'd party at Es Paradis or, on a good night, maybe venture a little further to Ku. We'd go for something to eat around 5am before dropping into bed until lunchtime.

We'd rise at a leisurely pace, have a coffee and ensaimada, then head over to Cafe del Mar for one of those amazing club sandwiches. We'd swap idle chit chat and gossip and relax in the ambient Balearic vibe created by music from the likes of Van Gelis, Clannad and Jean Michel Jarre.

Memories were created to last a lifetime. One evening Welsh rock band The Alarm came to play Es Paradis and Kenny, one of the guys from the Project Bar, was roped in as their drummer and I tagged along as his guest. The night ended down on the rocks in front of Cafe del Mar with me, Alarm frontman Mike Peters and his mate, television presenter Gaz Top. We had somehow sourced a couple of guitars and the three of us spent the time belting out the band's greatest hit '68 Guns'.

Slowly, Ibiza was becoming more and more popular as a holiday destination for Brits, but there weren't so many at that time working the bars. I revelled in the melting pot of nationalities, mixing with the

Swedes and Spaniards, Dutch and Danes. It was decadent, but there was also a style to the substance epitomised by the simplicity of the dress sense of Tony, or the local cheese Javier sourced to finish off a fine meal at his home.

Up in the hills there was a hamlet, Can Talaias, that mostly was known only to Spaniards. We'd head there after a night at Es Paradis or Ku and find its centrepiece, a tent in the middle of a field. Under the canvas was cooked the most amazing Ibicencan cuisine – fabulously rich stews, soft lentils, juicy roast chickens, home-made breads, sweet fruits and vegetables.

We sat in communion around the tables and chatted easily among each other, the warmth of the camaraderie at that moment as important a part of our experience as anything that had gone in the 12 hedonistic hours before.

And that, of course, included drugs. I was on cannabis and coke constantly – the latter helping maintain the rhythm of a hectic evening, the former as a mellowing agent on those lazy afternoons outside Cafe del Mar before we prepared to do it all again.

Tony clearly had a solid connection with a supplier for cocaine at the time, with the suggestion it was straight from Colombia and barely cut, its integrity hardly compromised when other lines were packed with bulking agents to help a dealer's profit stretch much further.

These were still virgin days for my drug taking and, truly, I believed I was taking sulph the first few times it was offered. Actually, I never asked for a line. In the midst of a frantic evening, Tony would simply tell me to go to the cupboard, a behind-the-scenes hidey hole where we kept our stock, and I'd find a line already laid out for me on a plate.

We had a relaxed and informal relationship in terms of payment. Tony was always very fair with me. I was on a cut of the bar's takings, around 10 per cent, and never wanted for anything. He may have taken a few pesetas off for the product I was consuming at the end of every month, but he was hardly profiteering.

The most difficult challenge facing hash smokers was sourcing decent skins. I was part of the mailing list for a London company called Rush Release, who sent records they hoped to break to prominent DJs and record stores. Kelson was also on its list. Paul Oakenfold worked for Rush Release. Every time an order was dispatched to Kelson, a stack of Rizlas was also included. It got to the stage we were as excited about the skins arriving as the next white label.

Bluntly speaking, I never felt in danger of dropping into the deep end of a drugs habit at that stage of my life, despite my daily use. It was all part of a crazy schedule that included partying, working, eating and the occasional bout of sleep. There was also plenty of relaxation and down time – I lost count of the people to whom I taught backgammon at Cafe del Mar – and at the age of 22 I felt I'd found the recipe for a contented life in the sun.

These were exciting times, adrenaline-fuelled, and the drugs came with a slice of danger that only added to the rush of being alive to such an awesome vibe. I was little more than 18 months into a drugs habit that would eventually consume 20 years of my life, but there was no time for self-reflection in those innocent beginnings.

We were sun-tanned and tranquilo and didn't have a care in the world. It wouldn't last forever because nothing ever does, but as I prepared to head back to Stirling for a new episode in my life at the end of that summer season, I was already preparing a return to an island I was slowly beginning to call home.

7

The 20 bottles of after shave kindly gifted by friends for my 21st birthday paled into insignificance when George Knowles offered his son a new nightclub for reaching the same, happy milestone. Talk about the sweet smell of success.

George was a retail tycoon who had earned his fortune from the Sterling furniture store in Tillicoultry, building an empire known to everyone in Scotland, not least because BBC sports commentator Dougie Donnelly never seemed to be off the telly advertising it.

George kept his stock of carpets in a draughty big warehouse tucked off Baker Street, slap bang in the middle of Stirling town centre. It went from storing shag pile to hosting a pile of… well, you get the picture, all in the space of six months.

The gig of running the whole kit and kaboodle came to me second hand, when I was still in Ibiza, after my pal Kenny Ritchie knocked back the offer to become manager because he had a well paid job in the (legitimate) chemical industry, as well as DJ commitments across the central belt of Scotland. Maybe he just didn't like the name George junior first proposed for the venture, Nosey Parker's. Who could have blamed him?

Approached about the new job in a telephone call, I returned home from the White Isle at the end of the summer season in October 1984 and went straight into a meeting with the Georges, senior and junior. I was immediately impressed with the range of their ambition for the enterprise, not to mention the salary and perks they were wafting in my direction – £12,000-a-year, an MG Metro Turbo and a two-bedroom flat in Stirling city centre.

But Nosey Parker's? It stank. As the warehouse was perched on top of the granite on which Stirling is built, I suggested calling it 'Rocks'. Knowles United were a formidable team. "Let's call it 'Rainbow'," they suggested. After much to-ing and fro-ing we settled on an uneasy compromise, 'Rocks Rainbow'.

The new name decided, we called in Danish flooring manufacturers Ege to design the bespoke carpeting that would feature the branding of the new nightclub throughout the venue. A few weeks later it came back, but there had been a mistake in the production process. The name 'Rocks Rainbow' had been turned on its head to 'Rainbow Rocks'. We let the error ride.

Stirling was crying out for a change. Le Clique was on its last legs and The Factory (now Fubar) had just opened, but the market could sustain another major player although the arrival of Rainbow Rocks, sadly, pushed McQ's to the fringes of the city's club culture, when once it had been its beating heart.

Hands up, I didn't exactly help my former employer when I took an ad in the Stirling Observer for Rainbow Rocks, ahead of its official opening on February 14 1985, declaring Fraser Hotchkiss as our new DJ.

There was one slight problem. Fraser didn't know a thing about it – and neither did McQ's owner, John McQue. Fraser's arrival was eased with the award of a hefty pay rise to commit to the new venture and, unsurprisingly, he jumped at the challenge. John McQue has never quite forgiven me yet.

The six month deadline to turn a warehouse into a nightclub was tight, but George senior also owned a building company and they cracked on, although we weren't exactly constructing the pyramids. The exposed brick of the warehouse interior was painted in simple primary colours but the owners wisely didn't scrape on the big ticket items – sound and lighting.

In the meantime, I got on with pulling together a team to do the new place justice, as well as a marketing plan and, crucially, outlined a strategy for musical and commercial success based on my experiences the previous months in Ibiza. Needless to say, as the key holder, several girls were also given tours of the property at a lot of strange hours during its reconstruction and we almost always lingered longest in the basement cellar, raising some heat in what was effectively still a cold builders' yard.

Management may have been new to me, but I had been bolstered by my experience in the Balearics and I also had some cracking records I wanted to share with a Scottish audience and which hadn't yet been broken in the country.

They included floor fillers such as Julio De Piscopo's 'Stop Bajon' and Sandy Marton's 'People From Ibiza'. My pal Colin Barr claims he brought 'Stop Bajon' to Scotland but he wasn't even in Ibiza that summer. It was me who returned home with eight copies in my suitcase, spreading the word on a record that would soon become a dance floor sensation.

I had a deep yearning to re-create the Balearic vibe in an admittedly unfamiliar setting and also to make Rainbow Rocks an event destination. The music alone would keep us going three nights a week, but we were a five night a week enterprise and that meant opening our doors to new ideas – gay nights, PR appearances from bands and personalities, including page three pin-ups, as well as band nights and stage hypnotists.

We had a capacity of 800 and on several occasions we squeezed in almost half as many paying punters again. We attracted an audience from across Scotland, including Old Firm football stars such as Mo Johnston and Ally McCoist. We became a cool, go to venue and soon we were taking in £35,000-a-week. It's a sum that Dusk, into which Rainbow Rocks transformed more than two decades later, must nowadays dream.

We cranked up the pre-publicity for the grand opening by advertising heavily, particularly in the local press. Management at the Stirling Observer raised eyebrows when we asked for our display ads to appear upside down, but I argued it made them more eye-catching. We printed car stickers, rainbow designs emblazoned with the word 'Discotec', and the buzz on the street began to build.

That capacity of 800 was stretched to 1,100 for the opening night, a Thursday – and I handed out every invite personally. On the surface I was working for fine employers and, at the age of just 23, I was elbowing James Cagney to one side for his position at the top of the world, ma.

The Knowles' knew business, obviously, but deferred the decision making on the nuts and bolts of running a club to those of us who understood it best. Interviews for jobs behind the bar became auditions – Gary Neill passed first time with that top hat ensemble, followed by Steven Croal, Tam Pryde, Rose McGowan, Gordon Crosbie, Vinny Doyle, Loraine Elder, Ann Haffey and Cha McPake.

The Knowles' insisted on employing a little Maltese fellow named Paco, who has since gone on to become a successful restaurateur with several highly rated places in Perth and Spain. Paco became my flatmate in the company apartment and also one of my closest pals, not least because I admired his ambition, enthusiasm and entrepreneurial zeal.

He arrived in Stirling with nothing, at the Beanstalk to be exact, on the back of a 'you must look me up if you're in Scotland' invite from a local policeman named Chopper when he was on holiday in the Med. Paco quickly found a home from home in Scotland and became the bar manager at Rainbow Rocks on the back of a willingness to graft, his exuberance, people skills and utter trustworthiness.

I wasn't naive. As much as I believed in the character of the people I had chosen to front our operation, there was no room for complacency when so much money was pouring through the tills every night. I had earlier decided the staff uniform would be blue and white dungarees, designed by Glasgow tailor Andy Dunn and emblazoned on the back with the Rainbow Rocks logo. Andy was under strict instructions. The dungarees must have no pockets. Temptation resisted is the true test of man – and woman.

The morning after our opening, the Knowles' accountant Gordon Mearns dropped a bombshell. The till was £800 light. Pockets or no pockets, it appeared someone had made off with a small fortune.

Unbelieving, I frantically scanned what seemed to be a mile long ticker tape of receipts from the tills. Got it! As a hair stylist, Steven Croal has long been a whizz with scissors but his usually nimble fingers had managed an £800 over ring on a round of drinks that should only have cost £8. Talk about first night nerves.

Actually, the opening night had been relatively stress free, not least because our preparation had been so thorough. It was a 'must have' ticket and confidence was boosted when I looked out an hour before the doors officially opened to see a queue snaking halfway down Baker Street.

Our door staff, under the careful watch of Andy McLean, were professional and on the ball. They looked the part too, in specially commissioned red jackets, again emblazoned with the Rainbow Rocks logo.

Andy had a smashing sense of humour, always a must on the doors. He handed me a copy of 'The Stud' by Jackie Collins in the build up to the opening, clearly expecting me to live the life of its lead male character Tony Blake. It was a caricature of a nightclub manager that wasn't so far off the mark of reality. Sadly, we only kept Andy for a couple of months before he went off for pastures new, with ultimately devastating consequences for yours truly.

In a nod to clubs such as Es Paradis, which refused to be musically stereotyped, we kicked off the new era with Van Halen's classic 'Jump'. It was an anthemic slice of rock and, more importantly, showed our new lighting rig at its very best as a blaze of colours spun, flashed and whizzed across the packed dance floor.

We'd forked out the best part of a grand and invited Steve Strange to officially open the venue. His Visage days were all but in the past, but he was still a cool and contemporary face. He turned up in a sharp suit with trousers that had one leg to the ankle and the other only to the knee.

It must have been the easiest money he ever earned. He mingled happily with the crowd, got drunk and then, at the end of the night, pulled a local hairdresser and they copped off to his pre-booked digs at the Dunblane Hydro hotel.

We didn't request a DJ set from him because, quite frankly, it wasn't needed. Fraser Hotchkiss and Kenny Ritchie were masters of their audience and the floor didn't empty once as they carried the crowd on the opening night euphoria. They played everything from pop to disco but, really, anything went.

One of the most popular records in those early days was another rock classic, 'She Sells Sanctuary' by The Cult. In homage to Ibiza, John Miles was replaced at the end of the night by Scotland's brilliant blues vocalist John Martyn singing 'Over The Rainbow'. It helped bring the crowd down but, behind the scenes, a natural high would remain for weeks.

These were heady times, with friendships made that would last a lifetime. At the end of a busy night the doormen would frequently club together and buy a bottle of spirits from the bar and we'd enjoy the comedown together for an hour or so after the doors officially closed.

We sometimes took it too far – two weekends on the trot I accidentally locked Tam Pryde in the toilets, with the police at my door at 5am to alert me to the alarm going off up the road. It was a toss up between me and Tam over who looked most sheepish when he was finally released to find a more comfortable bed.

We were determined to push boundaries and make Scottish clubland bigger, better and, dare I say, even more equal, although I must acknowledge also the premier drive for profit. The Golden Lion Hotel in Stirling, for example, had long been an informal hangout for the local gay community, small in number, but we wanted to bring it more into the open. Bill Grainger, who ran Fire Island in Edinburgh where I'd previously seen Eartha Kitt in action, agreed to promote a gay club night.

We attracted 300 paying punters on a Wednesday night, a terrific midweek trade, and the atmosphere was electric but, sadly, it would prove ahead of its time. Stirling was still far too conservative – with a large and small letter 'c' – and objections were soon raised by the public and local politicians in those darker ages.

We fought long and hard with the council to continue with the nights, but to no avail. It was an injustice, predominantly old folk poking their noses in where it didn't belong. To add to the absurdity of it all, the mother of one of our senior bar staff was among the councillors who rejected our pleas.

They were social and cultural Luddites. Stirling Council pushed its gay community back into the closet and turned a deaf ear to the subsequent banging on the door, demanding to be released to live the life it deserved.

God only knows, then, what the council would have made of one of our most popular personal appearances in those early days. Certainly, I was oblivious when a bald and overweight, middle aged American man, clad in polyester clothing and wearing tattered old carpet slippers, shuffled into my office one midweek afternoon.

"Are you lost?" I enquired politely, mistaking him for a tourist and ready to tell him Stirling Castle was another half a mile up the road. He gently informed me he'd been booked to appear at the club that evening and was here for his soundcheck. The penny dropped and after an hour a member of staff escorted him to the Golden Lion, where we had a room ready for his overnight stay.

A few hours later he strutted back through the door in size 12 stilettos, wearing a dazzling, gold and turquoise sequinned cocktail dress, outrageous make-up and a blonde, beehive wig with his quiet, reserved demeanour replaced by a sassy string of one liners. He had us eating from his hand.

Harris Glenn Milstead, aka Divine, walked on stage and belted out classics including 'You Think You're A Man' and 'Native Love (Step By Step)'. It was the work of high energy producer Bobby O at his very best, a brilliant sound that would soon be eclipsed by Stock, Aitken and Waterman, who were just beginning to emerge.

I had barely seen or heard a reaction from an audience like it before. It was utterly wild, the entire club went kinky for Divine. The stewards had to link arms to form a barrier and stop the crowd storming the stage in celebration of Queen D. He was a showman of exceptional talent and ability.

We may have banged the drum for sexual and gender equality with one hand, but we took liberties with the other. We were approached by an agent and offered what the tabloids would no doubt have described as a 'bevy of beauties' in the shape of the 'Sunday Sport Page Three Roadshow'.

Page three? My patchy memory of the Sunday Sport is the boobs started on the front page and continued all the way through to the football results on the back. They certainly gave us enough girls to fill a dozen pages, at least. It was cattle market stuff – again, of its time, not a period for society to look back on with particular pride. The girls paraded around the club in their swimwear as lusty local lads tried their best to dive in, most of the time to no avail.

The promoter had put the girls up in one of Stirling's most squalid hotels, The King's Gate at the foot of King Street, and maybe the quality of digs had something to do with the willingness of a couple of the models to accompany Paco and me back to our flat after their gig.

Or maybe it was the quality of our chat. No matter. My girl, it was claimed, was the pin up of a popular Athena poster of the time, in which she was pictured playing the saxophone, nude. I tried like a bear all through that night to orchestrate some passion, to no avail, eventually giving up all together before we fell asleep, listening to the occasional squeals of delight coming from Paco's room next door.

The girls made the coach to head to their next venue the following morning while Paco and I convened with the papers over a coffee in the manager's office back at the club. We opened up The Sun and, lo and behold, there on page three was the girl in all her topless splendour with whom Paco had just shared a night of passion. He strutted around Stirling with his head up like a prized bull for two months afterwards.

The PAs were readily available and generally cost effective, rarely more than £1500 a show. We paid northern soul hero Edwin Starr £500 to perform his classics, including 'War', 'Stop Her On Sight (SOS)', 'H.A.P.P.Y Radio' and 'Contact'. The club was an 800 sellout – and his backing tape blew. There was a deathly silence. Phil Collins and Philip Bailey were at number one at the time with 'Easy Lover' and Edwin lifted the microphone to his lips and nailed it word by word – acapella.

We also struck it lucky in April 1985 after committing, a couple of months earlier, to an appearance from a little known American soul singer. Phyllis Nelson was at number one with 'Move Closer' by the time she hit Stirling – and another capacity crowd gave us one of our best nights.

My old pal Tony Cochrane, who had started to dabble in PAs, even set us up with a new band who were desperate to bounce back from the flop of their first single – Erasure. Founder Vince Clarke, of Depeche Mode and Yazoo fame, understood the power of the personal appearance and wanted the sound of his new band to reverberate beyond London and the home counties.

Ever shrewd, he was keen to make an appearance in Scotland to increase the chances of a boost to his band's sales returns and chart position and Tony steered him in the direction of Rainbow Rocks. Erasure were on it the night they performed, as their subsequent success would prove, although vocalist Andy Bell turned a few heads by arriving on stage in a pair of leather cowboy chaps that left his bare arse exposed.

Perhaps with a nod to the previous ATOM nights at The Tamdhu, we also promoted the Gaga Club on a Thursday night, which gave new and emerging bands and singers the chance to make a breakthrough.

The most notable was eccentric Scots electro funk pioneer Jesse Rae, from the Borders. He had moved to the States as a teenager, working as a runner on Wall Street to fund his musical apprenticeship in New York.

He already had notable success under his kilt belt as the songwriter of Odyssey's worldwide hit 'Inside Out' but came to Rainbow Rocks to promote his single 'Over The Sea', the memorable video of which saw him swinging a six foot claymore from the top of the Brooklyn Bridge.

He turned up for his gig from his rural idyll in a Land Rover that still had two sheep in the back. He simply parked the vehicle around the quieter side of the club and made sure the animals had enough feed to last them the couple of hours he would be inside and onstage. Unfortunately, he tanked. The Rainbow Rocks audience didn't quite get him. In truth, he was too good for the crowd, musically too advanced.

At the risk of sounding arrogant, the decision to book him was me at my best. He was ahead of his time. Jesse Rae, like me, must have occasionally felt like a prophet in his own land. I couldn't feel too bad about it, however, as I had everything I could ever have hoped for at such a tender age. One or two booking mishaps apart, we got everything spot on at Rainbow Rocks, from the music we played, the crowd we attracted and the staff to the attention to detail on the sound and lighting.

It was even in the drinks we served – Schlitz and Red Stripe lager among them, which were relatively unknown in the UK. Few clubs in Scotland could match its Ibiza-inspired imagination – maybe only Henry Afrika's in Glasgow, a result of the three lads they employed and whom I'd come to know from the Project Bar in San Antonio.

I took my management responsibilities seriously – too seriously, many of my friends complained. I started work at 9pm and continued until at least until 3am and my role was to oversee everything. I was fortunate I didn't have to worry about the bar too much as it was in such capable hands with Paco and Andy also had the door and security staff covered.

I made sure we were in vogue musically but everyone in the club wanted a slice of me. Pals moaned I never stopped to talk. Others who didn't know me as well thought I was standoffish, but the truth of the matter was I couldn't give a lot of time to carousing, although I made one exception I never regretted.

It was another night of a capacity crowd and I made the mistake of stopping to look over the dance floor. Suddenly, I felt a tap on my shoulder and a petite girl, a class act with beautiful elfin features, asked me to dance. Jake. She was only 18 and it must have taken her some balls to be so bold.

I had met her once before, she later told me, but I couldn't recall the rendezvous. In fairness, it had been two years previously when Franny and I had been out cycling. Franny's then girlfriend Karen Ogilvie passed us in her car, then pulled over further down the road for a chat. Jake, her cousin, was in the passenger seat.

She clearly still had the memory of this lycra clad lad in her mind as she drew me towards the dancefloor – I was hardly a reluctant conscript – where Madonna was revelling in being touched by her lover as if for the very first time. After a couple of minutes Jake leaned in, whispered a raunchy joke and gave me a theatrical wink. I was instantly smitten.

However, as autumn gave way to winter in 1985 I began to feel uneasy, if not about the direction in which the club was heading, then certainly the pressure to keep delivering high line profits. Sadly, we'd gone from five nights a week to four on the back of the council's small mindedness over our gay nights and the Gaga Club on Thursdays wasn't particularly pulling its weight financially as it was expensive to hire bands and fork out for PA systems.

Rightly or wrongly I had the feeling the Knowles' accountant Gordon Mearns, who had flagged that £800 shortfall on the first night, didn't like me and maybe he sensed my antipathy towards the grey men of his profession, as essential as they are to every well run business.

The long and short of it is on a cold Monday morning in November, Paco and I were visited at the club by George Knowles junior who told us bluntly: "We're terminating your contracts. Hand the keys back."

I was stunned. Weekly turnover had taken a dip, but not outrageously so. We were still pulling in close to that £35,000-a-week headline figure from the opening few months, but it clearly wasn't enough.

I'm not ashamed to admit tears were shed as my world collapsed around me. How fitting, on the site of an old carpet warehouse, to have the rug pulled from under my feet. I was disconsolate, struggling for somewhere to turn to make sense of a decision I didn't truly understand and certainly didn't believe was fair.

I'd gone from the premier nightclub at the top of the town to the bottom of the heap, all in the space of an abrupt five minute meeting. Knowles was unrepentant. I held my dignity long enough to ensure I didn't beg for my position, but I forcibly stated our case to have our jobs re-instated. Knowles surely knew I was two years ahead of my time in nightclub trends and this was a relationship that would only flourish. I would have been as well talking to the brick wall that circled the dancefloor.

I left some time after 10am, dazed and punch drunk, and in need of advice and comfort. I could have turned to family and friends but I also needed answers and Knowles had become a closed book. I was struck by a flash of inspiration.

The mum of one of my dad's pals at the army supplies depot in Stirling was a spiritualist. I had never met her and knew only her name, Cathy Leitch, and the street in which she lived near the town centre. I made my way there and knocked nervously at the pensioner's door.

She invited me in, as if it was the most natural thing in the world, and made me a cup of tea. We exchanged little more than pleasantries, although she could clearly sense my distress. She sat down across from me on the couch and looked me in the eye. "I see a French-style bistro," she said bluntly. "There's a guy working there with a pencil thin moustache. You must go and see him now."

You could have knocked me over with a feather. The French bistro, I quickly realised, was my old haunt Ronnie's Bar, recently re-opened as The Pavilion and which did a nice line in casual dining ('Desert Island Discs' presenter Kirsty Young worked there are as a waitress). Even more pertinently, it was being run by Andy McLean, my former head of security at Rainbow Rocks, who had a pencil thin moustache.

By 11am I was at his door and told him: "Andy, I don't know why I'm here, but I've been told I've got to see you." He invited me in and dropped the bombshell: "Scooby, they've given me your job at Rainbow Rocks."

I loved Andy to bits and still do. I was crushed with disappointment, of course, but the spiritualist had at least helped me see the full picture. I couldn't have any bad feelings towards Andy. Business was business, but I still needed time away to recover and repair.

My drugs use, after the hedonism of the previous season in Ibiza, was consistent but not all consuming during my time in charge at Rainbow Rocks. I was dabbling four or five times a week, a few joints a day.

Occasionally, we'd head to the village of Kippen, where one of the Rocks' crowd had a caravan, and indulge in a Two Litre Toke, which was a makeshift bong crafted from a Coca Cola bottle. At other times we would pierce a plastic bag then hold it over our heads while one of the other boys blew smoke from a joint into the hole. It was eye-watering, mind bending stuff.

However, I went even further overboard for the next seven days in Amsterdam with my two mates, brothers Brian and Colin Roy. Decent, solid guys, they had previously booked the holiday as a hostel get away and didn't mind when I asked to tag along at the last minute as an escape from my employment woes.

They went out most days to see the sights while I ignored their offer to visit the museums and canals, preferring instead to sit in hash bars getting stoned out my tree. I slumped in a thick haze of marijuana smoke and minor depression.

However, my mood lifted when I heard Cherry Berry, Stirling's original punk, had turned up outside Rainbow Rocks on the first Saturday night after I'd been axed with a placard of protest. He was demanding my immediate reinstatement and calling on clubbers to boycott the venue out of sympathy for my plight. It all fell on deaf ears, of course, but his loyalty touched deep.

So too did the support of Jake, but not before I'd been left desolate and in despair when I returned from Holland to visit her at her student digs in Edinburgh, where she was studying accountancy and finance. I knocked on the door of her flat in St Patrick's Square only to hear a dull echo beyond, a sure sign of no-one at home. Was it an over-reaction, at that very moment, to feel utterly bereft?

I had gone from a clubland kingpin to nothing in the space of a fortnight and didn't even have the girl I cared about more than any other to console me. I slowly turned on my heels and walked back down The Bridges towards the city centre, scanning every face in the crowd for the woman I longed to find.

Suddenly, through the throng, appeared a vision in an oversized coat, so big for her skinny little frame I almost didn't recognise her. Her eyes gave her away and as they locked on mine, so too did her beaming smile. She was a vision. My heart soared as we embraced and headed back to her apartment, which I didn't leave for a week.

Depression soon gave way to determination as I made my way back to Stirling and, as it was a Saturday night, I decided to follow the lead of the rest of the town by heading to Rainbow Rocks. George Knowles junior stepped in front of me at the door and told me I wasn't welcome. Andy, in his new position, put a friendly hand on his boss's shoulder and told him to let me pass. Two can play that game Knowles, I thought.

The timing of my dismissal still rankled and at the back of my mind there was a gnawing question about why they had been so quick to let me go at that particular moment. It was answered when I went to see lawyer Roddy McKenzie, who was well briefed on employment protection.

Poor Paco had worked at Rainbow Rocks for less than a year and so had no statutory rights, but landed on his feet after being bagged when he was invited to work in a management position with Simon Littlejohn's infant chain of restaurants.

However, the Knowles' had boobed when they decided to fire me, wrongly believing I had also worked for the family for less than 12 months. They were out by four days. I was covered therefore by employment law and had been, in effect, unfairly dismissed.

Roddy was adamant. The Knowles valued their reputation more than the money and would settle with me before the case even came to court, he insisted. I only wish I shared his optimism. "You wait and see," he told me with a smile. He was spot on.

The night before we were due in court a gold Porsche 944 turned into Station Road, where I was back living with my parents. It belonged to George junior, who walked up the path, knocked on my door, and offered me a generous settlement. God knows where I got the strength to tell him: "Double it."

He returned to his car and sat pondering his options for the next 10 minutes. Eventually, he returned: "Okay, I'm prepared to do that." Again, gathering strength from who knows where, I told him I'd speak to him in the morning with my final decision.

Sod it, I reasoned, I might as well hand him an uncomfortable night for all the sleepless occasions he had given me those few weeks previously. We did settle, of course, for a sum of money enough to buy me an old Triumph TR6, a classic car to take from an experience that was far from vintage.

Fresh adventures, I consoled myself, would be right around the corner. On reflection, however, the first six months of 1986 were not halcyon days as I was forced to scratch for a living.

Joey Farquharson, one of the co-owners of McQue's, overlooked any misgivings around my poaching of Fraser Hotchkiss and offered me a Thursday night gig. I was on a percentage of the door takings for a club night called DV8 but was only just keeping my head above the water.

Dot, of Ronnie's Bar fame, took over the running of Raffles Bar across the street from our old hang out and gave me a couple of shifts. I set up a makeshift DJ booth on a Friday and Saturday night and Dot, a fabulous people person, went some way to recreating a Ronnie's Bar vibe.

Jake was my saviour. On our first date I had taken her to Kirkcaldy for an ice cream – a long way, but why not? I like driving and loved her company. She was so devoted she would even accompany me to gigs and sit in the back of the DJ booth with her nose in her university course books, studying hard despite the cacophony around her. She was full of surprises.

Jake even took a year out of her studies and worked in the Tap Room, a pub underneath Raffles so rowdy and rough her barmaid's apron should have been lined with Kevlar. She loved it. It was a working man's bar but drug taking was rife – and I should know, because I frequented it often enough and participated in several binges with customers.

They were very open about it and goodness knows why the police didn't move in and close it down. Most of the punters came from the Raploch and, quite frankly, were a bunch of rascals. However, they took a shine to Jake and also offered refuge to this scoundrel, which was appreciated at a time when my career had hit such a lull and I was on a significant downer.

There were glimmers of sunshine to occasionally burn away the low mood, but most of the laughs were unconscious. I sat with Sean Gentleman one December evening as he costed out every design-er label he was wearing and I frantically did the arithmetic in my head. "Scooby," he said: "My jacket's an £800 number from Katharine Hamnett, my trousers are Destroy at £300 and this shirt by Jean Paul Gaultier set me back £250." They were all from top Glasgow designer store Cruise, he added.

He awaited the cooing of a positive and complimentary response that was never going to come. Instead I told him: "Sean, you're a mug.

You're wearing more than £1,300 of designer gear and we're sitting in the Tap Room on Christmas Eve. Ho fucking ho."

Shortly afterwards, Franny's girlfriend Karen, who was training to be a dentist, suggested a foursome with me and Jake at a ball being organised by a group of Scottish orthodontists. Franny came to my house to get ready for the black tie event and as we caught sight of ourselves in the mirror in our tuxedo splendour he turned, without the slightest hint of irony, and asked: "Well Stuart, what do you think? Two local lads made good?"

I tell you what I was thinking – I had to get my head back in the game. And fast.

8

A barn dance? We were in danger of straying into White Heather Club territory, but Colin Barr was deadly serious. "Scooby, I'm telling you, the idea is a winner," he assured me. "We put one on in Howwood in Renfrewshire last year and it went down a storm. The punters loved it."

At that stage, my pal neglected to mention the night had ended in some disarray when they almost burned down the farm hosting an event more familiar to the wild frontiers of the United States than the wild west of Glasgow.

Colin's pal, Stevie Dick, was put in charge of the barbecue and all went well until 2am when a decision was made to sit the cooking grill on a pile of hay bales. For good measure, Stevie squirted lighter fluid on the charcoal with inevitable, and disastrous, consequences.

A youthful singer named Marti Pellow, minus his new band Wet, Wet, Wet, was the star turn that night but the strength of his raw vocals were a whisper in comparison to the siren howls of the fire brigade sent to restore order a couple of hours before the sun came up.

Colin was the Pied Piper of Glasgow in the eighties and nineties, setting trends and establishing clubs that defined the social scene in the city for a generation of revellers. He ran the iconic gay nightclub Bennet's in the early eighties, as well as the highly regarded Bar Luxembourg, before being headhunted by three entrepreneurs, including impresario Ron McCulloch, to open their new venture, Cuba, in Marbella.

Colin came from the Red Road flats in Glasgow and you could see for miles from the 30th floor of the Barmulloch high rises, but only he had the ambition to cast his glance all the way across Europe. He met his business partner out there, an English guy called Mark Woodhouse, and soon they were back in Scotland helping to determine the pub and club scene for a new era, aided by Colin's soon-to-be wife Kelly and his brother, Mel.

The first half of 1986, in the aftermath of my unfair dismissal from Rainbow Rock's, hardly represented salad days in my career but I was still determined to remain relevant and that meant keeping a close eye on emerging trends and fashions in music and clubland.

A buzz had begun to build around a Sunday night at Joe Paparazzi, a club housed in an old cinema at the top of Glasgow's Sauchiehall Street. It was a night called 'Fresh' and was unusual in itself because the idea of a club handing over its door to promoters was still something of a novelty.

The deal was straightforward – Colin and Mark were running 'Fresh' and were given the takings from the door, while the venue made its money from sales at the bar. It was no heartache to hand over a couple of quid in entry money, not least as the black haired girl on the till, moonlighting from her job as a hairdresser, was an absolute stunner – Sharleen Spiteri, not quite then of Texas fame.

Mark was the moneyman and Colin was the face of the enterprise and they used their pooled experience, particularly from Spain, to great effect. It was the coolest club, with a music policy that didn't always make sense but somehow worked.

It was the first place I heard Mandy Smith's 'I Just Can't Wait'. She may have been renowned as a wild child, but the Balearic beat of the 12 inch version was utterly authentic. Colin played Mory Kante's 'Yeke Yeke' and he pumped it out alongside the theme from 'Dallas' as well as Adrian Celentano's 'The Language of Love', which had first been introduced to Scottish clubland by my old pal Dave 'CL' Young.

It was a song released by Italian Celentano in 1972 and lyrically it was utter gibberish but the crowd went mad for it. It may have owed something to the club's licence restrictions but the music also cut out as soon as it went above a certain decibel level, which it did – frequently. The dance floor always erupted with joy.

On several occasions, Kelly also came into the club with Mandy Smith, who had married Rolling Stone Bill Wyman and was all over the tabloids.

The whole package was dynamite. One of the principal DJs was a guy named Michael McCrimmon, who forged his reputation and then went on with his brother Tony to own the legendary Sub Club. The place was jam packed with good looking guys and girls, who came from all over the central belt for their final big blow out of the weekend.

An idea quickly began to ferment in my own mind. Imitation, as they say, is the sincerest form of flattery. I had been lured back to Le Clique but the club was beginning to look pretty shabby after almost a decade on the go and was fairly drugs-fuelled, with dope and sulph the order of the day among many of the clientele.

Let's not be hypocritical, the bar staff also enjoyed chemical highs and I was as willing a participant as anyone, but discipline was somehow maintained and rarely gave way to disorder.

Let your vibe attract your tribe. I admired the mojo of Colin and Mark and pretty soon Le Clique had been re-branded into the 'Big House' on the back of the Chicago house music scene that was beginning to emerge and which the boys had exploited so successfully at 'Fresh'.

Le Clique had been under-performing financially, so I agreed with its new owner, a Pakistani guy called Raja, to run the club four nights a week for a percentage of the profits. I rounded up many of the old bar staff from Rainbow Rocks, who were gloriously loyal and agreed to throw their lot in with me at the venue down the road, no doubt to the annoyance of the Knowles'.

The first night was a riot. We took advantage of the club's greatest asset, a fabulous sound system, and blasted out Farley 'Jackmaster' Funk but, in a nod of respect to 'Fresh', we also dared to be different. I was pulling a stint as DJ, in addition to running the place, and mixed it up, filling the floor with Johnny Wakelin's 'In Zaire', as well as glam rock and funk classics such as New York Groove's 'Hello' and '(Are You Ready) Do The Bus Stop' by the Fatback Band.

It was November 1986, the height of the AIDS scare, and we used the opening night to urge our audience not to die of ignorance. We kindly included a condom with every ticket purchased on that sell out night and I stapled them together – right through the latex of the Durex.

There was a vibrant music scene around central Scotland and we attracted enough of an audience to slowly transform the fortunes of the club, although at times it was akin to asking the QEII to perform a three point turn in a bathtub.

Colin and I had become increasingly friendly and I offered him and Mark the chance to host 'Fresh' every Thursday night at our place, on similar terms to Joe Paparazzi. The nights were quite a success, even though someone tried to have a swing at Colin one night for no other reason than he was a big, good looking boy. The price some people have to pay.

His idea for a barn dance in Stirling, for the spring of 1987, was rejected immediately as utter lunacy. Well, wasn't it? However, after a couple of days his words had percolated through my brain and, lo and behold, if they didn't begin to make some sense. Let's face it, we were all running around at the time like Gary Cooper anyway, so we might as well go the whole hog.

One of my mates lived on a small farm in Kippen and had access to a shotgun. We used to buy jeans brand new, hang them from his washing line, then blast the crotch from close range with buckshot to give them a tattered, battered look. We wore cowboy boots and bandanas and faded leather jackets. The only thing missing was a stable of horses.

A fire was lit on the idea of the barn dance, thankfully this time only in our imaginations. I knew the Logans – son Kenny was a fine rugby player for Scotland – and their family farm, Blairmains, was perfectly sized and situated in the shadow of the magnificent Wallace Monument.

We came to a deal to hire a barn and field for a Saturday night in April 1987, at a cost of £500, and put the word out. It was a sellout before we even knew it, with 1,000 tickets snapped up almost instantly. Clubland went where Colin Barr went.

In those more laissez faire times, health and safety standards were less rigorous. We kept Stirling Council at arms' length by promoting the whole venture as a farmers' dance. Thankfully, they raised few objections, no doubt writing it off as young Tory toffs enjoying a knees up among their own.

It was a busy couple of months. We used contacts at a local electrical company to help us out with lighting and enough power for a decent sound system, set upon a flatbed trailer that doubled as a stage.

We sourced our supplies for the bar, predominantly cans of Schlitz that had just gone out of date. We snapped them up at 50 pence a time and knocked them out at £3 a go. We had a captive market as Blairmains was miles from the nearest off licence.

So many people were coming from across Scotland we laid on buses from Stirling train station to transport them to the farm, but when the night came around we were running late and our hopes of opening the gates at 7pm proved too ambitious.

We had roped in one of the locals, Tam Begley, to drive the bus. Frantically, we got word to him just before he set off that we needed to stall his arrival. "Tam, can you do anything to delay getting here?"

He didn't need to be asked twice and took the punters on a magical mystery tour, driving in the opposite direction towards Callander and delivering the full tourist spiel. Few were any the wiser when they eventually arrived at Blairmains almost an hour later. It really was a sight to see, my heart burst with pride.

We had pulled it off – almost. Up on the flatbed trailer, Colin had grabbed a microphone and was belting out songs under the stage name 'Bond is Back', living out 007 fantasies he must have been hard pushed to harbour growing up in the schemes of Glasgow.

Live music was also provided by Jalan 545, a Stirling band that included hairdresser Guy Grieve in its line-up, before the night gave way to the DJs.

Many of the punters sat on a wall in the middle of the barn for a better view of the stage and it nearly collapsed at one point, but thankfully held firm. The atmosphere was amazing. There were even few complaints about the price of the Schlitz and fewer moans about it being a month or two beyond its sell by date. The barbecue also did a roaring trade although this time we kept it well away from the Logans' stock of hay.

We quietly congratulated ourselves for thinking about absolutely everything except, crucially, where to store the money pouring into the tills. We had no safe, never mind a secure storage area, and there was nothing for it but to pop the trunk of the trusty TR6. Hour after hour bags of notes and coins were deposited within and with everyone committed to certain jobs on site, the car even sat for long spells with no-one guarding it.

The TR6 had cost me £2,500 to buy from an an old pal from McQ's, Ally Nimmo. It had been locked in a garage for a long, long time and

I had to spend a further £2,500 to make it roadworthy, including a set of fat, Jaguar tyres that made it sit up on the road and look really meaty. It was my pride and joy and eventually I moved it on to restaurateur Simon Littlejohn for £9,000, but it was never worth more than that night at Blairmains when it was stuffed with so much currency.

The barn dance finished without incident in the small hours and Mel Barr and I drove back to Glasgow wide eyed, alert and excited. We joined with Colin and Mark at Colin's place and emptied bag after bag of money onto his kitchen table.

Carefully, we set aside all the cash needed for expenses and bills still to be paid and then broke the profit into shares of three. My cut amounted to around £5,000, although for weeks afterwards I was picking forgotten fivers and tenners from the nooks and crannies of the boot.

I had handled sums of that size before, obviously, but never had it been mine to stuff into my own pockets. Spring would soon give way to summer. I had just bankrolled the next few months in Ibiza.

Like Sirens calling sailors to their fate, the White Isle continued to entice me towards its enchanting embrace, even though I hadn't visited for three years. After being offered the Rainbow Rocks gig by the Knowles' towards the end of the summer season in 1984 I reasoned it would be a while before I returned, certainly to work. The yearning to go back made perfect sense, certainly in my position – meat and two veg or tapas and sunshine? A no brainer.

Better still, Javier had used his contacts to line me up with with a gig at the Star Club, now Eden, after the original DJ, a guy called Simon, left only a few weeks into the season. The conduit was another Englishman, Peter Hankinson, a legend of San Antonio's west end who moved to Ibiza in 1971, opened his first bar, and is still there today.

He was running the Star Club and, with Javier's word and reputation holding strong, accepted me with open arms. The gig at the Star Club was a huge deal. My previous job at Maxim's had satisfied me, but only to a point. It was a pub. Great fun, but ultimately still only a pre-club stop off, however many happy memories we'd helped create for tourists. The Star was a proper club, with a capacity of 2,000. It was packed most nights. I'd won a transfer to the big time.

Candidly, if it wasn't a little tired when I arrived it was certainly set in its ways. Crucially, however, there was an appetite for Peter to change – a positive mindset that saw him prosper in senior positions at a string of San Antonio's most popular venues. To put it politely, the Star Club at the time was a little bit 'Oggy, Oggy, Oggy', English and somewhat laddish, lager loutish even, with an over reliance on mainstream soul.

My calling card – Javier's reference apart – was a boxful of records they had never heard before. It was a bank of rich assets, thanks to my relationship with Fraser Hotchkiss.

I may not have been in the DJ booth as often as I would have liked in the previous two years, but Fraser and I were always tight when it came to discussing musical trends so I knew the direction I wanted my summer sets to take.

I blew it up. I mixed modern sounds such as Steve 'Silk' Hurley's 'Jack Your Body', Marrs' 'Pump Up The Volume' and Nitro Deluxe's 'Let's Get Brutal' with earlier classics including Richie Havens' 'Going Back to My Roots', 'Jungle Fever' by Kinkina and Elkin and Nelson's 'Jibaro'. I had never felt more comfortable.

Peter witnessed the response of the crowd and let me get on with it. The Star Club was opened from 10pm-5am every night – a long shift – and I shared DJ duties with a Spaniard named Carlos who quietly resented being my warm up.

Thankfully, our relationship never drastically soured. During the day he worked the sunbeds on the beach, a lucrative trade. He spoke next to no English. He patrolled the sands telling tourists: "The funky music goes de bum de bah, it's not necessary." No-one had a clue what it meant, but it didn't stop him stuffing plenty of pesetas into the money bag around his waist.

Let's be candid, tempers and egos didn't overheat in the height of the summer sun because most of the time we were off our faces on drugs including, for the first time, ecstasy. It had arrived on the island that summer and the quality of the initial batch of MDMA was such the highs frequently lasted five or six hours (within a year its provenance would plummet).

It could get messy, but it was very liberating and I can still recall the overwhelming feeling of love and emotional warmth that coursed through my blood when I took it for the first time. I would have hugged King Kong and then sweet talked him down off the top of the Empire State.

For sure, my debut on the drug was in Amnesia but the memory of the specifics of the night, unsurprisingly, are hazy. The call generally went out: "Get right on one, matey." I was given the ecstasy by a close pal and I always took it towards the end of my shift in the Star Club, so I was coming up by the time we hit other venues, on my own personal time, when my set wouldn't be affected.

The connection between music and the drug went hand in hand. The vibe of the Balearic beat was enhanced and, let's not be kidded, ecstasy kept you up all night on an island where some clubs didn't close until 7am. It was a Disneyworld of drugs, a Fantasia of pharmaceuticals.

Ibiza wasn't then and, for many people isn't now, a reality. Everything was stretched to excess – alcohol, the sun, the opposite sex and, especially, the drugs. Ultimately, ecstasy is an hallucinogen and, like my first experience on sulph, I learned quickly to approach it with caution.

In total, that summer I maybe took it on half a dozen occasions but hash continued to be consumed on an almost daily basis, with coke chasers to pick me up and keep me fuelled to hit the pace of an existence I still couldn't envisage would ever take me over the penalty points threshold in the licence of a well balanced life.

It was a full pelt existence but I at least had the support of Javier and Wilson, who kindly put me up when I arrived that May in a big old house they were renting in the bay. Their boys, Christian and Alan, were still toddlers but my old pals threw their doors open and the warmth of their welcome was supplemented by the gentle nature of the family's new pet, a big friendly mutt of an English sheepdog called Gancho.

Slowly but surely the Star Club reinvented itself, as all the best clubs do, into a hotbed of house and the punters continued to pile in including, on the July night they had their famous musical epiphany, Danny Rampling, Paul Oakenfold, Nicky Holloway and Johnny Walker.

They stopped by while I was performing my set before heading to take in Alfredo at Amnesia, famously dropping ecstasy and being so overwhelmed by the experience and the brilliantly idiosyncratic music of the Argentine master mixer it directly led to the formation of acid house.

I never met them but Rampling and I went on to have a relationship of sorts. In 1996 he played my remix of the The Lotus Eaters' 'The First

Picture Of You' four weeks in a row on his Radio One show. It was released under one of my many musical monikers, Beautiful Imbalance, and in one of the weeks he even opened his show with it.

My relationship with Jake also continued to go from strength to strength, despite the distance. We were on the phone to each other on a daily basis and at some expense in the days before mobile technology.

She also pulled a fly one on a holiday to another Balearic island, Majorca, I didn't mind one bit. Jake was on vacation with her pal, Loraine Elder, who was also an old chum of mine, and word soon reached Ibiza that my girl was poorly.

She was on the phone constantly, several times a day, and it came as some concern to me as she was only a few days into a fortnight's holiday. What the hell. I hopped on a short flight from Ibiza to Palma to check out her health for myself. She didn't look too bad and, indeed, her mood seemed to brighten when I suggested she and Loraine return with me to San Antonio on the next available flight.

Amazingly, within hours of our arrival on Ibiza her previous fever, tummy bug and general wabbit condition were all things of the past. She'd thrown me a chunk of bait, of course, but I was happy to swallow it hook, line and sinker.

The summer seemed never ending, as it so often did in our youth, but an unexpected opportunity presented itself that left with me no choice but to willingly cut short my season in the sun and return to Scotland. My career was about to take a different turn, from drink and music into food but, determined to prove myself after the Rainbow Rocks fiasco, I was ready for the challenge.

It came from restaurateur Simon Littlejohn, who had been a regular at Rainbow Rocks and we had also become friendly on weekly skiing trips to Glenshee in Perthshire. He had opened his eponymously named restaurant, Littlejohn's, in Stirling and had also expanded into Perth, where he had made my former right hand man Paco the boss.

Simon and Paco shared a house in Bannockburn at the time and Paco was on 10 per cent of profits from the Perth enterprise. It may have sounded generous, but there was a method in the madness as Simon knew Paco didn't just provide a solid pair of business hands, but skilful ones too.

Pretty soon business was soaring. Further expansion was planned for St Andrews. Simon had watched the whole barn dance idea blossom and prosper and knew I had an entrepreneurial streak that chimed with his own. He offered me the same 10 per cent to run St Andrews that Paco was on in Perth. It was time to come home.

By coincidence, at the end of July it was Jake's 21st birthday party and I was determined to be there. There was to be no expense spared for Jake's bash with a marquee erected in the large garden of their beautiful family home, Endrick Lodge, as well as caterers, musicians, a disco and an open bar of champagne and wines.

I told her folks about my plan to return and they were delighted and reckoned my surprise appearance would give Jake's special day even greater resonance. Goodness Angus, her dad, even offered to send a limo to Manchester Airport – it was the only flight I could secure – to whisk me up the M6 in some style, refreshed and ready to party.

Admittedly, many of the arrangements had to be made at the last minute as there was a scatty system for purchasing flight tickets in San Antonio at the time that didn't always involve legitimate travel agents.

In the late eighties, tickets were still issued in paper form and the return portion could be transferred for sale, usually in the pub for a knockdown price by a willing seller who had decided to extend their vacation beyond the usual two weeks.

Lo and behold, I secured my Manchester return in a boozer in the west end, tucked it in the back pocket of my jeans and then, the night before my departure, set about getting wrecked after my final set at the Star Club.

I was out of my head on drugs – coke, cannabis and even, unusually for me, alcohol were consumed before Javier led half a dozen of us back up to Can Talaias. A guitar was produced from who knows where and a happy band of minstrels sang our way into the wee small hours and beyond.

I didn't so much arrive at the airport the following lunchtime as stagger and stumble into departures, but my thumping headache would soon become the least of my worries. Passport and ticket at hand, I approached the desk to check in and, within minutes, was surrounded by police asking quick fire questions even my improving Spanish could not comprehend.

Thankfully, Javier had accompanied me and translated almost as quickly as the cops were speaking, but the colour draining from his face as the seriousness of the situation hit home had nothing to do with the several large brandies he had consumed the night before. "It's your ticket Scooby," he explained. "It was originally purchased by a guy who's wanted by the police for holding up a hotel. He's been on the run. They think it's you."

I've never sobered up as quickly in my life as I desperately pleaded my innocence and explained, via Javier, how I'd purchased my ticket in the pub only the day before.

In desperation I lifted the box I was carrying, which contained all my records. I was a tradesman and these were my precious tools. I pleaded: "I'm a DJ, I'm a DJ." An order from the commanding police officer was fired in my direction immediately: "Open the box."

I breathed a sigh of relief. Surely now they would see I was a house aficionado, not a house breaker? Disaster. I clipped open the box and looked inside with utter disbelief at two bricks and a car jack.

For the first time, I noticed Javier looking a little sheepish and the police had seen enough, huckling me behind the scenes for further cross examination as the flight for Manchester was called and I knew I wasn't making it home for Jake's special day.

I was released without charge hours later – the flight had long arrived in England – and Javier at least had the good grace to look contrite and apologise for stealing my records. He knew the strength of my set at the Star Club and reckoned I wouldn't miss my inventory as I was heading home and would soon replenish my stock. He planned to play them at his own place, Bucanero, in a bid to mimic the success of the Star Club.

He was double wide, but what could I do? He thought I wouldn't let those records go, hence the car jack and bricks. Honestly? I would have gifted them had he asked. He knew the strength of their popularity. I couldn't really harbour any hard feelings – after all, he and Wilson had put me up for months at their place without rent, but I was still tearful that night when I called Jake, the party in full swing in the background.

I really wanted to make her happy, but she forgave me completely, which was typical. She hadn't expected me to be there in the first place so she didn't feel the loss, but my heart ached for weeks at missing out on sharing one of the biggest days of her life.

The bittersweet memory of my last 24 hours in Ibiza faded within a few weeks as I dived into my new career choice, with gusto. Understandably, Simon reckoned I would be best working the first few months in Perth with Paco, our roles reversed as I had been the gaffer when we were running Rainbow Rocks.

My first job was sweeping the kitchen floor. I did it willingly as it taught me humility and underlined my work ethic and enthusiasm for the new venture. Simon's words were wise: "Do everything in a restaurant. After all, you can't tell someone to take on a task if you haven't experience of doing it yourself." It was great logic, even if it did lead to me doing every shitty job going in the place for three months. Paco was a hard taskmaster. He may have been my mate, but he was the boss and he was fair.

Simon had been running the restaurant in Stirling, but had been in danger of taking his eye off the ball. After my speedy apprenticeship I was called to my home town to oversee operations. It was a right mess.

As manager, I didn't waste any time and sacked six under-performing members of staff in the first six days. Soon, the place was flourishing. Simon was pleased. I had passed his test, served my time. He promised to hand over the keys of his new place and, for the first time since Rainbow Rocks, I saw a positive future opening up in front of me.

9

It was all very well the criminal underworld in Dundee targeting me after they were banned from Fat Sam's but they were totally out of order taking out a £500 hit on my dog Doobie.

The poor thing was guilty of nothing other than looking occasionally mournful which is hardly a crime, especially in Dundee. In fact, it's what drew my assistant manager Vinny Doyle and me to him in the first place.

We turned up at the rescue centre in the city looking for a new pet and Doobie was a sad, dishevelled reprobate. Wouldn't you know, we saw something of ourselves in his personality and reckoned he would fit right in with our lifestyle. Scooby and Doobie, two peas in a pod.

We paid a couple of quid to the charity and took him back to my flat in St Andrews, where Vinny was also living at the time. We quickly decided it would be unfair to leave poor Doobie home alone while we nipped across the Tay Bridge to our nightclub – everyone called it Fatties – so we started taking him to work.

Doobie was a sociable dog, so much so it took to hanging out with the bouncers at the front door. In the absence of a steward's jacket we put a red bandana around his neck and he was so chilled, possibly because he was as stoned as we were, breathing in the hash fumes around the home he shared with me and Vinny.

Pretty soon, Doobie became a celebrity in his own right and the girls queueing for entry to the club put biscuits in their handbags to feed him as they waited. Unsurprisingly, Doobie never knocked back the offer of munchies after those second hand cannabis hits.

We even made him a star of our advertising campaign on local bill-boards and buses. Still looking glassy eyed, admittedly, he was pictured above a caption that read: 'You know where he's at.' A couple of weeks later we added another picture and caption: 'So go and seek him out.'

Sadly, a local group of hardmen from Lochee, one of Dundee's more notorious districts, took that command literally. Our head bouncer Rab Glennie also came from the area and was absolutely fearless, a point he confirmed when they all turned up at the door one night only to be told they weren't getting in. A couple of previous incidents in the club had made them personae non gratae and Rab decided to act, with our backing as management.

Arguments ensued and threats were made, but Rab had balls the size of Desperate Dan's chin. He refused to back down and they eventually sloped off into the night, muttering dark threats of vengeance. Within days the word was on the streets. Doobie was getting it – and there was £500 up for grabs for anyone who could take him out or cause him serious harm.

I wish I could say we called the police to report the threats, but we didn't even lift the phone to the SSPCA. Negotiations required tact and, in the meantime, Doobie stayed close to Rab on the door as it was the safest place to hang out, even if he was left a little exposed.

Rab took the lead in formalising a peace deal and Kofi Annan would have been proud of his diplomatic skills as he brokered a truce. We didn't have to retire the red bandana. Doobie survived and prospered.

In fact, Doobie lived on until 1995 after I had the presence of mind to gift him to my dad in a bid to give my old man exercise at a time when I was beginning to wrestle with my mental demons. Unfairly, perhaps, I went to the Bandeath Dog Home in Stirling in 1997 and, would you believe, if the spitting image of Doobie wasn't sitting there looking at me with the same perplexed and sorry expression.

I signed for my new pet there and then and decided to call him Groovy. I can't put it any more simply than to say I was fucked at the time, seriously unwell, and Groovy became as mentally imbalanced as me, following me around the streets of Stirling and beyond.

My dad eventually took Groovy off me and the poor mutt was medicated with canine Diazepam – jellies – for a year by the vet to chill it out. Seriously, my old man put a tablet in a bar of Milky Way every night and it was a full 12 months before Groovy could eventually settle down to a peaceful, less manic existence. If only I could have said the same.

Fatties was anything but serene and I wouldn't have had it any other way as I embraced a return to the sharp end of nightclub management for the first time since Rainbow Rocks, albeit I'd also enjoyed that short stint as boss at The Big House.

It was the spring of 1989 and we were in the middle of the two years that became collectively known as the second summer of love. Acid and ecstasy became the drugs of choice for a new generation of revellers and on the basis that if you couldn't beat them you may as well join them, I became a fully paid up member of the club.

These were raucous days and while cannabis and coke were still my drugs of preference, I began to dabble in ecstasy with greater abandon than in the summer of 1987 when I'd first been introduced to MDMA in Ibiza. In the summer of 1988 I even tried to hire the swimming pool at the Leisure Bowl in Alloa to host Scotland's first water-based rave in trunks and bikinis.

Stoned out my face, I printed up nonsense flyers, pictures of turn of the 20th century swimming baths with Edwardian gents in rubber caps and captioned them 'Bish, bash, skloosh, ploosh.' The party was planned between 7pm-10pm and I aimed to have everyone in the water, out of their faces on acid and E.

The council must have taken a look at the flyers and smelled a rat because they pulled the plug at the last minute, much to my disgust and annoyance. It would have been an evening to remember.

Fat Sam's had been a fixture in Dundee since 1983 and was established by the wily and astute music entrepreneur and promoter Stuart Clumpas, who went on to set up T in the Park and the V Festival. In truth, Clumpas and I never really saw eye to eye but there was a mutual respect. I thought he had a massive ego but admired his business sense and his organisation of the legendary Dance Factory, the gig nights hosted at Fatties on a Sunday night, was renowned.

The Dance Factory played a part in breaking some big names in music at the time, including Texas, Simply Red, Hue and Cry, The LAs, The Housemartins and Fairground Attraction. His instincts were spot on.

For his part, he recognised I was making money for his club. He was filling the place one night a week and on the other three nights it was open – Thursday, Friday and Saturday – I was playing my part in ramming them in.

Clumpas was originally from Glasgow, but had spent most of his adult life in Dundee after studying at the university, where he ran the entertainments wing of the student union. I wasn't a Dundonian so felt like an outsider. Really, Clumpas's protege was Brian Reid, a local lad, who had worked his way up through the organisation to become manager of Fatties.

I was given his job when Clumpas set up King Tut's in Glasgow and called for Brian to take charge. Brian would later succeed me as boss of The Tunnel. There was never any rancour between us. Brian moved Down Under a few years ago and we always got on well.

Clumpas was one of four directors at Fat Sam's – Ewan Webster, an accountant, was the only Dundonian and the others were Glasgow based, Mark Goldinger and Harold Ure. Mark and Harold had set up Colin Barr in the Cuba club in Malaga and were canny operators. I had my working week at Fat Sam's down to a tee – 26 hours, no more and no less, with maximum returns for the key hours invested. The place ran so smoothly it should have been sponsored by Rolex.

Mark drove up from Glasgow late on a Saturday evening to his pre-booked hotel room then checked in at the club to make sure all was well, grabbed a few hours of sleep, and was back home by first thing Sunday morning.

If not a licence to print money it was certainly a very lucrative venture. I was on a decent salary for the time and hours worked, around £18,000 a year, and had been poached, in part, because the club also had a restaurant. They knew I had done such a good job establishing Littlejohn's in St Andrews while, of course, my experience at Rainbow Rocks and in Ibiza hadn't gone unnoticed.

I bolstered my team by calling in my old Rocks' pal Vinny from Stirling, while Paco also agreed to look after the restaurant side of the business while he waited to establish his own place in Perth, which is still thriving today.

Unsurprisingly, I was no stranger to Fatties after moving to St Andrews in the summer of 1988 to take charge of Littlejohn's. Thursday nights at Fatties, which were known as 'Liquid Sky', were euphoric. Acid house had exploded and drug taking was rife which, combined with the music, left the bouncers on some nights scraping ravers off the ceiling.

The club's main DJ at the time was Ned Jordan, now sadly deceased, and while he wasn't the best mixer, he could read a local audience better than the editor of The Courier. They went crazy for Ned.

In the early days I naively took the group of punters who queued at the DJ booth as ravers looking to make a request for a specific piece of music, but I quickly realised it was the centre of another trade.

A particular member of staff always seemed to hang around there and, later on, I preferred to turn a blind eye to the obvious dealing. I knew it went on but there was an innocence in the early days more than in, say, The Tunnel, where the drugs were distributed on a distinct business model.

I was caught up in the ecstasy culture although, for the most part, I resisted the temptation to dabble in MDMA when I was working at Fatties, even if I continued to smoke blow regularly. Coke also remained a drug of choice throughout, admittedly even a line or two when I was 'on the clock' at the club.

In the months before I was put in charge of Fatties I had been running around with a bunch of local rascals including Jimmy Mackenzie, brother of Billy of The Associates fame, as well as DJ Ned, Wayne Dunbar, Cohn O'Dea and my mucker Zammo Simpson from Perth, who worked in a boutique called Valentino's and was always style conscious.

Wayne, Jimmy and Zammo went on to start the Rhumba Club in 1991, legendary house music nights held in Perth and still going strong today. I was also friendly with two smashing lads, the Taylor brothers, Dougie and Darren – Darren was appointed head of football operations at Dundee United in 2017. Talk about poacher turned gamekeeper!

The only United player we ever banned from Fatties was their fabled striker Paul Sturrock, who turned up on more than one occasion on a Thursday evening, when he was first team coach, demanding entry. Of course, he was desperate to see which players were breaking curfew 48 hours before games but I forbade the bouncers from allowing him through the ropes as first team players from big Duncan Ferguson downwards were left to party in peace.

Ecstasy had a bizarre affect on me. Dougie Taylor and I were off our tits in Fatties one night and he roared in my face with a huge grin: "Club Satan!" That just about summed it up.

Glasgow DJ Steven Sleepman, who had established his excellent reputation at city club Tin Pan Alley, teamed up with beer giant Schlitz in the late eighties and took 'Schlitz/Slam' on tour around the country, including Dundee. The gig also included a set by Electribe 101, a decent house music group with a stunning German vocalist named Billie Ray Martin.

I was so out of my face I stood at the front of the crowd all night waving at her. Literally. All fucking night. The gig ended but the punters still demanded more. Steven was already on his way back down the A90 to Glasgow and yet the punters refused to leave.

Riding the wave, DJ Ned jumped into his booth and fired up the anthemic 'Carino' by T-Coy, a dance act trio that included Mike Pickering of Hacienda fame. The place went mental, as did the bouncers, who were cracking up at the impromptu extension to their hours.

On another occasion I headed up the road to Fever nightclub in Aberdeen with a pal from Coatbridge, Gerry Gilmour. We were tripping out of our faces by the time we hit Montrose. Fever was amazing and in the midst of all the mayhem I remembered a huge basket of fruit in the boot of my car a wholesaler supplier had gifted me earlier that day at Littlejohn's.

God knows how the bouncers let me through the door with it, but I wandered around the club handing out plums, peaches and pears to grateful ravers. We chatted up two girls and one of them, a lovely lass called Jackie Angus, told me after some energetic thrusting to the house beats: "Aye, yir a bonnie loon Scooby, but ye cannae dance."

Officially, Jake and I were still an item but, in reality, we were as much off as on. She had departed for a year in London to build her fledgling career in the financial services industry and although we kept in regular touch, absence makes the heart go wander. Girls came and went, some leaving more of an impression than others and, occasionally, in more ways than one.

A pal from Falkirk named Gemma came to visit me at Littlejohn's in St Andrews at the end of one evening shift and, inevitably, one thing led to another. We went from fumbling in the kitchen to the full blown experience in the walk-in freezer, where she clamped her hands on the shelves at either side for additional support.

Unknown to her, it's where the head waiter had left two big cheesecakes, ready to serve the following day. They never made it to the table.

The confused member of staff approached me the next day: "Boss, I don't know what happened. Look at the state of these cakes. They were perfect when I left them last night and now they're all squashed." I rolled my eyes, kept schtum, and told him to throw them in the bin.

On another occasion I went through to Choice, Colin Barr's new club in Glasgow, and found myself chatting to a stunner from Bothwell. I invited her home for coffee and, intoxicated with each other's company, it was Cupar before she twigged I actually lived in St Andrews.

These were heady days of love and lust, a combination I felt in abundance for Rhona Hopkins, the only girl I went out with and felt, self-consciously, I was punching above my weight. I was best man at her brother's wedding.

Rhona worked in Avanti, my old Stirling clothes store, and later ran the women's department at Warehouse in Glasgow. She was a class act and it was as much a thrill to be dressed by her as undressed because she knew fashion and, more importantly, she instinctively understood style. I never looked better than the times we were together.

On one occasion I was driving back to St Andrews with Rhona, Gemma and another fabulous girl, Lucy, from a night at Fat Sam's and the sun was coming up on a glorious day as we pulled into St Andrews at 5am in my Toyota Corolla GTi. They were all planning to crash at the flat and they all knew each other's relationship with me and I was in a quandary, genuinely concerned about how the scene would play out.

In the end, Gemma and Lucy made it easy for us by bolting upstairs when we pulled up at the kerbside leaving just me and Rhona on the pavement with, of course, Doobie. We decided to skip the idea of sleep and wandered down to the Silver Sands, where I spent two of the most romantic hours to that point in my life just walking hand in hand with Rhona along the shoreline, my faithful four legged friend running around our feet fetching sticks.

Lucy was a hoot, funny and sexy as hell. She came from England, arrived at Dundee to visit family and made her way to Fatties. We bonded over a mutual physical attraction and a love of chemical highs.

The Open came to St Andrews in 1990 and in a bid to escape the claustrophobia – the town easily doubled in size for a couple of weeks – Lucy, Vinny and I decided to explore the vast expanse of our minds by brewing up a pot of mushroom tea.

Paranoia gripped as I skirted around the Old Course with Lucy and Vinny, only to be confronted with a convoy of 30 Range Rovers I mistakenly took as police cars. They were courtesy vehicles parked up for the night, being used to ferry the golfers to and from the course.

I panicked, flapped and bolted for the beach to escape the long arm of the law – only to run slap bang into a policeman on the sands, clearly on nightshift security duty. I recognised him from Fat Sam's!

He came from Kirkcaldy and cut about the club in a fur coat. I also knew he liked to dabble in substances that would not have met with the approval of his chief inspector. We greeted each other like long lost brothers and he immediately noticed I was out my face. He cut to the car chase: "Scoobs, you carrying a joint? I could do with something to get me through the night."

I was cannabis free for once and he was disappointed but soon brightened up as he shoved a pair of night vision binoculars into my hands and told me to check them out. Bad move. I put them up to my eyes and freaked. Green rabbits were running around in the rough of the golf course. I dropped his binoculars, turned and fled back up the road, where Lucy was waiting to lovingly guide me back to the flat.

We arrived and, bizarrely, pulled on a couple of ski suits that were hanging in the hall cupboard, attracted by their psychedelic colours and design. We danced around the living room for a couple of hours and then collapsed in a heap. I never took mushrooms again.

My reflections of St Andrews are bittersweet, in part because of the contradictory memories of my relationship with Simon Littlejohn. When he first approached me in Ibiza, he offered me the same deal as Paco in Perth, which included a salary and 10 per cent of the business.

Simon has acknowledged the deal with Paco, but refutes offering me the same terms. I maintain he did. Crucially – naively on my part – the deal was verbal. Generally, it was an arrangement that made sense for both parties.

The terms of reference may have appeared generous to me but, remember, I had given up a lot in Ibiza to come back and work for him. At the risk of sounding arrogant, he was hiring a 'face' to attract the young, upwardly mobile customer base he desired to make Littlejohn's a success.

The concept for Simon's restaurants was ahead of its time and has since been imitated by many others, although rarely bettered. He set his stall on casual, easy bistro dining; steaks, burgers, Mexican food and pizzas were part of an eclectic menu that attracted families but, importantly, a youthful crowd that had traditionally not been restaurant goers.

The interior was junkyard chic; Americana, old photos, train sets and musical instruments, items to grab the attention and maybe even provide a talking points for those who used the restaurant for a first date, of which there were many.

Simon knew I was a driven and motivated self-starter who would set standards for others to follow and that would reflect well on the business. I bought my first flat in St Andrews, a but 'n' ben in Bridge Street, and it cost me £20,000.

I converted it into a two bedroom apartment with money loaned to me by Simon – around £10,000, which I later re-paid – and it was exceptionally tasteful, with wooden floors, floor to ceiling free standing mirrors and bric-a-brac sourced from the Ken Myles antique store, which was situated behind his Perth restaurant. I sold it a few years later for £47,000 and so have reason to be grateful to Simon.

However, he also knew the value in keeping me happy. I was good at my job and had helped transform the fortunes of the Stirling restaurant before I prepared to move on and establish St Andrews. Remember, I had also grafted for three months with Paco in Perth, proving my willingness to make the Littlejohn's chain a success by doing everything from dishwashing to bar tending.

Simon taught me a lot. The way to run a successful business was set a standard and do all you could to maintain it. You had to be on top of it, especially staff. He worked phenomenally hard, 15 hours a day, seven days a week between Stirling and Perth. He could never be accused of shirking.

You could be a bastard I decided, but I soon learned to be a loveable one. In the Stirling restaurant, for example, I would eat at 10pm every night when the place was on wind down and staff were setting up tables for the next day's service. I would finish my meal and inspect the tables. If something was out of place I'd throw a knife or fork on the floor and they would set that table up again.

Undoubtedly, the staff cursed me under their breath, but they rarely quit. It was a fun, stimulating place to work and waiters received kudos from their peers for waiting tables at Littlejohn's, as well as decent tips.

Occasionally, I'd host a lock-in and get out my guitar – David Brent eat your heart out – and the kids were also guaranteed a place on the guest list for the 'Amnesia' events I had taken to hosting on Thursdays at Gates nightclub in the city centre, now Fubar. They were very credible nights and much sought after tickets. I wasn't quite the Glorious Leader, but the staff certainly knew I wasn't a dictator who lacked heart.

My commitment to the Stirling restaurant allowed Simon to oversee the kitting out of the new St Andrews venture, with the help of Paco, but a couple of weeks before I moved in a friend made a stunning revelation.

I had been knocking around with a girl who was close to his lawyers and she accidentally dropped a bombshell: "Isn't it great news about Simon selling the restaurants?" I was dumbstruck. I phoned Paco, who was equally taken aback. Neither of us knew a thing about it. The deal was rumoured to be £1 million for the lease of his three restaurants, signed with a significant Scottish company, CAC Leisure, who had interests in various cinemas, bingo halls and restaurants, as well as the renowned Flick's nightclub in Brechin.

I later discovered the motivation behind Simon's decision to sell up. His father unexpectedly passed away at the age of 57 and, with a young son at home and another on the way, Simon decided to put family first.

Ultimately, Paco received his 10 per cent, which allowed him to establish his own place in Perth and contributed to the creation of his successful group of restaurants, which he has worked long and hard to build.

I was left with nothing, much to my disappointment. Perhaps it was guilt that saw Simon, who's baptist, loan me the money to remodel the place I'd purchased in St Andrews but I felt let down, deceived even. Jake and I may have been on and off but I had harboured genuine hopes that in establishing St Andrews I could lay the foundations for our successful future together, both from a business and personal perspective.

Perhaps it was a fear of confrontation, but I chose to say nothing. I had put my trust in him and never thought he'd let me down, especially given his Christian background. I gave up a lot to answer his call. I was a DJ in one of the biggest clubs in Ibiza, enjoying the summer of my life, and I'd packed it in to hitch my future to his entrepreneurial wagon.

I've long wondered if I was wrong to keep my counsel but, in all honesty, I had been looking for a new challenge and had spent enough time in St Andrews to appreciate the quality of life that came with working there. I bit my tongue and focused on making Littlejohn's the very best it could be, my monthly salary now being paid by CAC Leisure.

We were busy from the very start, a 130 cover restaurant with big tables, often up to 10 or 12 diners, being turned over more often in the evening than a hospital mattress. I was working on my nerves and I loved it.

Every night was like playing a game of mental chess and, within weeks, I was touching grandmaster status. There were 24 tables and on a Saturday night there were three bookings confirmed every half hour and that was without walk-ins. Would that couple at table 12, who were on desserts, be finished within 15 minutes, which would allow me to place another couple of diners at the bar for a drink while they waited for places to become available?

Would that table of 10 students be finished within half an hour, which would allow me to break their tables into three settings of four and squeeze another 12 diners in before we wound down the kitchen at 10pm? My mind was a whirr of arithmetic and soon we were turning over up to £30,000 a week, phenomenal business.

Who would have believed it, Scooby in tie and dress trousers, directing staff and diners like an orchestra conductor? St Andrews took me so much to its heart customers even handed in new lines of natty neckwear for me to wear at work.

I may no longer have been waltzing around Bentley's in Kirkcaldy mimicking the style of Tony Hadley and the Kemp brothers, but I was still looking the part. Naturally, as a university town our customer base was mostly students and our most popular dish was a half CT – a cheese and tomato pizza, with baked potato or French fries and coleslaw. Carb packed and filling, it cost just £1.99 – and you'd be surprised at the number of cheques from Coutts and Co, the queen's bankers, written to pay such modest bills.

At Fat Sam's in Dundee I quickly got in tow with some local rogues and scallywags and there were some equally loveable characters among the students at St Andrews, all of them toffs.

They included Dougie Dick and his pal Dougal Fisken, whose family owned a car dealership in Forfar, as well as Maurice Forsyth Grant, apparently related to the royals, and Willie 'The Pig' Robertson, who family were, surprise surprise, pig farmers from Crail. We had some great nights together at Fat Sam's and, later, The Tunnel – the full VIP treatment for such exalted company, of course.

The explosion of the acid house scene had left me thirsting, more than ever, for DJ and promoter gigs. At Littlejohn's in Stirling I took every Thursday evening off, which allowed me to lean heavily on my Ibiza experiences when I set up those 'Amnesia' nights at Gates.

We attracted a really trendy crowd, drawn by music few others were playing. My Balearic adventures were paying off big time. We attracted an audience of cool kids, Adrian Rennie among them, a DJ who kicked off the night and later found even greater respectability at the 'UFO' nights hosted by Tin Pan Alley.

I took over from Adrian, using the records of my co-promoter and close pal Kenny Ritchie. It was the tail end of the summer of 1988 and Javier still had my vinyl collection he'd 'acquired' in Ibiza.

Unusually for me, I spent many of those nights in Gates stoned out my tree and I didn't handle Kenny's records as well as I might. I threw them around the DJ booth like a Greek waiter spinning plates, much to his chagrin.

Kenny was particular and precious about his vinyl – and rightly so. We took the takings at the door, while management at Gates relied on the significant spend at the bar on a night that would otherwise have been dead. Kenny's mumps and moans about the state of his records at the end of the night were usually silenced when we split a take of around £500.

My close pal Fraser Hotchkiss and I even returned to Rainbow Rocks in 1989, but the coast was clear as the Knowles had sold out to the Stakis Group, so all previous bad feeling was canned.

Once a month we hosted a night called 'Respect' – the name, in part, was chosen in an attempt to bridge the territorial differences that would often emerge on such occasions between kids from different towns such as Perth, Falkirk and Stirling.

The young teams from Falkirk and Stirling never got on but, in the end, we had to knock 'Respect' on the head because it was actually crews from Falkirk and Perth who were involved in one fracas too many.

I was also beginning to fight my own demons, particularly with ecstasy. Fraser and I split the takings on the door and also went 50-50 on DJ duties but on at least one occasion I got absolutely wasted on MDMA and spent the entire night standing in front of the DJ booth, waving to everyone on the dance floor below, just as I had with Billie Ray Martin and Electribe 101 at Fatties.

I even had the audacity to approach Fraser afterwards and claim I had made the entire night for the audience. He could and should have told me to fuck off, but he generously gave me a half the takings, to which I had absolutely no right.

My old promoter pal Tony Cochrane was also busy on the scene and I risked the wrath of my employers in Dundee once by nipping across the road to DJ at an all-dayer called 'Sweatbox', hosted in a club called De Stihl's, which was also owned by Stakis but really wasn't a patch on Fatties.

Tony, however, was a stunning networker who made it work, drawing his crowd to Tayside from as far afield as Aberdeen and Ayr. He offered me an hour long slot and I thought long and hard about its structure. The place had been resounding to solid beats for hours, so I decided to take a risk and finished my set with the Sister Sledge disco anthem 'Thinking of You'.

I chose it for the line, 'Now I'm living in ecstasy' and the place blew up in front of my eyes. It went absolutely gaga, taking the clubber experience to another level and the reaction gave me a buzz no chemical stimulant could ever reach.

Guru Josh was also riding high in the mainstream and dance charts at the time with his iconic track 'Infinity' and was supported in his set by a little known DJ named Carl Cox. They were both amiable characters and typical of the quality acts Tony could attract, although some had a higher opinion of themselves than others.

He gave us a PA at the time, MC Wildski, who was doing well on the back of a great record he'd released, 'I'm Talking To You'. He came into Fatties and we offered him a drink. He asked for two bottles of Bollinger and a large Jack Daniels and Coke. The round would have cost more than his appearance fee, a modest £50. We gave him a Bacardi and told him to like it or lump it.

Tony joined forces with Fraser and me in September 1989 to organise the first official rave in Stirling, hosted by the council-owned Albert Halls, and its legacy was added to life's chapter of 'What Ifs?'

On the same day at Ayr Pavilion a group of west coast dance music fans, under the name Streetrave, organised an event headlined by Mike Pickering and Graeme Park of Hacienda fame. They attracted several hundred to the venue, a decent turnout.

The planning of our event was as smooth as clockwork, no surprise with Tony involved, and we soon had a 900 sell-out and genuine headline acts including Radio One's Tim Westwood and Richie Rich, who had gained genuine traction on the scene at the time with his record 'Salsa House' which sampled Michael Jackson's 'Working Day and Night'.

Fraser and I did stints on the decks and the place was bouncing. We were in the right place at the right time. We had it covered from all angles. We had hired the venue so the door takings were ours and, unusually, so was the bar. We stocked it with a lorryload of seltzers, flavoured waters, and it was run by one of my life's true sweethearts, Nikki Cullis, and her pals from Glasgow.

I was aware many of the revellers were out their faces on acid and ecstasy. We took no part in any dealing, although we were not naive enough to believe it wasn't going on.

It was an all day event and there was no violence. Much of the scene was as concerned with fashion and looking good as the music – meaty house beats, Italo piano house popularised by the likes of 'Ride On Time' by Black Box and Wood Allen's 'Airport 89'.

They came from everywhere – Zammo, Wayne Dunbar and Jimmy Mackenzie from Dundee were joined by other ravers from across the central belt, Tayside and Perthshire. There was a great spirit to the event, really uplifting. We made several thousands in profit but, sadly, we could get away with it only once.

The writing was on the wall the following morning when the Daily Record called Stirling Council for comment on a story of 'acid house drugs barons using a council property to host a rave.' Barons? Fraser Hotchkiss and I were a couple of jack-the-lads. The closest we'd ever come to the Colombian drugs cartels was passing the coffee shelf in the local supermarket.

There was a touch of good fortune as the council official approached by the Record for comment was a relative of Fraser's and they did their best to set them straight. The bottom line is Stirling Council would have hired out wedding venues that weekend that ended in more violence than our rave was ever likely to see, but the public were spooked.

London sneezed and Scotland caught a cold. The UK national press was full of stories at the time of impromptu raves, particularly inside the M25, where up to 15,000 revellers turned up at carefully pre-planned venues including abandoned warehouses and countryside farms and fields. There was a moral panic, just as there had been with previous youth movements such as rock and roll and punk.

There was an unease, particularly as the first death attributable to ecstasy had been reported just two months earlier, sadly taking a 16-year-old girl as she partied at the Hacienda. Ultimately, the Record didn't run with their story but the whole experience gave Fraser a fright, an entirely understandable reaction.

He was a solid citizen, who loved his music and his young family. He had a responsible job and a mortgage and didn't want to endanger the life he had worked so hard to build. Our career as rave promoters was in serious jeopardy before it had really begun.

Meanwhile, over in Ayrshire, the Streetrave boys went from success to success. From their own humble beginnings they have built a phenomenal promotions company that later became Colours and now organises some of the best music events and club residences in the entire UK.

Call it sliding doors, but as one closed another one opened for me in Glasgow. I was about to hit club management, big time. However, in the end it cost me more than the 20 per cent of the business I stupidly gave up had I elected to stay at Fatties.

10

Talk about skating on thin ice.

Coasters Arena in Falkirk is a barn of a venue that has hosted sports events for more than 80 years, including ice hockey, basketball and indoor football. In the aftermath of that successful, if controversial, rave at Stirling's Albert Halls a couple of months earlier I reckoned there was still mileage in becoming a promoter.

Fraser, reluctantly given his personal circumstances, agreed to give it another whirl. We would have been fools not to have taken the plunge after a contact tipped the wink that Coasters Arena boasted a golden ticket in promoter terms, probably handed unwittingly to them by Falkirk Council – a 24 hour entertainment licence, which they never used.

I contacted a friendly lawyer, who confirmed the details. Alcohol could only be sold on the premises until 1am, in the licensed bar area, after which it had to be vacated, but we could use the rest of the venue for as long into the night as we wanted.

Ker-ching! An all nighter beckoned.

We packed around 700 punters into the disco area, with a bouncy castle and even face painters to help build the atmosphere. The music was banging with Italo house and the bulk of the crowd were out their faces on ecstasy as we approached 1am.

It was hot, damp, sweaty and smoky and the nearest thing to hell I'd experienced, but we still had our masterstroke to play. We emptied the disco and – here was our ace – pointed everyone in the direction of the more roomy ice rink downstairs, which had been converted for roller skating use. Gleeful clubbers swapped their shoes for skates and, tripping furiously, they were soon spinning around the floor at speed as well as on it.

It was the funniest sight I'd seen. We'd hired a little known band, TTF – The Time Frequency – for one of their first gigs. Scotland's techno pioneers went on to enjoy a string of chart hits under main man Jon Campbell with singles such as 'The Ultimate High', 'New Emotion' and 'Real Love' and they gave us an insight in Falkirk into the force they would become.

We also had PKA, riding high at the time with their single 'Let Me Hear You Say Yeah'. The place was buzzing, but we knew there would be a price to pay.

Inevitably, an hour or so in, the police arrived en masse, led by an officer of such seniority he had knotted braid like scrambled eggs along the peak of his cap. They weren't messing around but then again, neither were we.

He asked to see the promoter responsible for breaching the conditions of the licence and I stepped forward, thankfully with my lawyer on my right hand side. My brief had envisaged such a scenario when he had first scrutinised the paperwork I'd shown him a few weeks earlier.

Clearly, Falkirk Council had not issued a 24 hour licence to allow it to host all-night raves, but we were not breaking the law. Under its terms we had emptied the bar area by 1am and had simply moved downstairs to roller skate, serving the only thing the vast majority of our clientele wanted to drink at that stage anyway – mineral water.

My legal counsel caught my glance and said: "I'll take it from here Stuart," and invited the senior policeman into an office to study the licence in detail. The law were on the retreat within 10 minutes. They didn't like what they were seeing, but it was all above board and they could do nothing about it. A couple of police cars stayed outside the venue and kept a wary watch as we partied through until 7am but we knew our cards had been marked.

It was a shame as we'd grown fond of the venue over the previous few months. We had hosted several club nights at Coasters under the name 'Sueno' but, at that stage, were unknowing about the generosity of the licence.

Previous events, held every Friday night, had attracted several hundred punters until 1am and there was a decent mix of clubbers from the Stirling and Falkirk areas, many of them with allegiances to the football casual scene they thankfully left at the front door.

Our nights were all about the music and the fashion, not the fighting. There remained an undercurrent of tension which, thankfully, never flared but we had to keep a close eye on quality control of the acts and DJs we offered.

We were established enough that PA companies, similar to the one owned and operated by Tony Cochrane, would offer us bands hoping to break into the big time. On one occasion we were contacted and told we could have a five piece boyband out of Manchester for £100. Their manager was keen to emulate the success of American teen idols New Kids On The Block and they were undertaking a club tour the length and breadth of the UK, furiously plugging their first single.

Fraser and I took one look at a pic of the band, pretty boys in make up and lycra, and reckoned the Coasters crew would eat them alive. There would have been violence. We knocked back Take That for a pittance. The memory makes me smile today, but the call was correct. They weren't right for our club nights.

As a team, we would never pull the stroke of an all nighter at Coasters again as Fraser was mindful of sailing too close to illegal winds for those valid personal reasons and quit in the immediate aftermath.

We had been bobbing and weaving but the authorities were beginning to outsmart us with nimble footwork of their own. This was the height of acid house and the mainstream media were on high alert for the corrupting influence, as they saw it, of this damaging youth movement. Headlines screamed rebellion in England, where thousands would descend on fields and abandoned factories at short notice for all night raves.

It led to the Criminal Justice Act of 1994, a draconian piece of legislation by John Major's government that sought to outlaw outdoor dance festivals and 'music with a repetitive beat'.

Naturally, given its population, Scotland never hosted raves the size and scale of those seen in the south east of England, where up to 20,000 would regularly turn up to party. In fairness, Ingliston hosted up to 5,000 Scots at 'Rezurrection' in the nineties and Awesome 101 attracted 2,000 to their gigs in Livingston.

Scottish youth was determined to have its day and raves (legal and illegal) were memorably hosted in other venues including an industrial estate in Glasgow, organised by Desert Storm Soundsystem. The Desert Storm guys also put on 'Slam' at the Formakin Estate in Bishopton and the Rhumba boys even promoted a night on an old boat in Dundee.

At least I went out with a roar. In the summer of 1990 I had struck a deal with an old pal Gerry Coia, who ran Maxwell's 3D nightclub in Stirling and also held the franchise on the restaurant at Blairdrummond Safari Park. He may have needed some gentle persuasion, but soon agreed with my assessment it would be a really cool place to host a rave, which I called 'Beautiful Imbalance'.

I genuinely believe to this day the safari park owners didn't have a clue about the event. As far as they were concerned the restaurant, which sits in the centre of the park, had simply been hired out on a Saturday evening for a private function.

The numbers were compact, only around 150, but it suited the occasion as the restaurant area is small, although an overspill in the funfair area outside proved popular as we kept the shows open and, again, hired a face painter – unsurprisingly, tiger designs were the most popular choice among clubbers.

I DJ'd with my pal Steven McCreery and the night was an overwhelming success. Suspicions we were operating under the radar of the park's owners were only heightened when the three buses we'd organised to bring ravers to the event, which started at 7pm, were ushered in a side door.

There were peacocks running around the feet of clubbers but no-one dared venture as far as the enclosures hosting the lions and elephants even though security was so low key as to be non-existent. We piled out the place at 1am, ready to do it all again the following summer.

We almost made it too. I roped in my three pals from Erskine to PR the event – Paddy, Curly and Wee John, whose exceptional promotional endeavours around the bars of Glasgow had helped make The Tunnel such a force in clubworld.

Gerry Coia was in on the act again, figuring the previous year had passed off without incident so it would be madness to turn away the trade again. The 150 available tickets sold out immediately, most of them to clubbers from around the Glasgow scene.

The buses duly arrived at the side door of the safari park, but the punters had no sooner made their way inside than a squad of police arrived and busted the place. They'd been tipped off about the gathering and this time we were powerless to prevent them pulling the plug.

I'm still clueless about the official reason behind their decision, although no doubt concerns for the park's usual residents would have been uppermost in their thoughts. It's worth stressing again: no animals were harmed in this production. However, the action of the police left me in a quandary as I had 150 punters who had paid their money and were ready to rave.

I picked up the phone to Tracy McRorie and Steven Smith, who were running Maxwell's 3D that night. I gently asked Tracy if I still had a guest list on the go at the club and she confirmed it remained in place. "Any chance of getting 150 through the door in an hour?" I asked, cheekily. She laughed at my audacity and told me to bring them all in. She helped me save the night from the brink of disaster.

A couple of months later the nightclub changed its name from the eighties sounding Maxwell's 3D to Fubar, short for 'Fucked Up Beyond All Recognition' which was a phrase popularised in the Patrick Swayze movie of the time, 'Roadhouse'.

However, it was also a name that sounded more credible to the ears of the ravers who helped pack the place to the rafters that Saturday night. Their arrival en masse had alerted the club owners to the future and it was no longer Kylie and Jason warbling their love to the production values of Stock, Aitken and Waterman.

My career as a rave promoter was over – for the time being, at least – and so was my time at Fat Sam's. Long before Miley Cyrus found a job in demolition, we came in like a wrecking ball towards the end of 1989 when the owners decided on an extensive refit under the watchful eye of design guru, Ron McCulloch.

Fatties had promoted a casual, speakeasy style featuring dark woods and brass fixtures and fittings but Ron, a close pal of part owner Mark Goldinger, had seen the future. He drew up plans to install elevation decks and dance podiums and his vision was spot on for the new, rave-inspired crowd the venue was beginning to attract and hoped to nurture towards even greater profitability.

The club planned to close its doors for a week after one final, lucrative Saturday night, with the builders moving in first thing on the

Sunday morning. Willie The Pig, Dougal Fisken and the rest of the crew from St Andrews, along with staff such as Vinny Doyle and Danny Sweeney, accepted my invite to stay behind and give the labourers a helping hand.

So too did some of the boys from Dundee, including Dougie and Darren Taylor, Heath Bissett and Dundee United midfielder Ray McKinnon, who would later manage the club.

We allowed half an hour for the club to empty around 2am, poured a few drinks and rolled numerous thick, heavy joints – I should stress footballer Ray steered clear of the hash – and set about trashing the place.

We salvaged a nice mirror for Paco's new restaurant in Perth, but everything else was ripped out and piled high in the middle of the dance floor, which began to creak under the weight of it all. We said cheerio to a legend in style, working in almost complete darkness.

Someone finally threw open an emergency exit just as dawn was breaking and a plume of blow raced a cloud of dust to see which could hit fresh air first. We collapsed in a fit of giggles at the absurdity of it all. Fatties would never be the same for all of us ever again, in more than just design.

Ron McCulloch was a smart guy, with bold ideas that were on point for the developing dance trends of the time. He was a regular at Fatties in the second half of 1989 and as he drew up plans for the extensive re-fit I began to suspect he was measuring me up for a new challenge as he took an ever closer eye at how I managed a club that was running so well.

Ron had established a company, Big Beat, with my pals Colin Barr and Mark Woodhouse so he knew my reputation was solid and also, without blowing my own trumpet, I now enjoyed a track record of running successful and profitable clubs and restaurants.

He finally made his approach, pulling me aside one day to ask if I'd be interested in managing The Tunnel, the jewel in the crown of Big Beat's new and expanding empire. I was aware of The Tunnel – who wasn't? It was Scotland's first superclub.

Sure, places such as Flick's in Brechin were packing in thousands every month, but they were serving up so much cheese they should have been sponsored by Edam. Radio One DJ Steve Wright played there every weekend and the only cast member from Eastenders that hadn't made a guest appearance was Ethel Skinner's pug dog, Willy.

The Tunnel was different gravy. It was authentic and credible. I visited on its opening night when it hosted the after show party following a gig in the city by Soul II Soul and was in awe, utterly bowled over.

Clubs such as Flick's were the Akai of the Scottish nightclub scene. The Tunnel? It was Linn Hi-fi. The music, sound, DJs, everything was spot on. It was even the first Scottish club I can ever recall with toilet attendants, who handed out scents, sweets and soft towels for a small gratuity and provided management with sober eyes and ears in an area that wasn't always easy to police.

They appeared to have got the big things right at The Tunnel but, at that stage, I was equally as impressed with their attention to the small details that lifted it to another level completely.

The club was downstairs in a cavernous former snooker hall on Glasgow's Mitchell Lane and had been separated into three rooms, the main one of which would soon host a string of acts and superstar DJs that included Pete Tong, Danny Rampling, Paul Oakenfold, Sasha and Boy George.

The Big Beat boys had forked out a fortune on their sound system and got it right, big time. It was really meaty and pounding, but also crystal clear. The showpiece in the main room was two bass bins either side of the DJ booth that doubled as dance podiums. It was a thumping sound system, totally first class.

This old male ego is still boosted by the memory of Gemma and Lucy from my St Andrews days as well as a new squeeze, a sweetheart named Charlene, dancing their hearts out on the speakers above the crowd but with eyes only for yours truly.

The second room was more laid back and drew a discerning crowd to its musical menu of funk, hip hop, soul, jazz and house. The third room, which hosted VIPs, was the Blue Room, with a blue pool table and exclusive bar for those and such as those. It had its own doormen and was very elite. There was a guest list, but even that was no guarantee of entry. Your face had to fit. The selection policy of Saint Peter on the Pearly Gates appeared slapdash in comparison.

Surprisingly, perhaps, I demurred on an immediate acceptance of Ron's offer, not least because I was happy at Fatties. The salary on offer in Glasgow was exactly what I was earning in Dundee, £18,000-a-year. Fatties was the best club in Dundee by the length of the silvery Tay and, with it being revamped, things would only get better.

More than that, Mark Goldinger had dangled an offer under my nose the previous month, perhaps sensing Ron's designs on more than just the fixtures and fittings. Ron and Mark were best pals, with a string of successful business ventures already behind them, but it didn't prevent Ron making his play for yours truly. Mark moved to trump any offer, confiding in a plan to buy out the three other owners of Fat Sam's. How would I like 20 per cent of his new look enterprise?

I knew he was serious and not least because he had the financial clout and acumen to back his audacious plan. Mark was raised in Ayr and studied the flute and saxophone at the Royal Scottish Academy of Music and Drama, but dropped out of Leeds College of Music after a year to work as a bar manager for Peter Stringfellow, which was not a bad apprenticeship.

His family owned the Stockwell China Bazaar in Glasgow and he had also invested in a string of successful ventures that included Henry Afrika's and Nico's in Glasgow, as well as Club Cuba in Malaga.

He was a top bloke and really liked me. We regularly lit up a couple of joints and got stoned when he visited Fatties on those Saturday nights to ensure all was well. He'd stand at the back of his club, stroking his chin, master of all he surveyed. He was known as the quiet man of the Scottish club scene and there was genuine outpouring of grief when he died of a brain tumour in June 2011, aged just 55.

My ultimate rejection of his offer was dealt with in a cowardly fashion I regret to this day. Feeling the heat from both sides, I headed off alone to Tenerife for a week in the autumn of 1989 to gather my thoughts and decide the best way forward.

Quite frankly, it was a miserable few days all round. I popped my head into the famous bar complex, Veronica's, on the strip at Playa de Las Americas, reasoning I might pick up something to take back to Scottish clubland. An STD was most likely.

It was a horrible place, the 'Here we go, Here we go' brigade serenading a never ending stream of Sharons and Tracys. It made Skegness look like Las Vegas. I left after half an hour, but my mind was made up after a couple of days in the sun.

Shamefully, I chose to inform Fat Sam's of my resignation by fax before calling Colin Barr to tell him I'd take up Big Beat's offer to manage The Tunnel. Mark was a top bloke. I should have treated him with greater courtesy and respect and, with hindsight, should have stuck with him all along. Typically, he was sanguine about my decision, accepting it with a kindly mix of disappointment and good grace.

Why did I take the job, especially when I was so well settled in St Andrews and under no stress at Fatties? Undoubtedly, part of the draw was Colin and Mark and the opportunity to work with two good mates. There was also something in the air around Glasgow at the time. Pretty soon, the City of Culture tag would be hanging easily around its neck, like a label from the designer stores that were popping up all over the city centre.

I wasn't an Edinburgh boy, although I had enjoyed enough good nights out in the capital since my teenage years. Overwhelmingly, however, Glasgow was where I had socialised at clubs such as the Warehouse, Henry Afrika's and Panama Jax. It felt like home.

In truth, a wee bit of Rhona Hopkins also drew me to the west. The memory of that walk along the Silver Sands in St Andrews with Doobie the dog lingered long and Rhona was back working in Glasgow. Jake had returned from London and was part of my life again but I had been playing in the field when she was away and Rhona had left a lasting impression. I didn't so much struggle to shake it off. Rather, I was reluctant to give her up.

My relationship with the opposite sex has, until recent years, been complex. I was a high plains drifter when it came to women and never really officially finished with any of them. Rather, I just moved on. I was out every night as a young man clubbing all over central Scotland and it was easy to fall into relationships and liaisons that were rarely long lasting, never mind monogamous.

I'm not proud of the mess I made one Christmas when I bought seven items of lingerie for seven different women and handed out the baby dolls in all the wrong sizes. It insulted some to whom I presented a size 16, delighted others who opened a size eight.

They had been purchased on my behalf by Maureen Cullis, mum of one of the closest friends I've ever had, her daughter Nikki. We first crossed paths at Panama Jax in 1983 – I'm sure I had a thing for her big sister Gail – and established a bond that endured for years.

115

It wasn't just Nikki I adored but her entire family, who came from the traveller community. They lived in Glasgow and her dad Tom even gave me a van, free of charge, to help me back on my feet when I first went unwell. They were kind and extremely generous.

I could call Nikki at any time, day or night, and she would be there for me. Frequently, I'd phone at 11pm and ask if she fancied a drive to check out a club night in Paisley or Hamilton. She always responded positively. We attended weddings and social functions together. She helped run the bar at our raves and was a treasured friend and confidante.

Then I kissed her.

It was shortly after I had been put in charge of The Tunnel and it was the worst thing I ever did as it ultimately ruined two relationships, with Nikki and Jake. Jake had never been jealous of Nikki and, in fact, had accepted our friendship. If not warmth between them, there was certainly an understanding of our respective relationships – until the affair was uncovered.

Clearly, Jake harboured suspicions Nikki and I had moved beyond being pals. One morning, I was lying in bed with Nikki in my flat in Stirling when the doorbell rang at 6am. It was Jake, with a simple message. I had to make a choice. It was Nikki or her. I chose Jake.

Jake remained loyal and true to me but, deep down, I wonder if it was the beginning of the end for us, even after all the love and compassion she subsequently showed when I went unwell. The blame is entirely mine. In Buddhism, we talk often about the ability to change our karma. These last few years, I've had a lot of shit to acknowledge and try to resolve.

If The Tunnel was a woman I would have run a mile because she looked beautiful but I quickly discovered she was too high maintenance. Colin was the face of the club, Mark was in charge of the finances and Ron had built and designed the place, which he rarely tired of telling any pretty girl within earshot.

However, it was rudderless. No-one was actually running the business day to day, which is why they approached me in the first place. Fatties was 26 hours and easy peasy but I didn't realise how great a challenge The Tunnel would prove. I was up for most things, but this was a bomb scare.

The first thing I noticed was its 5am licence, granted as part of the goodwill afforded by Glasgow's City of Culture status, was more of a hindrance than a help. The drug of choice of many of its punters was ecstasy, so after MDMA had kicked in by 2am the bars did next to no business for the following three hours as the ravers danced to the beat of their own euphoria.

The club's hours were 10pm-5am and with 12 tills across the three rooms it meant a lot of cashing up. We were making money but those last three hours of the night ran at a loss because we had to absorb and subsidise staff and other costs with only pennies trickling through the tills.

We couldn't cut the hours because the attraction for many club-bers was the extended hours, which were also on offer at other places. I rarely left for home before 7am. At least nine hours a night over a minimum five days a week? It was fucking awful.

Stock checks proved another thorny issue. I arrived to find a monthly audit wasn't even in place, which was standard in any club. Put bluntly, it told you which staff, if any, were fiddling, either by dishing out free drinks to pals or pocketing money that should have been deposited in the tills.

At Fat Sam's, my guy Douglas was so good he could even tell me which optics were a measure light. There were no such controls at The Tunnel. I called in the ever reliable Douglas in my first month in the new job and he immediately highlighted a shortfall of £1200.

The boys told me: "If stock's short Scooby, then you're responsi-ble and will have to pay." Like hell I would. I hit back: "Colin, how many bottles of champagne at £60 a pop did you take from the bar on Saturday night and didn't pay?" He sheepishly confessed to three. I added: "And Woody (Mark Woodhouse), how many cases of beer did you lift from the cellar for that party last weekend because you needed a carry out?" He coughed up to two cases, another £40 from the business. And so it went on.

There was absolutely no malice from Colin, Mark or Ron. They were owners of the club that had quickly established its reputation as the best in Glasgow, on the back of their designs, dreams, vision and hard work.

They were enthralled and excited by the buzz of it all, but it was a beast from a business point of view. They had thrown me on its back and I was trying desperately to hold its horns and rein it into line.

I no longer had my trusted right hand man Vinny at my side but I inherited two bar managers who were first class and supportive. Yaz Faiz was sharp as a tack and John Reid was a brilliant operator who tragically passed away in 1992 aged just 25.

He died of liver failure after contracting Weil's Disease, the bacterial infection passed from rats' urine. There was speculation it could have been contracted by necking from bottles of beer that had been stored in our cellars but his family were, sadly, denied a definitive answer.

The Tunnel gave me several headaches and also, it must be acknowledged, countless highs. The club attracted a cross section of Glasgow society from the wealthy to young, hardened clubbers, gangsters, schemies and wannabes.

The place was dripping in Versace and Junior Gaultier from cool clothing stores such as Cruise and Ichi Ni San and the crowd wore Timberlands and Harley Davidson biker boots like a trend-setting army on the march.

I wore a 'uniform' of washed out jeans, paired with a white t-shirt and waistcoat, bandana and a black leather jacket and can only now confess to pulling on a pair of cowboy boots that added at least three inches to my height.

The Tunnel was the centre of the universe for a lot of people and the hype around the place was incredible. It was intoxicating to be one of the main men. I was looking good and attracting girls was never a problem, especially in a position heightened by more than just John Wayne's cast off footwear.

I didn't take ecstasy during my time in charge of the club, but lines of charlie were still hotwiring my brain regularly enough, along with almost daily cannabis consumption. I truly believed at that stage I wasn't a big drugs user, right? I still felt comfortable and safe in my recreational highs. I was also mindful of keeping my head screwed on to stay on top of an increasing workload.

We enjoyed our fair share of laughs. On Sunday nights we introduced karaoke. Ron was taken by the novel concept and we were among the first in the city to market it, hiring a fabulously funny wee guy, a little known actor, to MC the evenings.

He had the crowd eating from the palm of his hand with his constant string of Glaswegian patter and witty one liners before he invariably introduced the next punter up on stage to murder 'New York, New York'. Still Game's Ford Kiernan hasn't done too badly for himself in the years since.

We held a gay night on Mondays, never super busy but it still drew a crowd and unfortunately caused an old schoolpal some embarrassment. I hadn't seen him in years and in those less inclusive times he approached me at the bar and expressed surprise we shared the same sexuality and he would never have guessed I was gay. I had to explain I was actually working in the place, which left him a little red faced and tongue-tied.

John Crozier, still one of my dearest pals, paid me a visit one night and the daft sod walked into this ultra-cool club wearing a v-neck jumper. Everyone thought he was an undercover cop who had misjudged the dress code and gave him a wide berth. At least he found space to drink his pint in peace at the bar.

The St Andrews boys still visited regularly, although one Saturday night almost ended in disaster when a fire alarm forced the evacuation of the club.

Willie The Pig owned an Isuzu Trooper, which was vital for his farm, and had it kitted out with a top of the range hi-fi, including a huge beat box and matching speakers. He reversed his car into the middle of the street, opened the back door, and cranked out Westbam's 'The Roof Is On Fire' at top volume. The clubbers went loopy as they filled Mitchell Lane, dancing their hearts out.

On another occasion, a Sunday night, the place was flooded after a water drain collapsed in the street above. It was potentially very dangerous and we had to demand a quick evacuation, but the clubbers weren't for moving and not least as those boots they wore were utterly waterproof.

They stayed and kicked water around the main dance floor like gleeful kids in a puddle, belting out 'Singing In The Rain' at the top of their voices.

Friendships were made, even in just six months, that endure today. The Erskine PR team – Paddy, Curly and Wee John – were regular visitors to my new flat in Hyndland, in Glasgow's west end, and made it a home from home.

They knew every bar and member of staff in Glasgow city centre and their slick marketing and enthusiasm did as much as anything to establish

The Tunnel's reputation. We had some great regulars such as Gerdo, Swifto, Kendo, Pedro and Dara, wide-as-the-Clyde car dealers who walked into the sweltering club one night dressed head to toe in motorbike leathers.

They had come straight off tiny trial bikes they had bought on a whim earlier that day. They insisted on keeping their leathers on despite the heat and were promptly christened the Power Rangers.

We attracted many brilliant acts, some more memorable than the others. I did 20 minutes behind the DJ booth every now and again. I was still buying records and my actions in playing to the audience were driven mostly by ego as I sought to prove I still had relevance. For the most part, however, I was mindful of encroaching on the turf of in-house DJs Mel Barr and Michael Kilkie, both of whom were masters at controlling the crowd.

Guest DJs rarely flopped – Oakenfold, in particular, was a stand out. He has always been the daddy. However, American Frankie Knuckles, the Godfather of House, put on a set that was distinctly underwhelming. His mixing was seamless, technically flawless, but he stuck at 121 beats per minute all the way through. There were no highs or lows, but with the crowd out their faces on ecstasy they were soon 'gouching'.

The nondescript set induced a type of groggy drunkenness in the audience, who were denied the peaks and troughs normally associated with such appearances. In short, it was all a bit flat, hardly the most memorable experience for those in attendance.

Frankie finished his gig and in a desperate bid to salvage something from the night I leapt behind the decks and fired up 'Think' by DJ Stefy, a re-working of the Aretha Franklin classic and something of a Tunnel anthem. Finally, the place blew up and went tonto. We'd saved the day – but only just.

Rarely, if ever, in life have I been willing to portray myself as a hick from the sticks. Let's face it, Stirling is hardly Nowheresville but there was one aspect of The Tunnel's operation in which I was happy to step back and act as a small town boy and that was its drugs scene.

I knew the customs and cultures around dealing from previous experience, indeed my own personal use. I wasn't naive, I knew what was going down but there appeared to be a structure and organisation involving guys from Glasgow who were out of my league and I didn't need to get involved, even though I was part of management.

Colin and Mark were the faces of the club and had promoted themselves from their early days of 'Fresh' onwards. Everyone knew who they were. Everyone wanted a slice of them, or to at least bask in heat of their clubbing brilliance. Whatever the situation, their pride and joy ran smoothly from a security point of view and largely without incident throughout my time with Big Beat.

The Tunnel attracted the occasional arsehole, as all clubs do, but there was a positive vibe and energy in the place. It was never an intimidating atmosphere. There was an unspoken understanding. There would be consequences if the established order was threatened. In my time, it never was.

In huge part, that was also down to the influence of Cammy Bell and Kenny Mitchell, the two senior security staff who stood at the top of the stairs making the calls that mattered. They wore cossack hats and black jackets and wielded the power firmly, fairly and with the occasional favour. They knew the made men and also the madmen. They kept out the dross and knew which of the very well dressed still carried the potential to cause trouble.

Stripping fashions aside, crucially they knew which punters were loyal to the club, whether their jeans had cost £20 or £200. On the rare occasions they had to intervene to break up a rammy, they were also utterly brave. All aspects of security at The Tunnel were well covered.

I felt unsettled only once, on a quiet midweek night when I stood at the door downstairs and several known faces from the Glasgow underworld appeared. Their visit was for nothing more sinister than a late night drink and the two security staff on duty at the cash desk followed them into the club, no doubt to ensure their comfortable passage to the bar or maybe even the Blue Room.

It wasn't particularly busy so I wasn't unduly perturbed at holding the fort and a couple of minutes later an older guy, well dressed and in his sixties, made his way down the stairs. I stepped forward and politely told him: "Not tonight pal, I don't think it's quite your scene."

He looked at me with eyes I quickly noted were pleading, but also carried a hint of malevolence: "Please, don't let me lose face." A little more hesitantly this time, I responded: "I'm trying to do you a favour and save you eight quid. I don't think this is your type of place." His cold eyes remained fixed on mine: "I really would like to come in for a drink."

Maybe it was the tone of his speech, or perhaps it was my own inner voice calling on years of past experience, but I made a snap decision and stepped aside to let him pass. A few moments later the bouncers re-appeared and explained the visitor was a notorious crime lord, who had been walking a couple of minutes behind his friends they had just shown into the club.

Around 18 months later I was standing looking in a shop window on Renfield Street, minding my own business, and felt a tap on my shoulder. I turned and my face immediately went chalk white.

It was Mr Big, this time with a smile playing at each side of his mouth. He said simply: "Son, you made a good decision that night at The Tunnel," and walked off. I couldn't even muster a reply. The whole incident left me spooked.

It was becoming increasingly clear I'd wandered into the wrong movie. I'd taken the wrong job for the right reasons, but felt increasingly isolated. I was flying solo at The Tunnel. I was aware Colin, Mark and Ron, as well as Colin's brother Mel, were a strong and tight team and I wasn't penetrating their inner circle.

Our friendships would remain solid and none of us did anything untoward professionally or personally, but the chemistry for the long term management of the club had failed to develop. I knew how to operate, of that there was no doubt, and the other guys were experts in their own particular fields but the total wasn't greater than the sum of its parts.

I didn't feel part of a team and that shouldn't come as a surprise. After all, my previous jobs in club and restaurant management had allowed me to build my own squad of staff and as fabulous as most of the people I'd inherited at The Tunnel were, they weren't my hired hands.

Maybe the three partners felt I wasn't doing enough. Maybe I felt Colin and Mark, in particular, had eased off when I was appointed, happy to hand the bulk of the unglamorous work to me while they enjoyed its fruits.

No matter. It came as no surprise when Ron called me into a meeting just under a year after I'd started and told me it wasn't working out. Unfortunately, they'd have to let me go.

I didn't put up a word in argument. Instead, I breathed a big, fuck off sigh of relief.

tranzmitter
scoops, stories & chill-out options

EDITED BY ROB FEARN

Fight with Dario G wrecked my life, says producer

'Sunchyme' adversaries: Dario G (above) and (main pic) Stuart Cochrane

A SCOTTISH producer has ended a two year battle to prove Dario G's chart smash 'Sunchyme' was based his track. The fight wrecked his relationship with his fiancée and the resulting stress caused him to suffer a mental breakdown.

Stuart Cochrane rejected Dario G's out of court offer of one per cent of the royalties – around £60,000 – and it was later withdrawn. He said, "I wanted to prove it was my record, but now I just want to say sorry to my woman for what I put her through."

A musicologist's report found that both tracks shared the same tempo and musical key, sampled 80s hippy popsters the Dream Academy and featured piano solos. But it concluded that, while Cochrane's track, 'Yeah Oh', may have provided the basic ideas, 'Sunchyme' could not be seen as "an actual adaptation".

A spokeswoman for Dario G's label, Warner Brothers, said, "He's saying they stole the idea, and you can't really say that in dance music. Dario G uses the same sample but is a lot better. The guy feels like he's lost a lot of money but he was never going to make it because his track wasn't good enough."

Neil Taylor, from copyright body MCPS, explained that Cochrane would have to prove "a substantial part of the original song" had been copied. No ruling has been made on what constitutes a substantial part when the song is based on a sample.

Cochrane, 35, from Stirling in Scotland, cut his track in 1995.

Copies were mailed out in May '97 and it was played on the radio by Graham Gold. 'Sunchyme' was released a month later.
MARK WHITE

■ Copying of ideas in dance music isn't just an issue for unknown producers. 'Go' by techno nutter Moby – which used the theme from TV's Twin Peaks – was reworked for use in a Toyota advert. The judge in the copyright case ruled beats and bassline did not by themselves consist music, and dismissed the action.

Mixmag, April 1998.

The Modfather…front row, second right. The Stirling and Distric Gaelic choir, Mod champions 1972.

Cousin Jean with my faithful old friend, Cindy the dog.

Hair's one I should probably keep to myself;
my school photo from Bannockburn High.

Me and Vee, the love of my life.

Three's company … me with Alex and Mac, my beloved parents.

Everything starts with a 'D' … one singer, one song on the beach in Ibiza.

Scooby and Doobie … two of a kind.

Stone me … Rizla and hash to the fore as I prepare to skin up – again.

Fraser and I arrive for adventures in Ibiza, our bags packed with Irn Bru and square sausages.

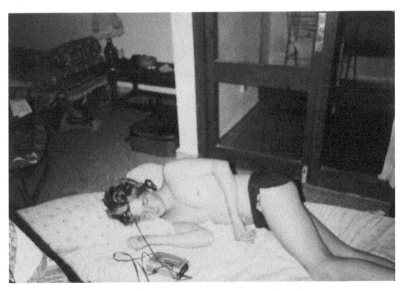

Wake Me Up When It's All Over … enjoying a siesta in Ibiza.

Mirror, mirror on the wall… Fraser, Caroline and I get ready for a big night out.

Ibiza young guns… from left Sean Gentleman, me, Franny, Brian "Trapper" Robinson and Fraser.

Taps aff…from left me, Sean, Franny and Caroline.

Another quiet night at Maxim's for me and Tony. The coke's just out of shot.

SCOT 'WROTE DARIO G HIT'

A SCOTS musician claims chart smash Sunchyme was based on a song he recorded two years earlier.

Sunchyme, performed by Dario G, made No 2 in the charts last year and was only kept off the top slot by Elton John's Candle In The Wind.

Stuart Cochrane says it was lifted from his tune Yeah Oh, recorded in a Glasgow studio in 1995.

Two years later Stuart paid £800 to press 300 copies on yellow vinyl with a sun motif in the centre and distributed them, hoping the song would catch on.

Stuart, 35, of Plean, Stirling, says: "The next thing I knew I was hearing a tune on radio and thinking, 'That's mine.' But the announcer said it was Sunchyme by Dario G.

Similar

"I thought it might be a coincidence that someone had produced something very similar to mine.

"But when I bought a copy I realised it was yellow, like mine, and where mine had a sun motif this one had the title

SHATTERED: Stuart

By EDWARD TREVOR

Sunchyme. I was absolutely shattered."

Lawyers acting for Stuart called in a musicologist who concluded four elements of Yeah Oh had been copied in Sunchyme.

Solicitors acting for Dario G said the star planned Sunchyme before Yeah Oh was written—but offered Stuart a one per cent cut of the hit's royalties.

It would have pocketed him £60,000—but he rejected the offer which has now been withdrawn.

Stuart said: "What I wanted was an admission it was my tune."

WILLIAM WALLETS helps the needy and bashes the greedy

PAGE 57

News of the World,
February 1998.

A working class lad done good? Me and Jake in our finest.

Cover stars…with Ross Waddell and Rhona Scotland, from Scottish rave
bible mag 'Club Scene'. We showcased a track as Area 51 called 'Let It Move
You'.

Beautiful Imbalance CD cover and track listing, one of five CD collections
I pulled together as I fought back from the brink of mental chaos.

Real Love...one of our publicity posters underlined the credibility of the acts we attracted to The Plaza.

We are not worthy...co-writer Gary Ralston and me with legendary DJ Alfredo.

Birthday greetings…me, Barry Fraser and Jok McPherson at my 40th.

Friends reunited. With the Mambo brothers in Bridge of Allan…from left Danny O, John Devlin, me, Leon Moodie, Bob Paterson, Alan and Christian Anadon.

Portrait of the artist as a young man ... on the decks at The Plaza.

Gimme Shelter ... me and long term producer pal Andy Haldane.

Always game for a laugh … me and Vee.

The best exercised dog in the district … my dad, Alex, with Doobie.

Making mischief and music: Calum McLean, Colin Tevendale, me and Jok at Apollo Studios in Glasgow.

Postcard from the edge…I was falling seriously unwell at this time, but Javier and Caroline always had my back.

Fantastic

HERE AT LAST.

HAPPY + TAKIN
IT EASY. CAROLINE
+ JAVI ACE SPECIAL
PEOPLE. THEY'VE TAKEN
YOUR JOB OVER.
DON'T WORRY!!

SCOOBS.

Alix Mac + Doobie
97 Station Rd
Bannockburn
STIRLING

Kitchen sink drama…Janice and I hard at work on our research for the book.

All our yesterdays…the fabric of Cafe Mambo hasn't particularly changed since 1994, but Javier and Caroline have transformed this part of San Antonio.

11

American superstar DJ Moby didn't ask for much when we lured him across the Atlantic to headline 'Love' at the Plaza, but we could at least have got his name right.

It's impossible to overstate the influence Moby had on the dance scene in the early nineties as he helped bring that style of music to the mainstream in a stellar career that also involved singing, songwriting and record production.

It was something of a coup to tempt him from New York to put on a set at the Plaza, a rundown former music hall at Eglinton Toll on the southside of Glasgow, just a mile from the city centre. Running and promoting 'Love' at the Plaza was the most hedonistic, thrilling, fun-packed 12 months of my life – and not without its dangers and challenges.

However, quietly-spoken Moby gave us no such issues. We picked him up at Glasgow Airport and he issued only two polite requests, for a church to pray in and a vegan meal to eat. We took him to visit Jesus in the west end of Glasgow and forked out a few quid on a specialist vegan caterer to provide him with a feast fit for a king.

He was in fine fettle later that night as he stepped onstage to DJ in front of 1,500 punters almost entirely off their faces on ecstasy. Goodness knows what our MC, the ever-ebullient Jim Ford, was on. He took control of the mic, walked to the front of the stage and shouted: "Ladies and gentlemen, give it up – a huge 'Love' at the Plaza welcome for tonight's star DJ, all the way from New York…BOABY!"

The crowd were so out their tits they barely noticed while Moby himself, cans clamped tightly over his ears as he lined up his first track, was oblivious. I groaned inwardly and then laughed, having long ago learned to treat anything Fordy did or said with a sense of disbelief.

I had a love-hate relationship with him when I first went unwell. We didn't always see eye to eye and there was occasional friction, but he was the only one who told it straight when locked wards in psychiatric units replaced my previously open roads.

Friends and family had a tendency to treat me with kid gloves when signs of my mental illness were first displayed. Fordy was blunt to the point of brutality: "The only person who can sort Scooby out is Scooby himself. He can get help, but ultimately it's down to him." He was dead right.

I first came across Fordy in 1986, when he was a DJ at Le Clique. He hung out beforehand in Raffles, the bar in Stirling town centre where I put on a pre-club set. He was always amused by the sheriff's badge I wore on the lapel of my denim jacket.

Fordy was a good pub and party DJ, up for banter and giggles. I was getting serious about mixing at that stage, which was a concept he grasped as easily as Japanese algebra. At one point he confided in me, quite innocently: "You make your money awful easy for someone who doesn't have to speak when they're playing records, Scooby."

Fordy came into my life again in the aftermath of my stint at The Tunnel, when I packed up in Glasgow and returned to live in Stirling. I wasn't saying goodbye to the Yellow Brick Road that led to the heart of the big city. I was still actively involved in several club nights there, but I was happy to establish my base in my home town again.

In 1991 the dingy, unlicensed basement under Ronnie's Bar that had previously hosted such bawdy social spectacles involving strippers, illegal parties and all night lock-ins had been transformed into an upmarket restaurant, the East India Company.

Always with an eye for an opportunity, I discovered Ronnie's Bar upstairs was available and took on the lease of the property, which had been lying empty. I named it Woody's Bar on account of the rich mahogany on its walls, but in agreeing to pay rent of £300-a-week I must have had sawdust in my head.

The bar was barely twice the size of my living room. It was screwed from the start. After Fat Sam's my trusted lieutenant Vinny Doyle had also made his way back down the A90 to Stirling and was running a popular bar and restaurant, The Courtyard, but he was up for joining forces again as a partner in the new venture.

We opened in the winter of 1991 and set about trying to re-create the success of Ronnie's Bar and there were echoes of the past in our boisterous 'Monday Club', run by Fordy.

As an MC with a big personality and quick wit, he perfected the concept of the phone call wind-up long before Scottish radio stations cottoned onto its comedic value. Every week he arrived from his home in Coatbridge with a phone and wired it to our sound system so everyone in the bar could hear a conversation from both ends.

Punters in the pub would step forward with tales of revelry and infidelity from the previous weekend involving friends and family. Fordy would quiz them about every aspect of events and then pick up the phone. Mayhem ensued.

Calls usually went like this: "Hello, is that Jim So-And-So? I'm Johnny Such-And-Such. I've been told you took my girlfriend out in Perth on Friday night and shagged her afterwards. Did you think I wouldn't find out? What the fuck you playing at?"

The call would always end in fits of outrageous laughter from the floor, while expletives were spluttered from the party on the other end of the line, who was invariably guilty.

On one occasion Fordy called a local lad, Billy Caddies, who lived above Raffles across the street. Billy's a good lad but Fordy fooled him completely when he phoned and claimed someone was threatening to jump off his roof. Could Billy go out onto the street and make sure the vulnerable person was okay and talk him down from the slates?

Billy raced downstairs and into the middle of the road and searched frantically above, only to be met with gales of laughter from the punters at Woody's, who were crowded at the bar window with their noses pressed against the glass.

In reality, the landlord had his heel stamped firmly against my throat. Mondays were jumping and at the weekend Woody's Bar became a popular departure point for the buses leaving for 'Love' at the Plaza, but

Vinny and I had taken our eye off the ball. He had met a girl and I was busy building 'Love' into a major player on the Glasgow club scene.

The pub was haemorrhaging cash which, for reasons that will become clear, I couldn't afford to lose. It was ultimately being run by Jake, helped by her cousin Susan, with my dad Alex taking on the role as cleaner. I looked at the books in the autumn of 1992, after less than a year in business, and was shocked to discover we were already £11,000 in debt.

Panicking, I went to see my lawyer. I had my own, very valid reasons to fret financially but I was more mindful of the position of Vinny, who was a full partner and had given up a solid position at The Courtyard to hook up with me again.

My lawyer was blunt and to the point: "Half the profit, but also half the loss – your partner owes you £5,500." My head was spinning. I could have done with that cash, but how could I hold Vinny to account when the bar had been my idea? I drove to the pub, asked Vinny for his set of keys, and told him to walk away. I absorbed the £11,000 loss alone.

My name was mud in Stirling for a while and still is among certain people. I'm the guy who made Vinny Doyle redundant after he had given up everything to join forces with one of his closest pals. Well, there's the truth.

I stumbled on for another couple of months and tried to make it work, but my heart wasn't in it. I dug deep into my limited reserves, paid off our debts in their entirety, and closed the doors for good.

The secret of being put out to grass is to never let it grow under your feet. I had been down at being dumped by The Tunnel, but was never out. In fact, I soon reconciled myself to an unyielding truth. If I wanted to make a success of my career as a DJ and promoter, I would have to carve my own niche and not be beholden to others.

If I couldn't make it work with good pals such as Colin Barr and Mark Woodhouse in Glasgow's top nightclub, how could I make it work with other people at all?

In the first half of 1991 an idea began to ferment that I could follow the success of Colin at Joe Paparazzi's, but on my own terms. Obviously, Colin was no longer hosting 'Fresh' on a Sunday night as he was totally absorbed in making The Tunnel a success and Joe's was lying empty on a Friday.

I had spotted my gap in the market. It was time to make a move. Best of all, I couldn't get bumped this time as it would be all my own, beautiful creation.

The idea came together over games of backgammon with the Erskine PR crew, Paddy, Curly and Wee John. Buzzy Wares bar and restaurant in Glasgow's Princes Square may have lacked the sunny, laid back sophistication of Cafe Del Mar in San Antonio to play my favourite board game, but it was a hub of activity I found equally as creative.

The influence of J and T Graphics in Glasgow's Parnie Street, next to the Tron Theatre, should not be under-estimated either. In fact, ask anyone who promoted clubs in Glasgow and the central belt of Scotland in the eighties and nineties about J and T's – I called it Jammy's – and they will tell a similar tale.

It was a printing shop owned and operated by two pals, Jammy and Tommy, and was used by everyone to print their flyers, from Colin at The Tunnel to Joe Deacon at The Metro in Saltcoats.

My relationship with Jammy stretched back to 1985. Who knows how we first met, but I needed flyers for an event I was promoting and was told he was the man to approach. During office hours they were as straight as a die, printing business cards, leaflets, letterheads, receipt books and the likes for a string of well established companies.

After 5pm? My Goodness, Jammy and I would sit and get completely stoned and creative, producing flyers that, even today, stand the test of time in terms of artistry and design.

Admittedly, as an outsider from Stirling I struggled initially to make my presence felt against the big boys of the city's nightclub scene. I paid for my flyers on the nose for the likes of Rainbow Rocks and Le Clique, which earned me respect but not a place on the pecking order above Henry Afrika's, Panama Jax, Tin Pan Alley, The Cotton Club or The Warehouse.

I made my breakthrough one night when Jammy confessed, through a hash fog of peasoup proportions, that he'd set his heart on a brand new Escort XR3i cabriolet. Didn't Jake's dad Angus own a Ford dealership? Better still, after a word in his ear from Jake, couldn't Angus offer Jammy a deal his rivals in Glasgow couldn't even begin to match? Jammy got his car and I was rewarded with a place on his list of favourites for the next two decades.

Along with the Erskine crew, I confided in Jammy about my idea for a club night at Joe Paparazzi's and we set about designing the flyers that would match the ambition.

Joe Paparazzi's remained a cool hang out and as I reasoned all of life spun off the feelings of the heart, it seemed fitting to call it 'Love'. I was an outsider to many of the clubland players in Glasgow but had made real progress, despite the ultimate rejection from The Tunnel, and was an inch away from the acceptance and affirmation that deep down I craved.

For years I'd lived on my wits, learned successfully on the job in bars, clubs and restaurants through instinct and hard graft. I knew I had the components to create my own special club night in a leading city centre venue. No compromises and no half measures. Everything I had achieved and created over the previous 10 years – I was still only 28 – had been building to this point.

We set a date, a Friday night six weeks in the future of early summer 1991. We plastered the city centre with advertising, all of it illegal.

Poster Davy was your man (we never did discover his real name). For a small sum, usually 50 pence per poster, he would stick your posters anywhere, probably even the front doors of the City Chambers if you were bold enough to ask.

He played a constant game of cat and mouse with the council and its official bill poster, Miles Cooney. Miles had a lucrative business advertising bands and concerts legitimately and also a heart of gold – when he retired he sold his profitable company to The Big Issue for only £1.

However, he was viewed by club night promoters and especially Poster Davy as a figure akin to the Child Catcher from 'Chitty Chitty Bang Bang'. In fairness, he could hardly stand by and see his official prime sites defaced by cheeky rivals.

Poster Davy was never caught and did us a great turn – writing the word 'LOVE' with 40 A2 posters on the Jamaica Street bridge, for example. Other posters featured our 'Love' logo and underneath was written 'Four weeks to go'.

We updated them every seven days and also hijacked every corner of the city centre with posters declaring 'Love is the drug', and 'Love is the message'. In the meantime, the PR boys had flooded pubs and even rival clubs, putting out the message of the new player soon to enter the scene.

The hype was incredible. On the first night I'd sourced a red carpet and a couple of Harley Davidson motorbikes even stood like silver sentries outside the entrance. It was a sell out. They were queueing down the street – well known clubland faces, a big crowd from The Tunnel, gangsters in Versace, DJs, promoters and club owners.

Inside, Fraser and Billy Kiltie, who owned the nearby 23rd Precinct record shop, ramped up the atmosphere still further with good house music from the DJ booth. I was mingling and tingling, high on something other than a line of coke for once.

The crowd were enjoying themselves, getting into the buzz. An hour in, shortly before midnight, I knew the punters and music were entirely on point. I saw the future and it dazzled brighter than the strobe lights throbbing on the packed dance floor.

And then … nothing. Literally, nothing. The music cut out and after an initial panic I remembered the breaker switch at Joe Pap's that silenced the sound system if it went above a certain decibel level. The crowd raised the roof when it happened at 'Fresh' but there was only a bemused murmuring this time. At 'Fresh' the music always kicked in again after a couple of seconds but 10 seconds passed, then 20, then a minute. Fuck. This was serious.

Fraser and Billy and some of the staff tried desperately to find the sound source and power outlets but all appeared in order. The lights in and around the club remained operational. It wasn't a power cut, but clearly a defect in the electricity supply going into the DJ booth.

I turned to the manager of Joe Pap's, who was equally as frantic. Five minutes stretched to 10. It felt like 10 hours. The conversation levels in the club plummeted to the stony sound of awkward silence.

My heart sank. Slowly but surely my A-list crowd made their way to the door and began trickling onto Sauchiehall Street. Soon it was a wave. Embarrassed, I quietly pleaded for the ground to open up and swallow me.

I don't believe it was sabotage, rather a surge of power that fatally compromised the electrics. I left the club soon after and drove a couple of miles to Whiteinch, where I had been offered solace by Nikki at her home.

I climbed into bed with her, utterly exhausted, and cried myself to sleep in her arms. You only get one chance to make a first impression. 'Love' at Joe Paparazzi's crashed and burned. So near and yet so far.

However, I couldn't fold, not least as a financial catastrophe was looming in the background. I wasn't ready to step out on my own again so soon, my ego and self-confidence still too bruised.

Soon after the setback of 'Love' at Joe Paparazzi's, I teamed up with promoter Steven Sleepman, who had just been bumped from his long-standing gig at Tin Pan Alley, where he hosted a club night known as 'The Orb'.

He had a brand that still had legs and, just as crucially, I had the PR contacts with the Erskine boys and my own marketing lads from Stirling that could give it a new lease of life. All we needed was a venue and our prayers were answered when a club owner from Paisley, Bill Baillie, stepped forward and offered us his place, Network.

It was lying empty, but he drove a hard bargain. He wanted the bar takings and would handle staff costs, but we reasoned his deal of £1-a-head per ticket sold would still net us around £1,200 on a capacity crowd.

We pulled it off and pretty soon every Saturday night busloads were coming from as far away as Stirling, Falkirk and Glasgow, as well as strong support from the Paisley club crowd. We had relevance, integrity and value.

One Saturday night in August 1991 we booked The Prodigy to gig at the club, 24 hours before their debut single 'Charly' crashed into the top 10. A couple of months later it was Belgian/Dutch dance group 2 Unlimited, who also shot into the top 10 the following evening with their first record 'Get Ready For This'.

We were cool, with our fingers on the pulse of musical, social and fashion trends. I enjoyed earning good cash again. No-one in my immediate circle knew just how badly it was needed.

We had it good for several months but, as always, greed took over. In an echo of what was to come at 'Love' at the Plaza, Baillie told Steven to get rid of me, no doubt reasoning he could split the takings more lucratively in his favour.

Steven represented 'The Orb' brand, but Baillie made the fatal mistake of underestimating the strength of good PR. The marketing guys were loyal to me and were working hardest to drive crowds through the doors every weekend.

Steven was keen to continue to milk the cash cow and didn't put up much of a fight to keep our team in place. His own squad were hardly whispering words of support for me in his ears. I knew his DJ group didn't like me or believe I was as credible. They were heavily influenced by techno. I came on for the last half hour of 'The Orb' and opened it up with Italo house, which was much more upbeat and enlivening for the crowd.

We split, citing the old chestnuts of 'musical differences' and 'conflicts of interest'. As is often the case, those terms were just a euphemism for overwhelmingly naked avarice.

It's an occupational hazard in the promoters' game. Cut throat? Some of those guys would have made Sweeney Todd look like Barber of the Year.

On too many occasions the club owner, in particular, plays his part in baking a lavish jam sponge then quickly decides the biggest slice still isn't rich enough. He gets rid of the chef, cuts back on the quality of ingredients, and still expects the finished creation to rise to the occasion. I've seen it a million times.

Ultimately, Baillie was left with stale crumbs. Nights at the Network didn't last long after I left and took my PR pals with me and Steven was soon back on the graft, scratching for his next opening. It was a role I knew well.

For my part, I returned to hosting a Saturday night at Panama Jax called 'Circa', the highlight of which was getting in tow with Manchester DJ crew Luvdup, who enjoyed chart success with a thumping remix of Corona's 'Rhythm of the Night'.

Mark and Adrian started out as DJs at events organised by indie band The Farm and were a couple of party animals, absolutely outrageous. The minute they received their fee for performing all they did was hand it straight back over for drink and drugs.

They had found a more than willing wingman to their mischief. They returned the favour, booking me to DJ at the nights they hosted in Manchester, known as 'Hell'. It was anything but. They only gave their club that name so they could plaster the city centre with advertising billboards that read 'Go To Hell.' Their devil had all the best dances.

As if to prove there were no hard feelings, The Tunnel even offered me the chance to host my own club night on a Sunday, known as 'Bounce'. The Erskine boys ramped up the PR – I ordered leather fliers to distribute, surely a clubland first – and Mel Barr stepped in to assist me on DJ duties.

It only lasted a few weeks, but was great fun. In the end I ran out of steam, in more ways than one. I flooded the dance floor with beach balls every weekend, but it was a bastard to blow up 300 of the things, especially when my lungs were inevitably burning from the glorious sting of good hash.

Friends came in and out of my life, relationships with most girls burned brightly then turned to dust, but cannabis was a constant throughout my adult years. I smoked blow constantly, every day, at least five thick joints, from the moment I woke up to the last remnants of the evening when I laid my head on my pillow to sleep.

As we moved into the nineties, coke also came into play more frequently. It was £60 a gram and on most nights out I would take at least a gram, occasionally as many as three. It was like paying £180 for a bout of flu with paranoia.

My nose was constantly sniffing as my worried eyes searched frantically around the room for confirmation in my racing mind that all was not as it should be. In the first few years I'd stuck to a gram a night, but coke makes you greedy.

There was always a ready supply in Glasgow, the quality dangerously variable. Sometimes it had been cut so much it was more baby powder than Bolivia but if it eventually hit the mark, who cared?

No Brownie points are sought for my confession I may have been a drugs user, but I was never a dealer. Mind you, I gave plenty of the stuff away. I wanted a recreational high, not a ropey business empire.

My life was dedicated to music. Drugs were a huge and influential part of my life, but I wasn't motivated to try and make money from them. Club promotion was safer – okay, only just, at times – and more legitimate. I've never been inspired by violence or the threat of it, which I suspected was never far from the surface of the dealer's lot. Love is the drug and all that.

I was arrested just once for possession, an episode so ridiculous now it makes me laugh. A group of lads from Stirling rented a cottage in Aviemore for a weekend in the early nineties. It was the stag do of my hairdresser pal Steven Croal and a string of sports cars, including my own MR2, made their way up the A9.

On the Friday night we piled into a local boozer, The Crofters, and they must have thought the Cosa Nostra had arrived for a sit down. On the Saturday night we took a mini bus to the same pub and it was madness. Lines of coke, poppers and an assortment of other drugs were being taken without much discretion and it soon got out of hand.

I wasn't drinking and so left early while the others waited on the bus. I strolled into the street and spotted a policeman eyeing up my licence plate, A14 LUV. We had an amiable chat about cars, but the pub doors flew open and the Stirling crowd fell onto the pavement.

It was all so messy 999 had been called and pretty soon two vans arrived, one full of officers and another with snarling alsatian dogs and their handlers. It was like the Wild West as the Stirling boys battled with the law and I will never forget the sight of Steven rolling around the pavement, physically fighting one of the dogs. In fairness, if it was a boxing match he would have taken it to at least the seventh round.

Three guesses who was the only one arrested? They impounded my vehicle and took me to the station. A quick body search revealed £600 in my back pocket and my admission I organised raves for a living was like a red rag to a bull.

They turned my car upside down and even looked inside the sleeves of every bit of vinyl in my record box in the boot. Finally, they found what they were obviously looking for – a particle of cannabis resin on the passenger seat, with a street value amounting to a magnificent 28 pence.

In the meantime, the revellers had gathered back at the cottage and, mindful of a raid, collected every drug in the place and buried it in the back garden.

After 20 minutes, their highs heading south, they clearly thought, 'Fuck it'. The shovel was brought out once more from the shed and used to dig it all back up again and to hell with the consequences. The police never did knock on the door.

However, they charged me and a couple of months later I attended Inverness Sheriff Court. The night before I checked into a local hotel and fingered through a Gideon bible, slowly coming to terms with the fact a conviction would sit on my file and make future travel to the United States, in particular, utterly impossible.

The judge was more forgiving. He took one look at the case notes, listened to the prosecution's threadbare case, and threw it out. I was a free man, without a blemish on my character.

My commitment as a promoter and DJ was to a club industry and rave scene that, brutally speaking, needed the drugs side of the night to work for the overall occasion to be considered a success. That's the honest truth, even though it may be unpalatable to many.

Was there a drugs scene at The Tunnel? Undoubtedly. Were drugs available at 'Love' at the Plaza? Unquestionably. We weren't running jamborees. I knew I was dealing with significant players from the time and moment I was approached and asked if I fancied organising raves at the Plaza.

The conduit was a friend, who shall remain nameless, and he ran a DJ agency. We always had a good and strong relationship, but he wasn't someone to be crossed.

Another player in the nightclub scene fancied a slice of his business, poaching a couple of his regular gigs to his new stable. As a consequence, he was invited to my pal's home for a cup of tea. Unaware, he arrived and was told to read the paper on the table while my mate nipped into the kitchen to put on the kettle.

He picked up the paper and an open razor dropped from within its pages. He scarpered, sharpish. The message had been delivered: Don't mess with me. The gigs were returned to their original agent shortly afterwards when his rival decided he'd stick to his own side of the clubland fence after all.

The bottom line, as naive as it seems, is I paid around £1,500 every month we hosted 'Love' at the Plaza not to have to worry or even think about the issue of drugs and their supply. That was my bill for security.

There was a dealer in each of the four corners of the Plaza, I understood. Don't ask me who they were or who they represented because I didn't want to know. All I wanted was the nights to pass without incident which, for the most part, they did.

Cowardly? Maybe, but ignorance was bliss. At least one of the buses taking punters to the Plaza offered the full package, I soon discovered.

You could get the bus to and from the southside of Glasgow and once on board you could buy a £20 ticket into 'Love', an ecstasy before the gig and Diazepam, or jellies, afterwards on the journey home to help bring you back down. Talk about a door to door service.

I can sound flippant now, but it was serious business back then. We sold tickets for 'Love' at the 23rd Precinct record store on Glasgow's Bath Street and my PR guys from Stirling, Roddy, Deek and Jason, soon found themselves accompanied to pick up the cash, as much as £15,000, by the same member of the security firm every time.

By the third month their curiosity had piqued and they sneaked a look inside the bag in which he carried the cash and spotted a handgun. Every month, before we opened the doors for 'Love', I handed my security boss £1,500 in cash for his services. I always paid in advance. Two long lines of coke were racked up, snorted greedily, and that was us – ready for anything the night would throw our way.

Were security aware of the sale of drugs? Most likely. Did I care? Not in the slightest. The promoters' take from 'Love' was between £10-£15,000-a-month while the operator of the licence to rave until 7am, Carnegie's Leisure Group, were coining it in from bar takings based on small bottles of mineral water at £2 a time, a mark up of hundreds of per cent.

This was a big cake, so sweet the jam wasn't so much spilling over the sides as dribbling onto the plate. There was more than enough for everyone to make a substantial profit – sadly and predictably, for a while at least.

If the all-night licence I'd uncovered at Falkirk's Coasters Arena was a golden ticket, 'Love' was like a win at the Vegas slots and not even those closest to me knew how much I needed to hit the jackpot. They should have hauled me in front of the Monopolies and Mergers Commission because never did a clubland promoter in Glasgow have it so good.

As a ballroom, the Plaza dated back to 1922 and enjoyed heydays through to the 1960s. It was the type of place your grandparents met, under art deco lighting, with a sprung floor supporting every dance trend through the years from waltzes to bops.

It also boasted a central ornamental fountain, which had long since stopped working when we got our hands on the venue. A few attempts had been made to revive it over the years – New Order played one of their first concerts there in 1981 – and it had also hosted a couple of gigs, promoted by the boys from Slam, although not all nighters.

It had seen better days and was really on its last legs. It held tea dances on Saturday nights until 10.30pm, with no more than 50 pensioners re-living their youth under fading lights, fuelled for their foxtrots from coffee flasks and with home made sandwiches. On Sunday mornings, a gaggle of schoolgirls used it for disco lessons under the watchful eyes of a couple of dance teachers.

It was bought by Carnegie's Leisure Group, who owned a string of pubs and restaurants in Glasgow, and I was introduced by my contact to one of its directors, a sneaky figure named Edgar Payne.

He outlined a proposal and initially I went into partnership with a long term pal and fellow stoner, John Carroll. John and I had first been introduced at Jammy's in 1985 and I was struck by his immaculate dress sense. Little wonder. He was a DJ and promoter and also worked with Ray Kelvin, founder of Ted Baker, in the company's first store, selling shirts in Glasgow's Princes Square.

He told everyone his name was Ted, but his confusion could be forgiven as he smoked a pipe constantly packed solid with top blow. John was a creative force and helped define the look of 'Love' in our marketing and promotions push but he marched to the beat of his own drum and quit after only a couple of months, a decision in keeping with his eccentric and endearing outlook on life.

That left a gaping hole and I turned to another old pal, Tony Cochrane, reckoning my experience as a promoter and his exceptional music industry contacts would make a winning combination. We kept it in the family with Tony's wife Gwen and Jake, who had become really good pals, in charge of taking the money on the door.

The licensing process, remarkably, turned out to be a breeze. Undoubtedly, we laid it on thick. We told the licensing committee on Glasgow Council we needed to protect one of the city's most prized architectural and cultural assets. We had to make the Plaza relevant to a modern audience and if it was to survive it needed to move with the latest trends – and that meant the award of a licence until 7am.

Quite frankly, we were chancing our arm as every other nightclub in the city was licensed until 3am at the latest. Give us a rave, we told them, or the Plaza was facing the grave.

Astonishingly, they granted our request. Our position was strengthened by the fact one of the tea dance regulars, an elderly councillor, was a member of the licensing committee.

Perhaps that explained the bizarre caveat that came with their decision to allow us to keep the doors open until 7am. We could have access to the venue, but only from 11pm, after the tea dances had finished. We also had to have the place in order by 10am the following morning to allow the wee girls to dance to their hearts' content for the next few hours.

In the long term, maybe our story wasn't too much of a concoction after all because the Plaza was a prized old gem of a place and deserved better than its eventual fate.

Heritage officials were careless and it was never granted listed building status. It was ultimately demolished in September 2006 and 77 apartments were thrown up on the site, with the development quickly voted by architects as the ugliest new build in Scotland. We at least brought new life to its final years.

We debuted 'Love' on Hogmanay 1991 although it headlined as 'Scotland the Rave' with the country's techno pioneers The Time Frequency and Q-Tex top of the bill. The Erskine and Stirling PR boys had flooded the city centre with flyers in the preceding weeks and looked the part too, with black flight jackets plastered with our 'Love' logo on the back, a brainchild of John Carroll.

The Time Frequency's frontman Jon Campbell would later make a red flight jacket his signature, but I beat him to it. Daring to be different, I walked around the streets of Glasgow in the weeks leading up to that first night with a crimson 'Love' flight jacket, like a strolling billboard.

I also took ownership of an old Land Rover, which did four miles to the gallon, and painted it white. Every month we would drive it around town plastered with A2 posters advertising the latest 'Love' at the Plaza. I did my stint as a resident DJ, along with Fraser and Michael Kilkie, Mel Barr and Joe Deacon, that legendary figure from The Metro in Saltcoats.

I knew Joe from Jammy's and he was an entrepreneur more skilled than many on the club and rave scene, but as a DJ he was no Carl Cox. Fraser and I went to his wedding and, for a laugh, bought him a Kenwood Chef for his kitchen so he could practice his mixing. Joe being Joe, he saw the funny side.

Hats off to him, he has made a fortune from the business. The early years of The Metro were cool – Chaka Khan once played there – and he was undoubtedly a populist DJ, with his strength a dedication to old skool anthems and cheesy dance floor fillers that drew them from far and wide.

Joe, helped by his assistants Tracy and Jo, also ran buses more efficiently than National Express. He organised transport to The Metro and 'Love' at the Plaza with great skill and profitability.

He also had a fabulous sideline selling tapes of his sets, but we used to wind him up he only slept at night for 45 minutes at a time. He didn't invest in the technology that would allow him to produce tapes en masse, so would take snatches of sleep before waking up to turn all the tapes over one at a time.

We took a few months to find our feet with 'Love'. Honestly? Our crowd was a bit rough. The whole scene was getting a bit more heavy, including the music. It was a little bit more banging, a little bit more seedy.

Our punters weren't wrapped in Versace. There were a few moments of anxiety, but rarely did it get out of hand. A guy from Barrhead, Rennie, followed my career around the clubs and was a bit naughty, but nothing too outlandish.

On one occasion I entered the all-night garage across the street from the Plaza for a pint of milk after a gig and found him stripped to the waist, standing in front of an open freezer with arms spread wide, trying to cool down.

By and large, that £1,500 was security money well spent. We were busy at the start of the night and then, when the city centre clubs emptied at 3am, we'd welcome a second wave. To my knowledge, city centre club owners never complained about the award of our licence and I don't know why as it gave us a position of commercial strength and advantage from the very off.

We refused to take it for granted. The turning point was arguably the deal we struck after three months that allowed us to hire the Happy Mondays' PA system from their holding company in Manchester. Their gigs were intermittent and we only needed it once a month, so it made sense to bring it up the M6.

It was a 30,000 watt rig, Rolls Royce standard. The sound was exceptional. Their crew arrived as part of the package to set it up, Shaun Ryder's dad among them. Most sound systems were tested with a soundman whispering the usual 'one-two, one-two' or playing a slice of music, but these guys used a CD of white noise. It gently hissed and they would walk around each speaker, one by one, listening carefully to its tone and balance. It was the real deal.

Tony and I were mining a rich seam and making good money, but we were giving our 1,500 clubbers a quality show that didn't come cheap.

We did it right, from the Happy Mondays' PA system to the most relevant and credible acts, the latter sourced by Tony. His music industry contacts were second to none and absolutely pivotal to the success we enjoyed. There were some big rave records out at the time and Tony lured the bands to 'Love' at the Plaza to showcase them all.

They included Toxic Two, riding high at the time with 'Rave Generator', Shades of Rhythm with 'Sweet Sensation' and 'Extacy', Praga Khan brought the house down with 'Injected With A Poison' and Utah Saints blew us all away with their biggest hits, 'What Can You Do For Me?' and 'Something Good'. We hosted a string of superstar DJs, with the likes of Pete Tong following on from Moby.

Those old walls of the Plaza never shook or sweated as much when Glenn Miller tributes brought the crowds through the doors half a century earlier.

The reality is most acts mimed and, mindful of the 'Love' at Joe Paparazzi's experience, we took extra precautions. The paint and plaster dripped with so much condensation from the pulsating beats and bodies of the ravers we had to wrap DAT machines in cling film because they were super sensitive to a change in atmospheric temperature.

We would only make our acts look stupid if the music stopped mid-performance and, thankfully, this time there were no mishaps. Punters didn't mind that Toxic Two, for example, mimed their way through their set. We kept a couple of mics open so they could engage with the crowd. Most of the punters were so out their faces they wouldn't have immediately recognised if it was Utah Saints or All Saints headlining anyway.

I was having the time of my life professionally, although a financial cloud was never far from casting its shadow. We picked up DJ

Grooverider, a drum and bass master, from Glasgow Airport before one show and lost him somewhere between arrivals and the main hall on his flight from London. We needed help, then cracked up as the PA announcer declared to the world: "Would Mr Grooverider report to airport information, please? Mr Grooverider to information."

One of our bouncers, Billy Mackay, was a more than decent dancer. At 3am one night, bang on cue, he walked on stage dressed as a policeman and proceeded to arrest me. The crowd were in an uproar, almost storming the stage in protest. Then, just before he slapped the cuffs around my wrists, he moved away and went into an impressive breakdancing set. We were scraping the punters off the roof.

Our DJs played fabulous house music, bang on for the time. The hype and buzz were incredible. I took the last half hour from 6.30am and my trademark became the piano riff from 'The Way It Is', by Bruce Hornsby and The Range. I also played 'The Best Things In Life Are Free', by Luther Vandross and Janet Jackson. The place had been jumping all night and the crowd also went bananas for that mainstream hit.

We cornered a market few had mastered thanks, in part, to the generosity of those licensing officials. The leading lights of the promotions scene at the time were the Street Rave guys, James McKay and Ricky Magowan, who have gone on to build such a phenomenal brand with Colours.

There was never any animosity between us. Ricky and Jamsy had their own strong following and had been established longer. They also managed to host their all nighters at such unusual locations, including Prestwick Airport. How did they pull that one off?

They were successfully attracting their punters to wild and wonderful events in the middle of nowhere, while we had our own advantage of a city centre base. The pie was big enough for us both to work our audiences.

We spoke once about hosting an all nighter together at the Albert Halls in Stirling as a fundraiser for the Dunblane Appeal, but unfortunately it didn't come off. The Colours boys were always more shrewd and streetwise as promoters and my naivety and openness would cost me dear.

All good things must come to an end and, in part, after around 12 amazing months I was the architect of my own downfall. An associate at the time nicknamed me 'Big Windaes'. I raised my eyebrows and he explained: "You're far too open with people, you tell them too much about the mechanics of your business."

True enough. I had never quite trusted Payne from Carnegie's, for example, but I was too quick to tell him and others how Tony and I put together 'Love' at the Plaza.

I would give open and honest answers to questions I didn't suspect were being asked for anything other than general interest: "How do you source sound systems? How much do they cost? Who are the best agents to approach for DJs and acts? Who'll do the best prices on lighting rigs?" All the time, answer by answer, I was giving away the secrets of the trade Tony and I had spent more than a decade establishing.

I should have been more business-like, discreet and professional. The Street Rave guys, for example, kept the phone numbers of every DJ and contact from the earliest days and formed long standing relationships to their mutual benefit.

They were in on the ground floor, hiring guys like Carl Cox, Judge Jules and Pete Tong before others cottoned on to their amazing talents. When those DJs hit superstar status, they were happy to still commit to Street Rave and Colours because friendships had been built and maintained from the days when they were all hustling for their coin.

Me? If I'd even bothered keeping their numbers, I would have given them to anyone who asked.

Two incidents ultimately ended my relationship with 'Love', one of which was a sinister episode that spooked and frightened me for a long, long time.

In the summer of 1992 I received a phone call at the Plaza from a friendly associate, but with influential and powerful connections. It was clearly a call made at great risk to himself.

He was short and to the point: "They know your car, Scooby. They know roughly where you live in Stirling and the route you take home after every gig. They know in three hours time you'll be walking out of there with 15 grand in a bag. They want it and they'll take it from you and there will likely be violence. Leave now."

I gathered up all the cash we'd taken that night and exited there and then. I jumped in the car, all the time checking over my shoulder.

I drove aimlessly for ages, zig-zagging across Glasgow until I was entirely convinced I wasn't being followed.

Exhausted, I came across the road signposted for Ayr, took it, and checked in for a few hours at a nondescript bed and breakfast. It wasn't only promoters and club owners who wanted a slice of the cake. Glasgow's major gangsters were also getting greedy.

An outsider, a boy from Stirling, taking so much money out of the city? It may have taken them a while to realise the profits involved, but the situation was far from acceptable to them.

Regardless of that unnerving episode, the writing had been on the wall after Payne approached me with the same ultimatum Sleepman had been handed by Baillie at the Network in Paisley.

This time, it was Tony who had to go, or both of us. Payne laid it on the line. Profits were good, but could be fatter still. I was devastated, caught between a rock and a hard place. Our set-up had been so sweet. Trust between Tony and I was implicit, our relationship was about more than business.

Behind the scenes, Jake and Gwen also got on like a house on fire. What could I do? Woody's Bar was failing, I had no monthly income and my financial position still needed badly bolstered. Tony at least had his successful company running PAs, I desperately reasoned. We spoke about it.

Shamefully, I decided to cut Tony loose. I can reason and attempt to reconcile myself to the decision I made, but it was the wrong one. I acted out of self-interest.

I should have quit and gone with him, my conscience clear. I carried the guilt of my selfishness for many years. Tony has never been anything but kind and supportive to me, ever since those early days at Rainbow Rocks when he put bands such as Erasure my way.

Understandably, he wasn't happy at my decision. The success of 'Love' at the Plaza owed hugely to the headline acts he sourced at the peak of their powers. It couldn't work without him, he told me – and he was right. It affected our relationship.

Typically, however, he forgave me. In the summer of 1997 he travelled to Ibiza, where I had established myself once again, with a business proposal. He was aiming to open a new string of lapdancing bars called Private Eyes, the first of which was set for Aberdeen. Did I fancy running it? I was loved up at that time, with a girl called Fiona. I reluctantly declined. I would have accepted like a shot had the circumstances been different. It meant a lot he sought me out.

In the end, Payne predictably sold me down the river but I was struggling to keep my heart in 'Love' anyway. He pillaged my contacts in the two months after Tony's departure, shortly after that frightening escape from those major villains.

Financially, I couldn't afford to walk away at that stage, even if I wanted-ed, because no-one knew the depths of my financial worries. Payne went behind my back after cutting deals with the links I'd established until finally he called me into a meeting. I was no longer needed, he told me.

From that moment on, he would take control of 'Love' at the Plaza. He was making a mistake, I knew, but no bigger than my error in ending my association with Tony.

'Love' at the Plaza limped on for a few months longer, but it was a shadow of its former self. He called it 'Real Love', but it featured shitty little local acts, who had no chance of making the big time. The glitz and glamour were gone.

I should have been able to console myself with a look at my bank account. It had to be in the black – and fairly substantially too, right?

Right?

12

In the early nineties Pablo Escobar and I found ourselves with more in common than a love of cocaine when the Bank of Credit and Commerce International collapsed and its financial tremors shook as violently in Main Street Bannockburn as they ever did in Medellin.

The boss of the biggest drugs cartel in the world may have lost considerably more than £90,000 tied up in my account, but you can bet he didn't bear even half as much of the emotional cost as £30,000 of the pot under my name came from my dad's retirement lump sum.

At least Escobar knew the skulduggery in which he was involved. Put bluntly, BCCI had been laundering for some seriously shady characters until liquidators walked into every one of its 25 UK branches in July 1991, including mine in Glasgow, and stopped the spinning cycle of criminality after a long and secret investigation by auditors.

BCCI had a black hole of debts totalling £10 billion and I was one of 120,000 small investors in Britain who would lose most of the money they had been saving for a rainy day.

Naively, I was completely unaware of the fate that had befallen the bank, despite the widespread publicity of its collapse. I turned up at my branch a few days later, looking to withdraw around five grand to pay a tax bill that had landed through my door with a thud the previous week.

The place was in darkness, the doors chained and locked. Unsurprisingly, staff were nowhere to be seen. A member of the public must have seen the bemused look onmy face as I stood on the steps outside and wondered what the hell was going on. "They've shut that place down mate," he said matter-of-factly. "It said on the telly they've been swindling customers for years."

I'd been with the bank for little more than 12 months, pointed in its direction by a reputable firm of financial advisors who, in turn, had been recommended by a solid business contact.

The attraction was obvious because BCCI were paying interest rates to savers at much higher rates than High Street banks. Call it greed or shrewd financial planning but the old adage was ultimately to hold: If a deal's too good to be true, it usually is.

I wasn't wealthy by any manner of means. DJs and promoters, by and large, are not salaried employees with pension rights. My decision to ring fence profits from a couple of flat sales, including St Andrews and Glasgow, as well as the money I had made hosting club nights were designed to give me, at best, a nest egg and, at worst, a cushion against a downturn in any later financial misfortune.

My dad retired early in 1991 and I urged him to throw his financial lot in with me, a move he was happy to make. Completely trusting, he didn't even know where his cash was invested, only that it was an overseas bank.

He understood I'd sought sound financial advice and his money would grow at a quicker rate than his usual Royal Bank of Scotland account, while remaining accessible if ever needed. Our money was as safe as houses, we thought. Little did we know the BCCI was built on pillars of financial quicksand.

I may have become known as 'Big Windaes' at the Plaza for being so open about my business, but I pulled down the shutters in the immediate aftermath of the BCCI collapse and adopted a position more akin to an ostrich with its head in the sand. I even kept it hidden from Jake.

BCCI had been placed in provisional liquidation with those eye watering financial liabilities, but there was still talk of a rescue in the second half of 1991 so I held firm and said nothing, hoping a wretched situation could still be salvaged.

However, by January 1992 the order came to wind the bank up, with the scant consolation the Bank of England's deposit protection scheme would at least net me £15,000. I cashed the cheque in the spring of that year and squirrelled the money away, praying liquidators Deloitte would soon claw back more than a couple of pence in the pound for creditors.

In the end, the legal wrangling lasted almost two decades, by which time my mental illness had caused me to lose track of the process and any rights I may have had to financial redress. My parents had long since written the money off. They had more on their minds with my periods of mental distress from 1993 until 2009 growing ever more prolonged.

My parents lived a humble life and quite comfortably with it, funded by a couple of small private pensions and the state's retirement provision.

Shamefully, I kept them in the dark about the loss of their money until a sunny summer's day in August 1993, three weeks before I was first sectioned, when the dam finally burst and I poured my heart out to them over lunch at the Pirn Hall Inn in Stirling. I was a babbling wreck.

Much of the profit from 'Love' at the Plaza had gone to pay off the debts at Woody's Bar and helped keep a roof over my head at the flat in Riverside where my friends and family would soon gather after that ill-fated trip to Gleneagles.

The £15,000 compensation from the Bank of England had remained untouched, but I withdrew it and managed to put in place the process that would see £14,000 go to buy my parents' house from the local authority, even if that surprised receptionist at Stirling Council initially refused my offer of hard cash on her desk.

The remaining £1,000 I used to buy two plane tickets to Canada, believing the gift of a trip to see my mother's sister Jean might soften the blow of their greater financial loss. Events the following month, when I was ferried by ambulance to Bellsdyke after my first breakdown, ensured the trip would never be taken.

I apologised and apologised to my parents, over and over again, as the lunch in front of us went uneaten. It should come as no shock their initial and enduring reaction was one of concern for my well being. The money was the least of their issues.

They held my hand over the table, saying time and again: "Don't worry about it son, don't worry," but their sympathetic response wasn't enough. I'd kept it to myself for so long I didn't feel a relief at unburdening my darkest secret. If anything, the weight seemed to sink even deeper in my increasingly troubled soul.

It was pretty much the last straw on a world that had been imploding since my departure from the Plaza. I was trying to fix things as best

I could in all areas of my life but, for once, the harder I tried the least successful I was becoming.

Everything I touched seemed to turn to dust in the immediate aftermath of 'Love' at the Plaza. The Queen famously described 1992 as her 'annus horribilis'. She should have tried cutting around Stirling with me in the 12 months following.

The loss of my father's money in the BCCI collapse was a killer because it represented 40 years of his working life, but initially I felt no such grief about my own financial setback. I'd earned the money honestly, through hard graft. I'd made it before, I could make it again I convinced myself.

My confidence was misplaced. In 1993, for the first time in my life, self doubt began to emerge as I struggled to make a living. There was something else there too, just beyond the grasp of my understanding.

Paranoia, perhaps? A touch of depression? For several months, slowly at the start, I'd felt a grey veil slowly dropping over my outlook, draining my life of much of its colour. I tried to shake it from my head, like a mental snow globe, hoping everything would eventually settle as it should be. Some hope.

It took me the best part of a quarter of a century to understand that feeling was the first signs of a chemical imbalance in my brain that had been building since, well, who knows when?

I had barely turned 30 and I told myself my use of drugs – I still didn't see it as an addiction – was not a problem to be addressed, certainly not at that stage of my life. Had I been 55 and still using hash on a daily basis, supplemented with coke two or three times a week, I might have told myself to act my age and knock it on the head. What damage was I doing?

A look inside my bathroom cabinet today reveals the stark truth. Plenty. I swallow a cocktail of prescription drugs every day that includes 600mg of Lithium and 2500mg of Epilim, or sodium valproate, which act as mood stabilisers. I'm on 2.5mg of Risperidone, an anti-psychotic, and all of them control the chemical imbalance brought on by smoking too much hash.

On a scale of one to 10 my chemical combination is categorised as level eight, heavy duty. It took doctors and psychiatrists a long time to solve the cocktail equation that best suited my needs – 16 troubling and anguished years of trial and error.

I actually gave up coke for a while in 1993, but only through financial necessity. I couldn't afford it, but was still working my way through between a quarter and half an ounce of hash a week. In the end, I needed to score.

I'd produced and released a dance track under the name Area 51 with Fraser and his nephew Ian Hotchkiss and another pal, Alex Milne, called 'Let It Move You'. We performed a series of PAs across Scotland, which even included a return to the arms of my old friend, Bentley's in Kirkcaldy.

I teamed up with another mucker from Stirling, who shall remain nameless, and a drop dead gorgeous local girl, Monique Ifla. My pal and I realised the £120 fee we picked up for miming badly to the track would be enough for two grams of charlie. Monique couldn't sing, but she was the only glamorous black chick we knew from Bannockburn and she was up for laughs and adventure.

Drugs were a no-no for Monique – if only we'd been as sensible – but she enjoyed the giggles of the new clubland experience. We all faked wildly, with me on keyboards and Monique commanding the stage with a microphone, lip synching furiously.

The highlight was supporting dance act N-Joi, who had significant chart success at the time with 'Anthem'. We even joined them on stage for their performance at Bentley's and in the background I jabbed and battered the keys of a synth with my index fingers, scared out of my wits. We just about pulled it off.

If there was a business I knew well it was club promotion, but I'd even lost my mojo in that area of expertise, to my complete and utter embarrassment after an initial triumph.

It came as no surprise, after the Plaza, to be approached by the Fubar. They confided they were on the brink of landing their first all night licence from Stirling Council. Would I like to replicate the success of 'Love' in my own backyard?

It was a no-brainer and we launched 'Love – The Rebirth' to public acclaim and commercial success. We wanted to do it bigger than the Plaza, even though audiences were capped at around 800, half the capacity of the old dance hall. So what?

We distributed A2 posters instead of flyers and our strong streak of integrity was underlined as we again called on credible and relevant dance acts to headline such as Awesome Three, Suburban Delay and The Bassheads.

The all nighters ran successfully under my control for several months before, as always, Fubar management decided to cut out the third party and take over promotional duties themselves. The shutters had come down on Big Windaes. Once again, I was on the outside looking in.

Fuck the lot of them. I was fed up being taken advantage of. It was time to pull out the big guns and blow all those sneaky bastards to smithereens. Calls were made to Ibiza, favours were pulled and deals were struck.

Striding to my rescue in August 1993 came the one and only Alfredo, the Amnesia legend, Godfather of Balearic Beat and Arch Angel of Acid House. I had lured him to Scotland from Spain and it was the clubland equivalent of signing Cristiano Ronaldo on loan for Stirling Albion.

The Fubar would have bitten my hand off for him, I knew, but they could whistle. It was Club SG in Falkirk who offered me a Friday night slot. I pulled in local PR and we swamped the town a few weeks before with flyers and put out word of mouth around the local pubs and clubs.

To keep costs down I teamed up with a crew of promoters from Cumbernauld, the Cool Lemon Guys, who had contacts with the Citrus Club in Edinburgh. It was agreed Alfredo would DJ a two hour slot in Falkirk from 10pm then head to the capital and gig for another couple of hours.

As arranged, he arrived at Glasgow Airport early on the Friday evening looking every inch the clubland Colossus, pulling what looked like a modified shopping trolley bag behind him, piled high with his record boxes. I've rarely been as excited about a gig.

No-one turned up.

I was completely devastated. We were paying Alfredo a grand, but I would have forked out 10 times that sum to have Club SG rammed and save myself the embarrassment.

We arrived shortly before 10pm to an empty hall and I started reasoning they would soon arrive en masse, or perhaps they thought it was a 10.30pm start. No-one came.

Alfredo, my pal Jok and I shuffled our feet for 15 minutes before the great man walked behind the decks and started mixing a few tracks. It was like hiring Michelangelo for a paint job, only to hand him a tin of Dulux emulsion and a request to freshen up the spare bedroom.

Why didn't they turn up? Was it a perverse take on the rivalry between Falkirk and Stirling? Was it to do with the gig being held on a Friday night, rather than a Saturday? Had our PR team simply failed to target the correct audience? It was probably a combination of all that and more, but they were answers to questions I couldn't fathom at the time as my face burned beetroot in shame.

In fairness, Alfredo was a good sport. He shrugged his shoulders. These things happen in the clubland game, although infrequently. We waited until 11.30pm, packed up and I drove him to Edinburgh. I took some consolation in seeing the Citrus Club packed to capacity, all waiting for the arrival of the great man.

A roar greeted his presence behind the decks that would not have been out of place in a football stadium. He got down to business, to the absolute delight of the punters.

I stayed half an hour, ensuring the handover to the Cool Lemon Guys went smoothly as they were seeing him to his hotel later and taking him to the airport the following morning. I returned to my flat in Stirling utterly dejected, not to mention seriously out of pocket.

I reached into the back of one of the kitchen cupboards, remembering a bottle of creme de menthe I'd found unopened behind the bar when I first turned the key in Woody's. I very rarely drank alcohol. I woke up the following lunchtime with a splitting headache and the empty bottle at my bedside.

The feeling crept up on me throughout 1993 that my life was no longer in order and I was stopping short of functioning as I expected. I wasn't contemplating my drugs intake or mental health in general, only that I'd hit a rut and, despite my best efforts, couldn't find a way out of it.

I had a lifestyle I enjoyed and for the first time in my adult life I didn't have the means to maintain it. It wasn't lavish but I had always managed to do the things I wanted and, of course, a daily diet of hash didn't come cheap.

Unsurprisingly, the BCCI debacle sat heavily on my shoulders, but I was in too deep. How could I confess to my losses now, a couple of years after its collapse? I didn't link the subtle shift in the breakdown of my coping strategies for stress and the daily bump and grind with my heavy drugs intake.

It's a conversation in my own head I never provoked. Things were fucking up for me and I knew it, but I couldn't quite put my finger on the cause. A streak of bad luck, most likely. I was trying any which way I could to find a way out and lift the grey mask slowly eclipsing my previously sunny outlook.

Diversification, I decided, was the name of the game. The pace of the thoughts racing through my mind began to increase. I thought I was Richard Branson, coming up with a list of amazing business ideas. I established a company called Destiny Management Services. The strapline under its name on my business cards read 'CBA – Conceive, Believe, Achieve'.

Impressive stuff, but I'm not even sure I was good enough to sell spring water in the Sahara. The owners of the Meadowpark Hotel in Bridge of Allan, Tam Sharp and Ron Cameron, gave me free office space above the bar. It was a kindly favour for previous good deeds done.

It lasted three months. Destiny Management Services was established as a printing broker. Printing and design were skills I'd learned over many years as a DJ and promoter and I gambled on drumming up business as a middleman, placing clients with companies and taking an agent's fee of 10 per cent.

There was no money in it. I was nickel and diming it, even for those who weren't sensible enough to approach design houses and negotiate their own contracts. I began to panic. Sure, I'd re-invented myself in the past, but back then I didn't have the loss of £90,000 weighing heavily on my mind. How could I get back on a winning streak?

Slowly, friends and family began to suspect all was not well. Jake approached her employer's occupational health department on the back of an unsettling incident at Duck Bay Marina, the well known club and hotel complex on the shores of Loch Lomond.

I had grown close to the owner, Russell Cawley, who had been a regular at Littlejohn's in St Andrews. He even offered me a gig as resident DJ, which helped keep the wolves from the door for a time, even if most of my profits went up in the smoke of the seven joints I got through heading to and from each shift behind the decks.

Tuesday nights were quieter at Duck Bay and I'd invariably head there for a chat with Russell, who had become a confidante, even if I was struggling to verbalise the emotions that would lead to my breakdown, which I still didn't see coming.

He told me bluntly, the week before I went unwell: "You're an angry young man with society, Stuart." I had grown quite intense by that stage, admittedly. I wasn't looking at life lightly.

A couple of months earlier a group of us, 15 in total, went for a day out at Duck Bay one Sunday and included Steven Croal and his daughter Lucy, then just a toddler in a pushchair. I disappeared for 20 minutes and arrived back from the jetty and urged everyone to follow me outside.

I'd sweet talked a boat owner, a complete stranger, into taking us out on the loch for a cruise. All of us were packed onto his 30 footer and I implored everyone to have a drink from his well stocked bar, an offer I had no right to make.

In fairness, the boat owner was sound and didn't appear to mind, but I was unaware of the troubled expression on Jake's face. I'd pulled a bold stunt. Too bold, she astutely reckoned. The episode left her unsettled and on edge.

Gary Neill, whose wedding I would soon move to arrange at Gleneagles, confided many years later of his concern when he turned up on his new Moto Guzzi motorbike to offer me a ride as pillion passenger around the country roads of Stirling.

It was a beast of a machine, an 850cc Le Mans, and he had so much respect for its strength and power he turned up in the height of summer kitted from head to toe in safety leathers. I bounded from the flat in shorts and a t-shirt and demanded he hit the road without so much as a helmet on my head.

The Stirling PR boys, with whom I'd enjoyed so many good times at The Tunnel and the Plaza, could also sense things weren't quite right. They couldn't say for sure, but kept me closer than usual. They invited me on nights out, spent time with me at the flat to ensure I wasn't on my own. They were good friends.

I found it increasingly difficult to turn off. Shortly before I went unwell I hosted a night at The Outhouse, the popular club attached to the Meadowpark Hotel. Perhaps there was a subconscious nod to my own sense of mortality, but I called it 'You're Dead A Long Time'.

I turned up without one item of kit essential for any DJ, his record collection. It was soon retrieved from the flat and I cranked out my set, with a heavy emphasis on a new record from Rozalla, an acapella version of 'Are You Ready To Fly?'

I was behind the decks for three hours and every 10 minutes mixed in a slice of Rozalla. In my mind I was mixing the upbeat line 'Are you ready to fly?' over the sounds I was playing, working the beat and the crowd to a crescendo.

In fact, I was actually mixing the second line of the track, the slightly more sombre lyric 'colours are black'. Colours are black, colours are black, colours are black. It barely drew the punters onto the dance floor, never mind lifting them to the ceiling.

I finished the gig and was absolutely drenched in sweat, another first. I asked my pal Ross Waddell how it had gone, genuinely expecting glowing compliments. "Scoobs," he said flatly. "That was a load of fucking shite."

I looked outside my immediate community for the key to unlock the door to happier times and invested money I didn't have on that mind bending course I didn't need in that hovel of a Paddington hotel.

There was only one other place I knew I could seek solace from my mounting worries – Ibiza. Talk about zippin' up my boots and goin' back to my roots. Maybe I just needed to empty my head, I told myself. Two weeks of hedonism was just what the doctor ordered, I convinced myself.

As always, Javier and Wilson threw open their doors. They still had the Bucanero so I hung around there most nights, before heading to party at Es Paradis and Amnesia.

I was grasping at straws. To some extent, my everyday behaviour was rational and not out of place among the bedlam of San Antonio, but my last night on the island suggested it had moved beyond the eccentric.

Javier and I attended a foam party at Amnesia and 2,500 punters were out of their faces and up to their ears in Fairy Liquid. I had an early morning flight and walked out the place soaking wet and still covered from head to toe in soap. I took my bag and passport from a dry, safe spot in the club and jumped in a taxi to the airport. A few hours later I was back in Stirling, still popping soap bubbles in my hair.

A couple of weeks later and everything fell into place. I locked myself in the flat at Riverside and for two days solid smoked hash and catalogued my extensive record collection until I moved beyond a period of stupor to what I felt was a state of enlightenment.

The anger and frustration subsided. There was an epiphany. It all began to make perfect sense. I knew exactly what I wanted to do with my life and the new direction it should take became crystal clear. I awoke early on the morning of Friday, September 3, sparked up a joint and threw a putter and a sand wedge in the boot of my car.

I had a wedding to book at Gleneagles but not, of course, before I'd played a round of golf at one of my favourite courses.

13

The plunge into a week long state of Catatonia was bad enough without eventually coming round to a lurid colour scheme of lime green walls and turquoise curtains. The interior design was pure Laurence Llewelyn-Bowen but this was not an episode of Changing Rooms and my life could never be transformed with a 60 minute makeover.

I had been sectioned and placed in the Endrick ward, an ICPU – Intensive Care Psychiatric Unit – of 10 beds, a mixed dormitory locked tighter than the prison cells at Alcatraz and part of the larger psychiatric facility at Bellsdyke hospital.

It used to be known as the Stirling District Lunatic Asylum and was first opened in 1869. It closed its doors in 1997 as the lamentable move towards Care in the Community – I would later have first hand experience of that appalling legislation – became official government policy.

It has long been demolished but when I was first admitted it housed around 800 patients, most of them elderly and long term residents and many of them suffering from Alzheimer's and dementia-related illnesses.

Admittedly, for the first seven days I didn't know if I was living in Bellsdyke or Beverly Hills. That injection straight into my arse on my arrival from my flat in Stirling turned out to be a drug called Clopixol Acuphase, an anti-psychotic used to treat schizophrenia and other psychoses.

I didn't find out until years later it was used to keep patients heavily sedated. It's no wonder so many wandered around the ward like the walking dead, saliva drooling from their chins – a cruel side effect of that particular treatment. They only administer the drug these days as a last resort – and not without first giving patients a full ECG.

It turns out it could have induced a heart attack, although I wouldn't have known a thing about it and probably wouldn't even have cared. A 50mg dose would have brought an elephant to its knees. I settled for dropping into deep sedation for several nights, before slowly clawing my way back to a reality of sorts over the next few, weary days.

I slowly grew accustomed to my environment and the rules, written and unwritten, in which we all lived, most of the time in our own separate, zombie worlds.

Those vivid, intense colours on the walls were the least of my problems as I noted a television bolted high up near the ceiling, out of reach of grasping hands.

If paranoid schizophrenics hear voices in their heads they most often come from the television, with Noel Edmonds and other kings and queens of light entertainment issuing the instructions. If their demands were not to the liking of the patients, the set was frequently attacked, ripped from the walls and thrown across the room.

Similarly, there were no happy pictures framed on the walls, perhaps to take us to a Highland idyll or a warm beach on the Mediterranean. They were also subject to attack and were potentially weapons of choice, not just against unsuspecting nurses but also as self-harming tools, with sharp pieces of glass or plastic capable of inflicting maximum damage to jugular veins.

To that end, we weren't allowed to wear belts, carry anything in polythene bags and even watches, bizarrely, were banned. We were allowed radios, but not at night as the electrical cords were assumed to be weapons in the making.

There were no wardrobes or bedroom furniture because it could also be thrown hard and dangerously and, for the most part, we slept on mattresses on the floor.

There was an absence of privacy because none of the beds were curtained off as every patient was considered a suicide risk and had to be in full view of staff as they slept.

Double glazing specialists CR Smith came one time and fitted new windows of unbreakable glass. A few weeks later a patient still managed to shatter them in a futile attempt to break free.

Everything given to us by friends and family was checked. Attempts to smuggle in drugs for patients were not unusual. Staff were alert to most tricks, including bids to hide hash, coke or heroin inside the hollow funnel of a packet of Polo mints.

Throughout my first admission, which lasted three months from September to November, I formed no friendships or bonds with fellow patients and remain unaware, to this day, with whom I shared such intimate spaces.

I later learned several fellow patients were prisoners, in on a treatment order known as a 52D. Ultimately, it was a bid to assess if murderers and the likes were simply bad or really mad. I was also aware that many of the patients appeared to have issues with alcohol dependency, one of the most common reasons behind the decision to section.

For the most part, patients were kept in pyjamas as the nursing staff reasoned it made them less likely to make escape attempts. Trainers were allowed but shoes were not because they could cause more damage when patients kicked out at nursing staff, which happened frequently.

In the centre of our ward was an off-white plastic couch and there was an unofficial pecking order that stated whoever sat on it was considered the ruler of the roost. I lay on it for three months but never knew of the significance until later, although being alpha male in Endrick ward was hardly the pinnacle of life's ambition.

As the effects of the sedative slowly eased I began to grow more aware of my environment. It was a locked ward, but we were allowed access to a small garden outside and one day I met an old friend from the McQ's scene, Linda Stronach.

Linda is a beautifully kind, compassionate woman and was working the kitchens at the hospital (she would later become a top class nurse). She was devastated to see me in such a state. Built like a jockey's whip anyway, I had lost even more weight in my first weeks at the hospital and my grey jogging pants didn't so much hang off my waist as droop down to the top of my thighs.

I felt terrible at seeing her, embarrassed, as if I had let her down, an emotion that would stick with me throughout my stay. I could handle visits from my mum, Mac, and Jake, who came every day with that meal cooked by her dad but it was tougher to see close friends, even though I was swamped with more than 200 'Get Well Soon' cards.

Fraser Hotchkiss visited regularly and his appearances later reminded me I was surrounded by lime green when I should really have been basking in silver. I had been shortlisted as Kensitas Club Scottish DJ of the Year for 1993 and the awards ceremony was pencilled in for September 5 – two days after I was sectioned.

It's fair to say the award was in the bag before my breakdown. Not only was the ceremony taking place at my former club, The Tunnel, but Fraser and Colin Barr were on the judging panel. The whole competition had been organised by another close pal, Katriona Tasker.

The stars were aligned, only for my world to turn upside down. In the end the trophy went to another Stirling DJ, John Pryde, but it was the least of my problems. My pal Steven Croal visited me after a week and left the ward in tears, visibly distressed at how quickly I'd gone downhill since he'd seen me into the ambulance at Riverside.

Gary Neill also dropped in regularly – Jake had to suffer the embarrassment of going to Gleneagles to cancel those two weddings – but for the most part my friends were kept at bay to give me time and space to make a complete recovery.

Music had been a huge and influential part of my life to that point, but now only one tune went round and round in my head. I stood at the door of the locked ward most days and repeated the line from the big Urban Cookie Collective hit at the time, 'The Key, The Secret'.

Goodness knows what the nurses thought as I stood there, telling no-one in particular: "I've got the key, you got the secret?" The song is actually about taking magic mushrooms, so maybe it wasn't so out of place after all.

Officially, I was given a formal diagnosis of bi-polar disorder which, they decided, was a result of my extensive use of cannabis and the shock of the loss of our life savings in the collapse of the BCCI.

I saw a psychiatrist once a week and after the effects of Clopixol Acuphase wore off I was switched to Halperidol and Lithium for the remainder of my stay at Bellsdyke, which allowed me to engage more consciously with my world around me, although only slightly more lucidly.

Days stretched to weeks, with little variation from a Monday to Sunday. Breakfast was a continental offering of bread and jam, followed by soup and a sandwich for lunch before an evening meal, served

175

through a hatch from warmed trolleys as the main kitchen was on the other side of the hospital.

For the most part the main meal was inedible, certainly in comparison to the home made offerings from Angus Kerr, but taste buds hardly tingled against such strong and mentally deadening medication.

For up to 10 hours every day we played cards and dominoes, although I could never get to grips with those 800 piece jigsaws. When it hadn't been thrown against the far wall, we also watched the television, although it was mostly turned on to give a soundtrack to an existence many of us feared was already in danger of becoming meaningless.

If the atmosphere crackled with tension and the threat of violence, I barely noticed it. As Russell Cawley at Duck Bay Marina acknowledged a few months earlier, I had become an angry young man with society, but I rarely succumbed to bouts of aggression.

I was restrained a few times – they increased my dose of Halperidol on each occasion, which helped – but the frustration Russell identified could not be turned off in only a couple of weeks.

The ratio of one nurse to two patients helped, particularly the presence of my favourite medic, Stewart McNeill. He became a regular presence in my life as my mental health declined further over the next decade.

I'm sure Stewart won't mind me saying I wish we had never met, or at least in different circumstances. He was a kind, genuine and calming presence always and I warmed to his style of care, so much so I was allowed into the garden for a walk after a month and breathed deeply at the fresh air, as if it was life's first.

Generally, however, I felt zonked. I was heavily medicated and had no yearnings, certainly not for dope or coke, but something deep within urged me to cling to a sense of normality.

Really, I didn't take my diagnosis of bi-polar to heart. In truth, it didn't mean anything to me, beyond the prescription of those new drugs. I never said, 'poor me'. I came to terms with my illness, but was never happy to stick a label of mental illness around my neck.

I can see that reaction now as a pure defence mechanism. Once I got to grips with the situation in Endrick I actually became a little cocky, refusing to admit I was part of the patient programme. I wasn't as badly off as those around me, was I?

Apparently, it's a common reaction. I addressed doctors, for example, by their first names. I was over familiar with staff because I was anxious to be seen to relate more closely to them, rather than the patients on the ward.

Only in recent years have I started to appropriately refer to the psychiatrists with whom I'm still in regular contact as 'Doctor Smith', for example, rather than Michael, Colin or Mhairi.

Throughout my time in care I've had three diagnoses – bi-polar, schizoaffective disorder and, most recently, chronic bi-polar. Some people have three or four episodes of mental breakdown that causes them to be sectioned. I've had 23. It's safe to assume I've come to terms with telling people, when asked in the relevant circumstances, that I suffer from chronic bi-polar.

Fittingly, my reintegration into mainstream society began slowly and cautiously. It grew from those visits to the garden until, a couple of months in, I was allowed to visit Jake for a couple of hours at night, so long as I was returned to Bellsdyke by 8pm.

A tremendous sense of freedom came from walking from Endrick ward to the main entrance of the hospital, where Jake would pick me up in her car. It was a move, psychologically, many of the patients, particularly the elderly, would never make. They had become institutionalised in a home from home that had everything from a sewing and snooker room, budgie breeding club, bowling green and even its own general store, not to mention regular dances every Friday night.

Jake's presence was a Godsend. I was her first love and she couldn't half make me laugh. I used to tell her to make a monkey face and she would contort her features and it cracked me up every time.

By coincidence, her family home was also called Endrick Lodge. Towards the end of my stay in Bellsdyke she would take me to Endrick Lodge for the weekend and her sister, Sandra, would give up her apartment for us in the old maids' quarters. I just lay cuddled up, watching television.

Sometimes I would go to bed at 3pm, often to lie, not even sleep. It must have been so hard for Jake, who had been used to her boyfriend being full of such get up and go. My illness was provoking new feelings and yet she stuck around, too full of love to ever contemplate walking away.

Eventually, my release was confirmed and I moved back home with my parents, having entered a legal agreement known as a voluntary sequestration that saw my car and Riverside flat repossessed.

It was organised by the health authorities as part of my care package. It left me free of debt but I would effectively remain bankrupt for the next three years. It was the least of my issues but a weight off my shoulders nonetheless.

Old friends rallied, but I wasn't ready to embrace again the life we had all known just a few months earlier. The Stirling PR boys, such as wee Roddy and Deek, as well as James Kilgannon, Jake and her cousin Susan decided to throw me a party on my release from Bellsdyke and 200 people flooded into The Outhouse in Bridge of Allan.

The place was rammed to the rafters and the evening was organised with the very best of intentions, but it was too claustrophobic, physically and emotionally. I was overwhelmed, embarrassed even, and I lasted 20 minutes before making for the door.

I had always been viewed highly in and around Stirling, dare I say I was even someone to look up to, but in my new straitened circumstances I felt fraudulent. I'd lost my car, my home and all my money. Fuck, I'd lost my mind. I found it hard to reconcile the kindness around me with feeling so uncomfortable in my own skin.

Amazingly, I have no recollection of leaving Bellsdyke with a prescription for drugs that may have controlled my bi-polar. I moved back in with my parents and have no memory of Mac or Alex making a weekly pilgrimage to the local pharmacy for any meds.

It seems improbable today, inconceivable even, but perhaps doctors felt the 'short, sharp shock' treatment of the ICPU was enough. For sure, over the next few months I did not touch drugs. For the first time in my adult life, I did not have the appetite for them nor, in the case of coke especially, did I have the money.

I also felt dabbling again, even a joint or two over the course of a week, would have been disrespectful to my parents, whose love and support of their son in such harrowing circumstances was absolute.

Nevertheless, despite all they did, I could not shake the feeling of isolation. My life appeared to be going backwards as I moved upstairs into the spare bedroom. The room that had been mine as a kid had been hastily re-arranged into a store for all my furniture from my Riverside flat that had just been repossessed.

Lying in that back bedroom in the dead of night, I felt as if I'd been hit on the head with a mallet. Where was the life I recognised? I didn't even have a car, but my mum allowed me to borrow her Ford Fiesta for occasional trips around Stirling. I was stopped by the police for going over 30mph through the village of Strathyre and their checks revealed I wasn't actually insured for the vehicle.

I was summoned to court, with Mac. How utterly bizarre to stand in the dock at Stirling Sheriff Court with my old mum, supporting herself with a walking stick, as the judge put three points on my licence for the misdemeanour and gave the bemused Mac eight. There was black comedy there, somewhere, but I was struggling to see it.

Of course, the reality was that I was still a stricken man emotionally. My self-esteem had taken such a battering in the months previously that a period of withdrawal was only to be expected, surely.

I remained broken, but knew in the short term I had to make the best of a bad situation. My confidence had been knocked and I was still largely retreating from the friends I knew best and loved me most, but I reconciled myself to the fact it was a stage through which I needed to pass on the road to a fuller recovery. I knew the time would come when I could re-invent myself, I just never expected to be given the opportunity so soon after my release from Bellsdyke.

In Ibiza, Javier and I had spoken frequently in the past about a desire to launch a new style of sunset beach bar, maybe one that in time would even come to rival the famous Cafe Del Mar.

The Bucanero was doing great business for Javier, but it was a pirate themed bar. Lucrative, but a theme bar nonetheless. We reckoned an upmarket, fashionable bar would be a hit, particularly if we could attract the new wave of cool British tourists who were increasingly making their way to the White Isle on vacation. It was a daydream at that stage, nothing more and nothing less.

Towards the end of January 1994, Javier called out the blue: "Scooby, get your ass over here. That sunset beach bar we've always talked about … do you really think it could work?"

14

Javier Anadon and I always considered ourselves Braveheart conquistadors.

He came from Navarre, a medieval Basque region in northern Spain, where they famously run the bulls through the streets of its capital, Pamplona. Talk about cojones. Javier could have been chased by those angry beasts through the narrow alleyways and still convinced onlookers he was leading a parade.

Me? Well, an upbringing in Bannockburn was always going to inspire a fighting spirit of sorts. It's said Robert the Bruce was outnumbered three to one by the English in 1314. After all that history in my own backyard, what could be so challenging about opening a new bar in Ibiza?

Javier and I had spoken often in the previous years about creating a venue to take advantage of the spectacular sunsets off the west coast of San Antonio.

He has kindly credited me with the original idea and, true, I had hung around Cafe Del Mar long enough to appreciate the easy ambience created by the combination of laconic vibes pitched against the lazy slide of the fiery orb over the horizon of the Mediterranean.

If the tempo of the music matched the pace of the setting sun it was as if God himself had placed his hands on the Technics decks.

Our discussions, mostly over cortado coffee and ensaimadas at places such as Pikes, went quickly from pipedream to the planning stages when Javier called and asked if we really could make such a venture work.

He must, I'm sure, have known about my breakdown in the previous months. However, the offer of 10 per cent of the new business was heartfelt and was not made entirely out of sympathy, although Javier had the type of personality that leant itself to giving a mate a dig out.

Without sounding boastful, his call to Stirling also made pure business sense. Javier recognised I was rarely happy following trends, which appealed to his sense of entrepreneurship and risk.

I recall a small, but significant, detail from the mid-eighties when I turned up in Ibiza one summer wearing cycling shorts. Why not? I liked them. They were comfortable, hard wearing and washed easily. The following year, everyone was wearing cycling shorts. Javier pulled me aside one day and asked who had told me to wear the shorts in the first place. I told him, honestly, it was all my own idea. He was intrigued by someone who could set fashions, not just follow them.

Admittedly, the blatant truth is I had visions of our new place – Javier had already decided on its name, 'Sunset Cafe' – and if my ideas weren't carbon copies of Cafe Del Mar, then they were at least next door neighbours. What an irony that would prove to be.

As I was still bankrupt and penniless, my parents fronted me the cash for a flight to Ibiza and some pocket money and in the days leading to my departure, in January 1994, I set about compiling a playlist for Sunset Cafe.

The list was extensive and covered every musical genre, from Clannad to Ennio Morricone. I was keen to capture the Balearic vibe of Cafe Del Mar and that meant a songlist that included Carly Simon's 'Why?', Jon and Vangelis' 'I'll Find My Way Home' and It's Immaterial's 'Driving Away From Home', a fabulous little track from 1986.

Cafe Del Mar was without equal at that period. Established in 1980, its design was timeless, typically Spanish with lots of white tiles, brilliant blue trims and cool marbles. As a package it was complete and it had soul. The tempo, music and the sunset from Cala Des Moro bay, as well as the melting pot of nationalities, united to create something far bigger than its individual parts.

It did not attempt to be something it was not. It was not uncommon even for classical music to be played by the resident DJs. It had a groove and it had gravitas. You could spend millions trying to create that type of bar experience and never get anywhere near it.

I played a set there only once, soon after my arrival to help Javier with his new bar. I played one of my own tracks, 'Cathedral Song' and the experience was a box ticked. In truth, even then it felt as if I was sleeping with the enemy.

For Sunset Cafe we could afford no such financial extravagances, which at least forced us to think outside the box. We were counting our pesetas or, more specifically, Javier and Wilson were watching every one of their centimos as they scraped together everything they owned to put into the new place. As the opening loomed they couldn't even afford to buy a new fridge for drinks and had to beg, steal and borrow one, second hand.

Bucanero, their themed pirate bar, was doing well but it was a raucous tourist joint. Of course, tourists would provide the custom base for the new bar but we'd already decided it would be more upmarket, discerning even, with fashionable music and drinks.

Javier still needed some convincing, however. He struggled to see the vision in its entirety but I stressed, with as much self-belief as I could muster, the market was ready to welcome a new player, a change of direction.

The super clubs were already established and were only growing more powerful. Javier recognised we could tap into that increasing popularity by attracting a pre-club crowd, maybe even with the DJs coming down to play short sets at our new place, a marketing advantage to the benefit of both parties.

The Sunset Cafe would serve food and although we were still undecided in the early days about the style of eating we'd promote, we knew the venture's selling point would be those fabled sunsets.

We didn't have its identity completely pinned down, but trusted it would grow organically from our previous experiences. My hospitalisation at Bellsdyke had been a dent to my confidence, but slowly I felt my self-esteem return as I settled back into island life, relishing the chance to re-invent myself after such a troubling 12 months.

Again, I was invited to stay with Javier and Wilson in their house in the bay and by this time Christian had been joined by his little brother, Alan, to complete the family.

I taught Christian the rudiments of music mixing, practising on a couple of old decks owned by Javier. He used to catalogue my vinyl for me, noting the beats per minute of the tracks I'd brought to the island that summer.

He wasn't as confident as today, of course, when he and Alan tour the world as the Mambos Brothers, but he was really into his music, even though he was just a kid.

There was a great track at the time by Voice of Africa, called 'Hoomba Hoomba' we loved to play and it will always remind me of him. Alan was sports daft, crazy for basketball, and was a determined little grafter, even as a kid.

When the bar eventually opened he was regularly up to his elbows in soap suds, helping my cousin Roddy in the kitchen, washing pots and pans in a tight little space with no ventilation, sweat dripping from his forehead.

The walk between San Antonio harbour to Cafe Del Mar, along part of what is now called the Sunset Strip, takes around 10 minutes. There were plenty of bars available for sale further around the cove, a further 10 minute walk, but I wasn't convinced enough tourists would trek out there to make it a viable business proposition.

However, I was intrigued by a family home only 100 metres from Cafe Del Mar. It was a two storey house, split into four apartments and, next door, there was a working man's bar called Rey De Copas, a real spit and sawdust joint which Javier and Wilson later purchased to become the restaurant Mint.

The house intrigued me. It was owned by an old woman from Valencia, possibly with links to the Bohemian crowd who flooded the isle in the sixties, and was being used as a holiday home.

Thinking outside the box, I was hit by a flash of inspiration. Javier looked it up and down and, crucially, we noted the wide open views they enjoyed over the bay. With extensive remodelling, it would make a terrific bar – and I gave Javier my thoughts.

Nothing ventured, nothing gained. "Why don't you ask if it's for sale?" I asked him. An idea was beginning to ferment, but I sensed a reluctance from Javier to make the approach.

I urged him to make the move. I knew it was the perfect spot. "Go for it Javier, you won't regret it. I promise." Our eyes met – and stayed fixed. He broke the stare, turned, walked to the front door and gave it a loud knock.

Understandably, the nuts and bolts of the financial negotiations had nothing to do with me. This was Javier and Wilson's territory, it was their money on the line, but the owner agreed to sell.

It transpired there were others interested, but the deal was concluded in her front room with Javier and Wilson present, along with me and the two boys. I literally jumped from the chair and punched the air with delight when she said it was theirs. It almost cost us the deal.

The owner turned to Wilson and claimed the price agreed was clearly too low. Wilson quickly explained my pleasure came from the vision we could now realise, not the fine details of the money on the table. The owner smiled and accepted the truth of her statement.

Done and dusted within a couple of weeks, we met for dinner in San Antonio and there was an air of excitement around the table as we discussed the new venture, the drinks and food we'd offer, the staff we'd hire, music we'd play and vibe we'd work hard to create.

Only one thing rankled with me – the name. I didn't like the idea of The Sunset Cafe. I got the sunset bit, but it sounded a bit greasy spoon (I'd later hang out in a mental health charity cafe in Stirling with the same name).

Javier sensed my discomfort and asked for my suggestions. Always with an eye for fashion, I'd taken to wearing a new range of Aussie surfwear. I dropped my chin to my chest and looked at the logo on the t-shirt I had pulled on that night. With complete spontaneity, I innocently asked: "Why not call it Mambo?"

A legend was born.

The name also fitted and chimed with Javier, in part, because of the resonance of the move at the time, 'Mambo Kings', which gave Antonio Banderas his big break in Hollywood.

It captured a sultry groove based around the Cuban music scene in Havana and New York and epitomised the cool credibility we wanted to create at the new bar, but the name was only the beginning.

We set about fulfilling our vision and, with Javier's permission, I called a pal in Scotland, Kevin McLachlan, who had worked closely with Ron McCulloch in designing The Tunnel and the new look Fat Sam's, both to great acclaim. He agreed to come over and share his design ideas as the house would have to be extensively re-modelled and, in parts, demolished to make it into a bar.

Even today, if you look closely at the front of Cafe Mambo, you can still see signs of the house it used to be. By April we had been joined by wee Roddy, formerly of my Stirling PR crew, but this time we needed his hands to do the work, not his sweet talking tongue.

He was a bricklayer to trade and even offered to bring over the Technics SL 1200s, along with his trowel. The decks cost him £150 in excess baggage charges, but they would prove vital pieces of kit in the months ahead as Mambo set about establishing its reputation as a major pre-club venue.

Sadly, despite the initial optimism, cracks soon began to appear in relationships. The problem, as I saw it, was a project manager called Bernardo, who worked as a builder for Javier. He could not even see Kevin's vision for Mambo, let alone share it. Their relationship quickly deteriorated, souring the atmosphere around the project.

I believe Kevin's Gaudiesque design ideas for Mambo were outstanding, but no sooner would wee Roddy build a wall then Bernardo would arrive the next day to demand it be broken down.

It pitted me against Bernardo and so, by association, one of my closest friends, Javier. I felt Bernardo was full of bluster. He talked a good game, mostly to impress Javier, but I felt he didn't have the know-how to deliver a stylish bar that needed to make an immediate impact.

I wasn't a fan of Bernardo and, it must be said, the feeling was mutual. I pushed hard for Kevin's vision, but Javier seemed increasingly to side with his man and I couldn't accept it.

I found myself in the Steeler's Wheel position – stuck in the middle, although it was hardly clowns to the left and jokers to the right. Everyone involved in the project was utterly determined to see it thrive and prosper, but too many people were beginning to pull in too many different directions.

In hindsight, Javier deserved the final say. After all, it was his financial future on the line, but I struggled to understand why he had agreed to let Kevin come from Scotland in the first place if he was not going to buy into his ideas.

For those first three months my mental health had been good but as the stress and pressure began to build I could feel myself losing a grip again on my reality. Kevin quit the job and returned home and as my relationship with Javier began to fray I decided to leave the home he and Wilson had been kind enough to share with their boys.

I had been in Ibiza for almost four months and drugs had been a no-no, but I found myself slipping into my previous bad habits after I rented a flat in the bay towards the end of April.

I had lost my appetite for coke, but my cannabis consumption was soon almost reaching the same levels as the weeks leading up to my Bellsdyke admission eight months previously.

The one-bedroom flat I leased was quite cool and I kitted it out with a set of decks. Soon, I was hosting parties for no-one but myself until all hours of the morning. It was a vacation property and the apartment block was sparsely let at that time of the year, which is just as well because the noise coming from my new place would have seen me thrown out on the street at any other time of the year.

Inexplicably, I also purchased a 250cc trials bike from a hire place that had shut for the winter. I had never owned a motorbike in my life but I failed to view that as a setback.

I lived dangerously, quite literally at times. I didn't go to the trouble of buying a helmet and played a crazy game of chicken with myself, frequently turning the headlight off and hitting 50mph in the rain, just to feel the wind in my hair, replicating the stupid scenario I used to play out in the car at Castlecary arches on my way home from Glasgow's club scene many years previously.

Wee Roddy was a willing accomplice to my nonsense. Equally frustrated with the way the job was going, he used to ride pillion and we'd head into the fabled nightclub Pacha a couple of nights a week, just 20 minutes along the road in Ibiza old town.

On one memorable occasion we were playing pool when a group of fat cat sheikhs arrived and attempted to take over the table. We bluntly told them it was 'Bannockburn rules' and the winner stayed on and we ended up in their company until 4am, defeating all comers.

They plied us full of champagne and we all eventually staggered outside, where they had a fleet of limos waiting to take them back to their yacht in the bay. They were a great bunch of lads. Wee Roddy clung to my waist for dear life as we zig-zagged back to San Antonio on the bike, though this time we were lucky if we topped 30mph.

Quite frankly, I was becoming a pest. My mind was beginning to race again, a sure sign of imminent mental distress. Every morning I took the bike into Ibiza old town for coffee at the Gran Hotel Montesol, arguably the best on the whole island.

I stopped en route and bought a copy of the Daily Record and the English edition of The Sun. I would flick the pages of the Record with one hand over coffee, the pages of The Sun with the other. My head would dart left and then right, reading both papers at the same time on the table in front. I must have looked a strange sight.

Sadly, my behaviour also impacted on Javier and Wilson at a time in their lives when their stress levels were already through the roof. Every traveller or tourist from the UK I met and who confided a plan to extend their stay on the island would be sent to Javier over at Mambo.

Slowly, the bar was beginning to take shape, but I was promising jobs to strangers I had no right to offer and which weren't even available at that stage anyway. My behaviour must have been a huge distraction for my friends. It wasn't clever.

Unbeknown to me, Javier and Wilson had been making frantic phone calls back home to alert family and friends to my worsening mental state anyway. This was my first relapse, so I hardly considered my behaviour out of the ordinary and knew little then of the trigger points that would become a signal of an imminent breakdown.

I must have known I was living on the edge, even subconsciously. I had purchased 10 copies of my favourite record of the time, being played constantly at Pacha. It was 'Crayzy Man' by Blast and featured the lyric 'Crazy men don't live for long'. I related to the sentiment.

I was a loose cannon and with psychiatric facilities on the White Isle almost non-existent, not to mention the pressure of having Mambo ready for the summer season, I was a distraction Javier and Wilson didn't need.

The situation must have been serious because I had left a case full of records at Javier's place and this time he didn't even try to nick them. He handed them to my cousin Roddy to return when he arrived back in Scotland at the end the the summer season.

Javier may have promised me 10 per cent of the bar, but unlike the previous episode with Simon Littlejohn, the loss of such a handsome slice of what would become a booming business did not concern me in the slightest.

After all, I soon had other issues on my mind. I was eventually persuaded to return to Scotland in May 1994, on a Saturday evening flight to Manchester. As always, Jake was waiting for me at arrivals after a three hour flight I spent forensically examining a set of cheap earphones handed out by the cabin crew.

I was completely gone by the time we touched down, a fact that was recognised as soon as my girlfriend set eyes on me for the first time in five months.

She drove back to Stirling that night, the four hours spent in almost complete silence, and dropped me in the early hours of the Sunday morning at my parents' house. They called my GP, Dr Flanagan, almost immediately and I was sectioned for the second time in nine months.

This time I was taken to Stirling Royal Infirmary where its new psychiatric unit, Ward 30, had replaced the acute unit at Bellsdyke and was less than a week old. They took me to see a psychiatrist and as I sat outside his office I noticed a sign on the door, which could be slid between vacant and engaged. I shouted: "Vacant doctors, what's that all about?" They kept me in for four weeks.

Javier and Wilson opened our dream bar in June 1994. I may have named it Cafe Mambo, but on its opening night I was back in the land of Ga-ga. As they all watched the sun going down over the Mediterranean, back in Stirling I was already wondering if it would ever rise for me again.

15

Ward 30 of Stirling Royal Infirmary was built in a circle but all roads inevitably led to the smoking room.

The psychiatric unit was super new and fresh, opened only a week when I was first guided through its doors that Sunday afternoon in May 1994.

The Endrick ward at Bellsdyke reeked of institutionalisation and fear, but this time there was only the whiff of gloss magnolia, with the paint on the walls barely even given time to dry before the first patients moved in.

Slowly, they were dismantling the facilities at Bellsdyke as part of the Care in the Community programme, although the elderly residents with dementia and Alzheimer's would continue to call it home for another few years.

Psychiatric services were moved to the local hospitals and Ward 30 at Stirling and Ward 18 at Falkirk Royal Infirmary were effectively puppy farms. The daddy of them all, Guantanamo Bay crossed with Colditz? That was Ward 19 at Falkirk, a locked door facility that unfortunately would become my home for home in the years ahead.

If Enid Blyton ever wrote about bi-polar or schizophrenia then the smoking room would have been the garden shed of the Secret Seven.

That's not to trivialise mental illness in any form. However, it served as a gang hut for the patients, a neutral space away from the prying eyes of staff, who rarely popped their heads around the door, although whether they would have been able to see anything through the thick haze from Benson and Hedges and Golden Virginia is open to debate anyway.

It was all a big game – albeit with serious consequences – and if the rules were bent, we were only doing to them what they did to us.

It took me the best part of two decades to understand the mechanics of a 28 day section. Once the jungle drums started beating and a psychiatrist was called, you were invariably asked if you wanted to go into hospital voluntarily.

If you agreed – and I never did – you might spend a few days less than a month in the mental health unit. If you didn't agree, you were still sectioned and you served the full 28 days. It was a case of damned if you do, damned if you don't.

The approach at Ward 30 was softly, softly. The doors to the unit were only locked at 8pm and the staff were still finding their feet around a client base of approximately 24 patients.

I received counselling and psychiatric assessments and, for the first time, I was prescribed Lithium for the long term to balance the chemical inequality in my brain caused by my excessive cannabis consumption. There were arts and crafts and the television was never off but my abiding memory, as it is with most of my stays in psychiatric units, was the smoking room.

Like Neil Sedaka's greatest hits, all of life was there. It was the room in which we schemed, plotted, cut deals, told our stories, shared our dreams and formed friendships that were as haphazard as the wiring in our heads at that moment in time.

At Ward 30 the smoking room opened at 7am and I was up and out my bed like a kid on Christmas morning, drawing so heavily on my first cigarette of the day I almost always fainted and fell to the floor.

I once traded a girlfriend's Cartier watch for a cigarette and if I lost a couple of grand on that deal I almost made four grand on another.

I came up with an idea for a nightclub speed dating game and even went so far as to trademark a logo for 'Love' with lawyers. I excitedly laid out the plans to a fellow patient from Stirling, Abie Bennett, explaining how customers at the nightclub would be given a red sticker, which meant they were out of bounds for an approach, or a green sticker for go.

An hour of each night would be given over to music dedicated to love, at which point you could approach someone with a green sticker who had caught your eye.

I reckon it had franchise potential and, ever the salesman, Abie was so excited with my pitch he demanded his missus go home that night, take four grand from their safe, and bring it in the following day to provide seed funding for our new venture. She humoured us and played along, but never turned their combination so much as an inch.

You learned everything in the smoking room – who was up to what, the best new medicines on the go, the most malleable staff, even the menu for that week. The nurses occasionally tried to catch snatches of conversations, but we were all double wide. It was like the Boston Tea Party, with reasoning frequently thrown overboard from a cargo heavy with mischief and mayhem.

We didn't half form some dodgy friendships, which meant everything to us at that period in our lives. In later years I met a kindred spirit, Brian from Falkirk, and we played off each other like a black comedy double act.

He had bumped American Express for 25 grand and was paying it off at a pound a week, which wasn't a bad rate of interest. We whooped like native Americans every time we set eyes on each other.

Later on, after we'd been released, I picked him up from his house for a day trip and discovered he slept in a tent pitched on top of his bed.

Along with another good pal, Henry Coyle, we set off at 5.30am for the Perthshire village of St Fillans. Every time one of us shouted: "Up!" we had to stop the car at the side of the road, get out and do 50 press-ups. We screeched to a halt eight times on the road there, then caused a tailback in Callander after stopping in the middle of Main Street to exercise in front of bemused summer tourists on the way back. It was madness. Literally.

I was released from Ward 30 after four weeks with that prescription for Lithium, which had levelled out much of my mania from the weeks previously. I came to the conclusion I needed a break with my past so decided on the ultimate move for anyone who comes from Stirling – I found a flat in Falkirk.

Actually, the flat found me – an old pal, Nick Tahoo, had a place in Bainsford rented from the council and couldn't stand to let it go. He'd split from his wife, moved down the road and then reconciled with his better half, but kept the second property as an insurance policy against any future domestics.

He sublet the place on an ad hoc basis and threw me the keys for little more than a peppercorn rent. The first thing I did was paint it yellow throughout, reasoning it was a happy colour that would only serve to enhance my mood, which was holding good, even though I had quickly returned to smoking hash on a daily basis.

The house didn't have any curtains, but the bed was comfy, the central heating ticked along nicely and the living room boasted two stout room-mates Nick and I quickly tagged PK1 and PK2. They were two Parker Knoll recliners and once we'd added a telly and a set of decks I told him I couldn't have asked for more.

In hindsight, it was a decompression chamber from the stresses of the previous year and while Christmas 1994 was one of the most spartan I'd experienced, the time in my own company seemed to do me some good.

I can see now it was little more than a crash pad. I was all but down and out and yet the crucial difference, absolutely pivotal in mental health assessment, was I kept myself clean. I never lost pride in my appearance, which is often one of the first things to go when an individual suffers a period of mental ill health.

I even wrote a diary, which only lasted a couple of weeks, but I enjoyed the discipline of monitoring my own moods. Nikki Cullis was no longer in my life but her dad, Tom, generously gifted me that second hand van, a 10 year old Renault, and it kept me mobile.

Jake and other friends visited regularly but part of the reason for moving to Falkirk was a yearning to escape from a fear and dread I had let everyone down – including my girlfriend.

I had gone from owning all the material trappings, including my own place and a decent car, to absolutely nothing. I began to distance myself from Jake in such a cruel and cowardly manner. After more than nine years I stopped returning calls and didn't pick up the phone to ask how she was doing.

I was weak. As with every significant female relationship in my life I didn't have the balls to end it in a mature manner. I never met her, told her my thoughts, asked for time out or requested we go our separate ways for good. I just…let it go.

It was shameful behaviour and so unfair on Jake, who had always been a loving and positive influence on my life. She had been there in the good times, but was even stronger and more resolute in the bad.

In recent years I've been drawn to Buddhism and one of its most compelling teachings is the concept of changing karma. I had a lot of negative energy to confront, especially around my relationships with some wonderful women, not least Jake.

It took me four years of chanting to alter my karma. I've since said sorry to many of the women who agreed to share my life, even for a time, for my bad behaviour. I don't know if it will ever be enough but the apologies offered have been genuine, heartfelt and sincere.

In total, I spent seven months in Falkirk and in that time I also picked up the thread of a few gigs, although money was hardly pouring into my coffers.

Previously, I'd held my talents as a DJ and record producer in high regard, which was reflected in the money I could charge from club owners, usually around £150-a-night. In the aftermath of my two periods in psychiatric units at Bellsdyke and Stirling Royal the gigs were still there, but the money was not.

I started to DJ at Duck Bay Marina for £50-a-night, likewise The Outhouse in Bridge of Allan. Duck Bay Marina was rammed on a Saturday and they were queueing out the door at The Outhouse, 200 people on a Wednesday night, which was unheard of.

Once upon a time I'd scoffed at bar owner Chris Morris when he opened the Beanstalk, but he and business partner Vivien Lafferty graciously didn't take it to heart and at least paid me the going rate, £150 a night, to DJ at their new Stirling venue, Behind The Wall Too.

The money situation didn't rankle so much at the time as the gigs boosted my self-esteem, which had taken a battering. I was still relevant as a DJ and although my hash consumption remained high and a blifter was never far from my lips, the Lithium was doing its job in keeping me on an even mental keel.

By February 1995 Stirling was drawing me home and an old school pal, Alex MacDonald, offered me one of two flats he had recently refurbished above the pub he owned in the village of Plean.

The Plean Tavern was a hub of the community, known to everyone as The Billy, and Alex lived in the other apartment upstairs. Alex is one of the most pleasant guys you'll meet – and also one of the toughest.

One Sunday morning I was wakened by a kerfuffle outside and opened the curtains to find a scene straight from a Sergio Leone western developing on the street outside. Across the road were spread 10 angry men, remonstrating with Alex, who was standing outside the pub.

He calmly told them: "Come over here, one at a time, and we'll sort this out around the back." To this day, I don't know what caused the argument, but I do know not one of the guys moved an inch to take him on.

The Billy had a function suite that did little business, so when Club SG in Falkirk – scene of my embarrassment with Alfredo – announced it was closing its doors we bought up half its fixtures and fittings.

We brought in Billy The Brush, a South African who was a dab hand at painting, and he transformed the interior so it looked like a blue sky, with fluffy clouds on the ceilings and walls. The look was completed with cherubs in the shape of Paul Gascoigne, a nod to the Rangers roots of the boozer.

Alex invested a few bob in a decent sound system and I named it Es in honour of Es Paradis, but it would have been easier persuading Celtic to host their player of the year night in the club than attracting a regular clientele to come so far out of town to party.

Our hopes for a prosperous future were hardly helped when Cream, the fabled Liverpool nightclub, threatened to sue us for nicking their logo to promote our own place. In fairness, they had a point.

The Cream logo was little more than the universal sign for an electrical fan I decided, but instead of saying 'Cream', ours said 'Plean'. I made up stickers and Cream would never have known but the record label, Deconstruction, regularly sent me new releases as I was on their mailing list. The vinyl I didn't fancy I sent back in an envelope, sealed by our cheeky tribute.

One afternoon the phone went and it was James Barton, owner of Cream. He cut straight to the point: "Are you trying to pass yourself off as my company? I'll sue the arse off you." I let his legal threats fly over my head and responded: "We're just a wee village on the outskirts of Stirling, pal. Sue away. The only people holding any brass around our place are the darts team." I never heard from him again.

We were naughty, but never malicious. An old pal from the Glasgow clubbing days, Dave Ross, promoted the controversial militant Irish republican band The Wolfe Tones on a tour of Scotland. Dave had a date free and asked if I fancied putting on a night in Stirling. They went down a storm at the Albert Halls – and The Billy boys made a fortune from running the bar in the venue.

Our Plean tribute to Es didn't do much business, but it hosted a party to remember in Hogmanay 1995 when more than a hundred of us held a lock in until 7am and then continued the new year celebrations upstairs in my flat.

It was the first time I got together with another great love of my life, Fiona, a girl I had spent months trying to woo at one of the local cafes where she worked. She was built like a racing snake and had the most amazing blue eyes. I was so infatuated I turned up at the cafe four times a week, just to watch her work. On each visit I ordered a kiwi fruit milkshake and by the end I had swallowed so many I was in danger of turning green.

She eventually agreed to start seeing me that Hogmanay and perhaps she was attracted by my latest get up, a Burberry waistcoat and trousers gifted to me that Christmas by my parents. I added a duffle coat to the ensemble and walked around like Paddington Bear.

My Burberry collection would leave a lasting legacy. In the years ahead the triggers for another looming mental health episode included less than six hours sleep, an increase in tobacco intake, a quickening and repetitive speech pattern – and an appearance of the Burberry from the back of my wardrobe.

If pals saw me out and about with my Burberry waistcoat and strides, they knew another breakdown was just around the corner.

Alex and I were so tight at The Billy he even confided an ambition to sell it all up and run a bar in Ibiza. We went as far in the summer of 1996 as heading to the White Isle for a week, splitting our time between Javier and Wilson's place and a couple of nights at Pikes hotel.

We scouted a couple of venues but nothing really caught our eye, although the visit remains memorable for the wrong reason. We headed into Ibiza old town for a night out and, for the first time in a couple of years, I snorted a line of coke.

Javier shot me a look as if to say I hadn't changed a bit and it was a glance laced with disappointment, which made me uneasy. It was a rare return into Class A territory, but my daily consumption of cannabis was back at previous levels. Hash didn't do me any favours. It's a gateway drug that often opens the door to something else which, in my case, frequently included recreational carnage.

At the time, one of the most popular movies in the cinema was 'Things To Do In Denver When You're Dead', starring Andy Garcia, Steve Buscemi and Christopher Walken. It was a gangster flick in which the bodies piled up at the same rate as the references to 'boat drinks'.

I became obsessed with this concept, which centred around a group of friends hiring a boat on a pleasant Sunday afternoon and kicking back to shoot the breeze over a few beers. I quickly called a company based on the Forth and Clyde Canal and took one of their vessels on a day long charter from Kirkintilloch, with a skipper and waitress thrown in to steer the barge and serve any food and drink we brought on board.

A mini-bus was hired and 12 of us piled in, but the day started badly when Jamie Masterson revealed he'd baked a cake (he'd even frosted it with cream) into which he had sprinkled an ounce and a half of cannabis resin.

I've rolled a fair number of joints in my life, but even I recognised that amount of blow would have brought down a Clydesdale horse.

We weren't so much stoned by the time we staggered off the bus after a 30 minute journey from Stirling, with half the cake still uneaten, as tripping out our nuts.

Steven Croal and Gary Neill were hallucinating so badly they didn't even make it as far as the canal. They crossed the road from the car park and hopped on the next available bus back to Stirling, where they got off and ate two lunches each at a local restaurant.

It went from bad to worse. The young waitress who was serving our food and drinks accepted the offer of a slice of cake, as did the skipper. It was a low blow and should never have been offered in the first place.

After 20 minutes she phoned her partner in a panic, stoned out her face, and he arrived soon afterwards from their home in Cumbernauld, swinging a baseball bat like Babe Ruth.

Meanwhile, my mucker Jok was giving another guest mouth to mouth after they collapsed on deck and the skipper was so out of it the barge veered from one bank to the next while the guy from Cumbernauld tried in vain to jump on board to save his girl and knock our heads in.

We had chartered the barge for the day, but after three hours it had travelled less than a mile. Earlier, we had brought a couple of decks on board, but we couldn't get them to work and the CD player was stuck so the soundtrack to the whole afternoon became Bob Marley's 'Could You Be Loved', which was played constantly on repeat.

The damage already done, we ditched the last chunk of cake overboard, but it only served to attract a herd of swans and they gorged on it hungrily before swimming in perfect circles for the next 40 minutes.

A DJ and record producer pal, Colin Tevendale, turned up with a singer he was promoting in Glasgow that night, a classy act called Grace who was signed to Paul Oakenfold's Perfecto label. They looked on shell-shocked from the sidelines at the scenes of devastation that had unfolded before they turned and fled.

We eventually made it back to the jetty, but didn't know if we were in Kirkintilloch or Kazakhstan. Our big day out had started in Stirling at 1pm and by 6pm I was back in my bed in Plean.

A year later Lee Masterson, Jamie's brother, was recalling the story with Colin at the 23rd Precinct record store in Glasgow. A stranger, listening in, turned and asked: "The barge? Did that really happen? Man, we all thought that story was an urban myth."

The truth is often stranger than fiction.

16

I have been privileged and blessed to know many good times in life. On March 13 1996, there came the very worst when evil visited Dunblane Primary School and took with it teacher Gwen Mayor and 16 other precious young lives including Emma, the beloved daughter of my close pal John Crozier and his wife Alison.

I was John's best man and had even hosted a night at Fat Sam's for the boys to celebrate Emma's birth. I told the bouncers to cut them some slack.

When the lights went up at the end of it all, Steven Croal was hanging upside down from a metal support that ran the length of the club and John was on his way to Dunblane on the back of a milk float after persuading the driver to make a 40 mile detour.

John worked with my dad in the REME, the Stirling army supplies base, and we first got to know each other in the days of McQ's. He was, and continues to be, a rock in my life and we still speak every other day.

He was always there for me during my darkest, most troubling times. Many a stay in hospital was brightened by his cheery presence, a packet of 20 menthol cigarettes in one hand and a copy of FHM or Loaded magazine in the other.

This time, it was my turn to reach out for him. I heard on the radio of a shooting at a school in Dunblane and initially reckoned it must have been at the educational establishment in the town called Queen Victoria, which teaches the sons and daughters of senior British military personnel.

I turned on the television in my flat above The Billy and when it became clear it was Dunblane Primary School my first thoughts were for John and Alison – and, of course, Emma; a wee smasher, a beautiful picture of innocence, just five years old and with a knack of bringing a smile to your face with her presence in the room alone.

I raced to their home and was absolutely unnerved. Time appeared to have stood still. Doors were lying wide open, dishes were still out on the table, the radio was playing and the television was on.

I walked from room to room, calling for John and Alison but no-one was home. News had clearly been delivered and they had fled towards the school immediately, abandoning everything.

The next couple of days remain a blur. I recall the house becoming really busy with family and friends that first afternoon, but there was nothing anyone could say or do. What words could possibly have made sense, let alone offered comfort?

The following day I returned to the same emotional scenes and there stood John, operating on autopilot, making tea and handing out biscuits to visitors. Every part of me ached for him and Alison. They were living on their nerves. It hadn't hit them fully at that stage, but how could life ever prepare anyone to deal with an act of such utter wickedness?

Their story isn't mine to tell, but I know the birth of Ellie, born after Emma's passing, brought them joy and she has grown to become a proud, loving and loyal daughter, as well as a good sister to big brother Jack.

Emma was laid to rest after a service at Lecropt Kirk in Bridge of Allan, where John is an elder. A stained glass window there honours the memory of Emma, her teacher and her little classmates and a set of hymn books was also bequeathed in her name.

It still doesn't make sense. Jake came to the funeral with me and gripped my hand tightly on a cold, dark morning that seemed somehow fitting and yet also so much at odds with the little ray of sunshine who lit up so many lives in her five short years.

It was and still remains the saddest, most heartbreaking day of my entire life.

17

A track that took less than an hour to produce ended up consuming 20 years of my life.

Shamefully, I even sent heavies to the door in Liverpool of the producer and manager of Dario G, so convinced he had ripped me off and robbed me of my chance of the big time by stealing my inspiration and using it to create the worldwide hit 'Sunchyme'.

The fury burned within me for years, a chip on the shoulder that grew so heavy even Atlas was carrying a feather pillow in comparison. Then remarkably, early in 2017, I found out I had been so stoned and disengaged from reality in Ibiza in the summer of 1997 the narrative of events I'd allowed to build in my head was substantially incorrect.

I got it so wrong, all along.

I owe Jon Barlow of Three Beat Records in Liverpool and Paul Spencer, the man behind Dario G, a full apology. As manager of the band and producer of 'Sunchyme' I called Jon, in particular, several times to vent my spleen.

A clubland associate had connections in Liverpool and offered to send a couple of heavies to pay him a visit. Stupidly, I agreed and they did – a friendly word to the wise, I stress, no violence – but the police were soon at my door in Bannockburn and, knowing my delicate mental state, settled for a strong word in my ear, telling me bluntly: "Leave the guy alone, Scooby. No more contact – or else." I heeded their warning.

Jon, if you're reading this, I'm sorry it ever went so far.

My frustration poured out in an article in the News of the World on February 22, 1998. Under the headline, "Scot 'Wrote Dario G Hit'", it started: "A Scots producer claims chart smash 'Sunchyme' was based on a song he recorded two years earlier. 'Sunchyme', performed by Dario G, made number two in the charts last year and was only kept off the top by Elton John's 'Candle In The Wind'.

Stuart Cochrane says it was lifted from his tune 'Yeah Oh', recorded in a Glasgow studio in 1995. Two years later Stuart paid £800 to press 500 copies on yellow vinyl with a sun motif in the centre and distributed them, hoping the song would catch on.

Stuart, 35, of Plean, Stirling, said: 'The next thing I knew I was hearing a tune on the radio and thinking, 'That's mine'. But the announcer said it was 'Sunchyme' by Dario G.'"

The following month Mixmag, the DJ bible, featured me in a full page article, including a picture with my yellow vinyl and the identikit yellow CD from Dario G. It revealed I had rejected an offer of one per cent of royalties from Warner Brothers, a sum of £60,000.

It also quoted from a musicologist's report that said both tracks shared the same tempo and musical key. It concluded that although 'Yeah Oh' may have provided the basic idea, 'Sunchyme' could not be seen as "an actual adaptation" which is notoriously difficult to prove in dance music.

For me, the offer from the record company was a vindication of my position, but I wanted more than a 'point', or one per cent, of the deal.

Strangely, after all I had been through financially, it wasn't actually about the money. Perhaps I should have taken their cash and paid back my dad from the BCCI debacle, but I felt my credibility was on the line and there was no price on integrity.

Arrogant, maybe, but after two spells in the psychiatric unit I was really happy again and felt the big boys of the music industry were in danger of damaging my fragile mental equilibrium.

My relationship with Fiona was flourishing, I had a good thing going with Alex in Plean and I had found a level of contentment I could never have thought possible even a couple of years previously.

I ploughed on, even hiring top London music lawyers Clintons, who represented U2, to fight Warner Brothers but half a dozen letters at hundreds of pounds a pop soon took their financial toll. I threw in the towel and silently stewed every time I heard 'Sunchyme' over the following two decades.

The origins of 'Yeah Oh' grew from the spring of 1995, when I was in the Apollo studios in Glasgow city centre with my pal Andy Haldane, a producer with whom I'm still making music today.

We had been commissioned at a grand a time by German dance label ZYX to re-mix several tracks and had been working on a cover version by a fine singer called Justine Earp of 'Ooh La La La', originally recorded by The Fugees.

Andy and I never messed around in the studio, certainly not when it cost £300-a-day to hire, and we still had an hour left in our session after we'd put Justine's track to bed. There was no way we were calling it quits with lucrative studio time still under our control.

Instinctively, I raided my memory banks for a couple of ideas that had been whirling around in the back of my head for several years.

I had long been captivated by Dream Academy's 'Life In A Northern Town', one of the most iconic singles of the eighties in which the haunting vocals of Nick Laird-Clowes and Kate St John merge beautifully. (It's also a tribute to folk singer Nick Drake, another hash addict who suffered mental health issues. A coincidence?)

Three minutes into the track, St John sings one line acapella 'Ah hey ma ma ma ma', and that was the sample that stuck in my mind. I had also been a big fan of 'Hill Street Blues' and loved the piano heavy theme tune, which reminded me so much of my younger days.

In my head, it made sense to mix them together and I asked Andy, who plays piano, if he could improvise a few bars in the style of my favourite cop show while I isolated St John's vocal.

All in, it took 60 minutes to mix and produce and while the track was understandably rough around the edges, we committed it to a digital audio tape, or DAT, for posterity, where it would have stayed had my pal Colin Tevendale (back talking to me again, despite the high jinx with hash on the Kirkintilloch barge) not stepped in.

A few months later, he was rummaging around in the shaving bag in which I kept my DATs, which were little more than musical snapshots, musings and works in progress, and came across my master copy of 'Yeah Oh' (it didn't even have a name at that stage).

202

Colin was a producer and DJ at a string of popular clubs, including The Tunnel, and an eighties music freak. He loved the track and asked to send the DAT to London, where he was willing to pay for a one-off test pressing, known as an acetate, which would give him the track in record form and, as a result, exclusivity in playing it around the clubs.

I really rated Colin, both musically and as an individual, and agreed. Within a couple of weeks he was playing 'Yeah Oh' at his gigs in and around Glasgow and it was blowing the joint up.

The story would have ended there, but early in 1997 I headed back to Ibiza and was determined to arrive with the summer's big hit under my arm. It was a challenge DJs regularly set themselves ahead of the season on the White Isle and I was no different in looking for that self-produced track that could translate from club floor filler to mammoth mainstream success.

Under my latest moniker, DJ Sueno, I'd roped in Andy to help produce 'Ibiza Cultura', an ambitious, 11 minute epic that sampled everyone from The Beatles to Ian Dury and the Blockheads.

I lined up a deal to press 500 records, but needed a 'B' side and quickly decided 'Yeah Oh' would fit the bill. In total, I took 200 records to Ibiza to play, sell and distribute and left 300 with my pal Barry Fraser, who had established a record store, Uber Disko, in Edinburgh, specialising in dance.

He sent the bright yellow vinyl, pressed to resemble the sun, to a London distributor, Amato – and they sold out within two days.

A strange thing subsequently happened, about which I had been unaware (or had forgotten) since 1997. Firstly, Pete Tong called Barry expressing an interest in the track that had been sent to Amato and which he was keen to release on his own record label, FFRR.

Secondly, he wasn't fussed at all with 'Ibiza Cultura', but was intrigued by the 'B' side 'Yeah Oh', my Dream Academy/Hill Street Blues mix.

Tong and his people called a couple of times a week for several weeks and was quickly followed by Warner Brothers, the original publishers of 'Life In A Northern Town', who were also keen on my re-make. For the first time in my career, I had two major players battling for one of my tracks.

Sadly, they would have found it easier to hunt down the man on the moon. In the early days of mobile technology I didn't own a phone and Barry called the hotel where I was staying in Ibiza every second day to inform me of my impending good fortune and the desire of Tong and Warner Brothers to meet and speak about my track.

Unfortunately, I was so stoned and having so much fun all I could think to say was 'manana'. Barry contacted mutual friends on the island to try and stir me from my sun and drug-induced apathy, but to no avail.

Tong made strong and serious attempts to work with me, as did Warner Brothers, but I was so out of it and enjoying my Ibicencan experience I didn't even want to know. Tomorrow, tomorrow, tomorrow, I promised Barry. But tomorrow never comes.

Barry informed me of that angle to the story when I went to see him in early 2017 for research into this book and I was absolutely gobsmacked, oblivious to it all.

Dario G released 'Sunchyme' on Warner Brothers later that summer and it was selected by Pete Tong as his record of the week on his Radio One show.

I was raging, believing I'd been turned over by the music industry when, in truth, I had once again been the master of my own missed opportunity.

Did Warner Brothers approach Dario G when they failed to communicate with me? Undoubtedly 'Sunchyme' is beautifully produced, slicker sounding and more polished than my track, but never forget 'Yeah Oh' was put together in minutes, not days or weeks.

Dario G disagree, but I maintain the roots of their track can be found in my original, although it must be remembered I'd also stolen that acapella line from Dream Academy in the first place.

It's par for the course in dance music, like it or not, and that's how great music is made. I've come to believe and accept the £60,000 I would have earned from Warner Brothers wasn't to buy my silence after all, but was offered as a sweetener and reward for a great idea that, ultimately, was brilliantly executed by another artist.

My principles – others would call it pig-headedness – had also cost me a tilt at the big time in 1996 when I walked away from a £20,000 album deal from Pulse 8 records after they reneged on a promise to acknowledge the kids of Dunblane in the linear notes of one of my remixes.

Pulse 8 were the label of Rozalla and also the Urban Cookie Collective, quite a coincidence after I'd stood at the locked door of Bellsdyke and belted out their biggest hit, 'The Key, The Secret' to no-one in particular.

Rozalla had taken 'Everybody's Free (To Feel Good)' into the top 10 soon after its release in September 1991 and Frank Samson, owner of Pulse 8, was keen for a release of remixes five years later.

My relationship with the track was established in 1994, not long after I had first teamed up with Andy at the Apollo studios, which were situated next door to Rab Ha's bar in Glasgow's Merchant City.

I was keen to construct credentials as a serious producer and I found a home from home with Andy and his production partner Calum MacLean, who played in a local covers band, The Johnny Sevens.

I quickly learned there were two sounds in the studio, which suited me to a tee. Andy was a master at producing poppy, mainstream music and if you kept him fuelled with a chocolate bar in the morning, a sandwich at lunch and a cream cake by mid-afternoon there was nothing he wouldn't do for you.

Calum? Musically, he was so far out you met him coming back. He produced tracks equally as amazing as Andy's, but they were really wild mixes. If you wanted the best from him you left him with five joints in the morning and brought him a fish supper when the munchies kicked in at 3pm.

I saved hard for my first day in the studio and, in hindsight, £300 was a snip as it came with Andy's expertise. I've always had a soft spot for Rangers and decided to make a track called 'Coop' as a tribute to one of the club's most famous wingers, Davie Cooper.

Andy later confided amateurs and hobbyists would hire the studio for a day and stand over him for hours demanding music that was impossible to make.

He must have groaned inwardly when I first walked through the doors with a bagpipe sample from the Strathclyde Police Band, a snatch of Runrig from their famed Loch Lomond concert, a drum sample from Paul Oakenfold's Perfecto label and a VHS cassette of Hollywood hit 'Highlander', from which I wanted to isolate Sean Connery's killer line, "You've done well."

Andy told me later I had handed him the equivalent of a strawberry, a stick of liquorice, some wasabi peas and a clutch of iron filings and he was at a loss how it could all be mixed together into something musically palatable.

I walked through the door at 10am and within 25 minutes the Akai sampler was loaded with my unique ingredients, but I knew Andy needed more. I handed him a copy of the DJ Ricci mix of 'Pacific Symphony' by Transformer 2 and politely asked if he could use the track as a road map for what I hoped we could achieve.

I got up and moved to leave the studio and he looked at me with some astonishment as most clients pulled their chairs closer to his mixing desk, rather than pushing them away.

I explained: "There's no point me being here, I'd only get in your way." I wandered around Glasgow city centre for the next few hours, did some shopping and treated myself to lunch, and returned to the studio at 3pm.

Andy had worked diligently on the track and played the finished version. It was so spellbinding the hairs on the back of my neck stood to attention. A partnership, which soon became a close friendship, had been formed.

Admittedly, even Andy was flummoxed when it came to Rozalla. A couple of months previously I had released our Rangers track under another pseudonym, this time 'True Blue', and earned a P and D – press and distribution – deal for my track 'Coop'.

It was awarded by one of the dance industry's major players, Mo's Music, and netted me a grand. I was keen to follow it up, this time under the moniker 'Espirit', but even Andy was scratching his head when I turned up with four big samples for 'Everybody's Free (To Feel Good)'.

I cut the word 'everybody's' from the B side of Rozalla's original track, which was an acapella version, and with musical rainbows shooting back and forth in my mind requested it be mixed with The Who's 'Won't Get Fooled Again', Simple Minds' 'Changeling' and 'Here Comes The Rain Again' by The Eurythmics.

At one stage, Andy wanted to give up but he persevered and delivered another fabulous track, which we called 'Sueno Ibiza'. I dedicated it to Jake and my DJ mentor, Alfredo, and Mo's were happy to distribute it on the same terms as before, early in 1995.

The remix enjoyed modest success, selling its 500 copies, but I'd forgotten completely about it when the phone rang in my flat in Plean on a miserable winter's night towards the end of the year.

On the other end was Frank Samson of Pulse 8, a respected music industry figure who had worked in the past with the likes of Genesis, Peter Gabriel and even Monty Python.

He was calling from MIDEM, a major music industry conference being hosted in the south of France, and had just heard my Rozalla re-mix. He loved it and asked me to come to London to discuss an album deal.

He offered me £20,000 and I reasoned 10 tracks, recorded with Andy over 10 days at Apollo, would leave me £17,000 in profit. We batted details back and forth for the next few months and Frank asked for my Rozalla remix to be included on a four track package he planned to release in the summer of 1996.

I agreed to allow my version, the 'Mambo Pacha Remix' to be part of his release, in return for that dedication to Emma and the Dunblane kids in the sleeve notes, which was met with approval.

Rozalla's 'Everybody's Free 96' made the UK top 30 and peaked at number two in the dance charts, a phenomenal effort, but I was so saddened and disappointed when Pulse 8 went back on their original promise, overlooking our previously agreed tribute to the Dunblane kids.

The subsequent success of the track meant less to me as a result. I told Samson to stick his £20,000 where the sun doesn't shine. An over-reaction? Maybe, but what price trust?

I was a relatively naive DJ from Scotland, which was reflected in the deal I accepted for my Rozalla re-mix, a flat fee of a grand from Pulse 8, rather than a point – or percentage – of sales.

It would have made better business sense to accept the latter, but I didn't know any better. Perhaps I could have approached it with greater maturity, but I felt my integrity – that word again – had been compromised and even today I have no regrets about not pushing ahead with that album contract.

In truth, I wasn't looking at making music to earn big money, or even as a job. It was fun. Re-mixing and production elicited within me the same joyful emotions as that moment when, as a 15-year-old,

I cautiously looked up from the decks at Bannockburn youth club and saw the other kids nodding their heads in time to the music of the Climax Blues Band.

Strangely, music was never as much of a craft for me as it was for others, even if I wanted to be taken seriously. A day at the Apollo studios was as much a £300 party as it was an expression of a creative process.

We smoked umpteen blifters, ate fish suppers, enjoyed lunches at Rab Ha's and frequently reached for our guitars and had impromptu jam sessions with Andy, Calum and whoever else happened to stumble into the centre of it all on any given day.

I had been involved in the chaos and creativity of record production since 1992, when I first teamed up with Michael Kilkie, who worked at the 23rd Precinct Record store on Glasgow's Bath Street. He was one of the country's best young DJs and has gone on to enjoy even greater success today as one of Scotland's leading chefs and restaurateurs.

The 23rd Precinct became a home for home when I was a DJ and promoter and Michael and Colin Tevendale, who also worked in the store, really looked after the regulars. Theirs was the best place in Glasgow to buy dance music, so much so within a few years I was spending £150-a-week on records.

The guys made it easy. They knew their customer base so well they would frequently divvy up new releases that arrived in store into different bags, based on musical preferences. They worked like a late 20th century Spotify and their keen ears saved guys such as me from having to sift through hundreds of tracks a week.

It was always a pleasure to head into the store every weekend and be given a musical dip bag of tracks they reckoned I might like.

Those of us lucky enough to have an 'in' would even be ushered into the back, where they had set up a couple of decks to play the new releases, with those tracks you didn't fancy simply returned back into the shop floor stock mix.

The store also had its own record label called Limbo and Michael and I, in a fit of inspiration, decided to team up as a duo named Skonk (The 23rd Precinct's co-owner, Billy Kiltie, refused us permission to call ourselves Skunk) and we released a track known as 'Banjo'd'.

We went into the studio with a big bag of grass and took the bass line from Talking Heads' 'Psychokiller' as the spine of a mix that also included the chimes from an ice cream van and a sample of banjo music.

As a label, Limbo were really credible. Michael was part of a duo on their books called Umboza who took 'Cry India', which sampled 'All Night Long' by Lionel Ritchie, into the Top 20. He even turned up on Top of the Pops playing the bongos.

The critics hated our track. Dave Calikis, the reviewer for Mixmag, described 'Banjo'd' as "the worst record ever released by Limbo." The public didn't disagree. Our first royalty statement declared a return of 23 pence on a letter than cost 25 pence to post, but there was something about our track I couldn't let go and I would re-visit it a couple of years later.

The vibe at 23rd Precinct was amazing. Everyone who was anyone in the Glasgow club scene hung out there and deals were made on a daily basis as plans were plotted for worldwide domination.

When that nonsense English track by eccentric Italian Adriano Celentano, first popularised in clubland by Dave 'CL' Young, went big in 'Fresh' everyone rushed to 23rd Precinct in a bid to buy a copy. The store phoned contacts in Italy, but the track was released in 1972 and no copies were available.

Celentano himself even called to find out what all the fuss was about. An Italian label called Clan Records asked Dave 'CL' Young to remix the track for a nineties audience but he rightly refused, correctly reasoning it would only spoil its authenticity.

In the end Clan Records simply re-released the seven inch track, but put it on a 12 inch disc and sold hundreds in Glasgow alone.

Dave, Andy Haldane and I paid tribute to Celentano when we were asked by ZYX for a remix of a track called 'Hablando' by Italian musician Ramirez. It was heavy on the squeeze box, so we called ours the Will Starr Remix after the famous Scottish accordion player – and added a wee sample of Celentano's track to the mix for good measure.

I had also dabbled with record production in the early nineties when Fraser Hotchkiss, his nephew Ian and our pal Alex Milne joined forces with me to mix a couple of tracks. We worked from a studio that was attached to the house of a mutual friend Davie Paterson in Tullibody, a village on the outskirts of Stirling.

Our tracks were really credible. Working under the name of Area 51, our first release 'Let It Move You' was even played on Radio One by Pete Tong and my house phone almost rung off the hook with excited pals calling to offer congratulations. It also made top 20 of the Radio One club charts.

As La Rue, we also produced 'Cathedral Song' and it was even released by Stress Records, part of the Mixmag empire. Dave Seaman, one third of respected music producers Brothers In Rhythm, accepted my invite to play The Outhouse in Bridge of Allan and stayed the night at my place in Riverside.

We were chilling at my home after his set and he was listening to some of the DATs I had in my collection and came across 'Cathedral Song'. He loved it enough to recommend it to Stress Records and it was released to positive reviews, even if it enjoyed little commercial success.

However, as a producer I knew collaboration with three mates could only work in the short term. Four producers meant four opinions and a camel is only a horse designed by committee.

Fraser, Ian, Alex and I worked hard to produce records that were relevant and we did really well, but going forward I knew I needed my voice to be most dominant in the expression of my own musical ideas.

In that respect, I felt most creatively comfortable at the Apollo studios, where Andy and Calum were happy to work under instruction. Crucially, they were also strong enough to offer their own take on my point of view and rarely was their advice anything other than sage.

It was the most creative time of my life, although my fragile mental health around 1997, after three years of wellness, caused a couple of issues, even if I refused to allow Iggy Pop to send me over the edge.

I had re-mixed a copy of his iconic track, 'The Passenger' with the trusty Andy, but couldn't get a clean sample on Iggy's vocal. Thankfully, Calum had the answer. There was a guitar shop upstairs and one of the staff, Jim Brady, played in The Johnny Sevens with my producer pal.

Jim performed under the pseudonym 'Rick Flick' and for the cost of his lunch and a bung of £30 he agreed to play the famous riffs from 'The Passenger' and mimic Iggy's 'la la la la la la la las'.

My take on the track was re-mixed again, this time by Calum, Colin Tevendale and Barry Fraser, who called themselves Fool Boona. I had established a relationship with Andy Thompson, head of dance at Virgin Records, and he released it on his label under the title 'Popped', handing the boys a £7,000 advance. They kindly gave me £1,500, even though I wasn't due a penny.

Their cut even made 'Now That's What I Call Music, Volume 42' which netted them an extra £25,000. However, an advance is only ever that – an advance.

As a result of its inclusion on 'Now' they needed a video to go with the track and it cost £30,000 to film. The song ended up in debt, which had nothing to do with me – but a letter from Iggy's lawyers in New York most certainly did.

They threatened to sue us for lifting their client's vocal unchecked, as well as the original riffs. Jim Brady, aka Rick Flick, had done such a professional job he had even convinced Iggy Pop's management team he was their man.

We wrote back and told them it wasn't Iggy Pop who was singing on my version, nor had we used the original riffs. It was all the work of Rick Flick and would they please give us peace? We never heard from them again.

I wasn't in the least concerned with burning that bridge, but I ruined a couple of professional relationships as my bi-polar began to bite again – and one, which had also developed into a good friendship, I still regret today.

My version of 'The Passenger' was doing the rounds in 1998 and it came across the desk of Radio One DJ Judge Jules, who played it on his show several times. I had paid for 500 copies to be pressed and it was made known he would love another copy for his collection.

I was in London at the time and made my way to Radio One, where I managed to talk my way into the studio when he was on air. Everything was agreeable, but as I handed over the vinyl I told him I wanted a fiver for it, which was the selling price in record stores.

There were bemused looks all around – not, I stress, that Judge Jules was refusing to pay, but it was clearly not the done thing. I turned belligerent, demanding the cash. I'd been bumped by everyone else in the music business, I told them, and it wasn't happening again.

There was embarrassment all around as the atmosphere around the studio chilled to freezing point. I still can't recall to this day if Judge Jules ever did hand over a fiver, but I was huckled out the door by security – and I headed straight to see my pal, Solomon Parker.

I had an incredible relationship with Solomon. His dad, Louis, was the owner of Concorde International Artistes, the main agency for The Prodigy and Nirvana, among others. As a kid learning the music industry ropes, Solomon even used to make the tea for Curt Cobain.

I can still see Solomon nodding, 'Go on, go on,' as he listened to my extravagant chains of thought on musical issues and ideas of the day. I always felt he was one of only a few London-based lads in the business who got me.

I stayed with him occasionally at the family home on the outskirts of the capital – his old man had a life sized Dalek in the hall, gifted to him one Christmas by The Prodigy.

Solomon gave me the absolute highlight of my career as a DJ when his record label, Solid State, asked to release a re-mix of 'Banjo'd' by Skonk. I had never lost faith in the track and went back into Apollo studios in 1997 to re-work it with Calum.

Michael Kilkie and I were a couple of rascals so we put the latest version out as Dos Piratas – two pirates – and re-named it 'Sonrisas' after my old friend and mentor in Maxim's bar.

In the summer of 1997 I was back in Ibiza and pulled a gig as warm up DJ at Il Divino, a nightclub in the old town. On my first night, the owner showed me the ropes, how the decks were set up and the likes, a really pleasant guy.

In many ways, the warm up man is more interesting to listen to because he can't play the big pounders so early in the evening, so his music tends to be a little more experimental and left field.

I played 'Sonrisas' on my first night and the owner ran straight up to the booth and demanded excitedly: "What's that?" He added: "Mark Moore from S'Express was playing here last night, put that track on and it blew the place up. They went mad for it." I took the record off the turntable and told him: "I made that." It was my greatest moment as a DJ.

Sadly, however, a relationship with Solomon that really should have flourished ended in the rubble of my poor mental health on that night I was thrown out of Radio One.

Earlier in the day I'd made fruitless trips around countless record companies, trying to convince them of my legitimacy as a producer and re-mixer. I wore my Burberry suit, so should have known a crash was just around the corner. The unhappy episode in the studio with Judge Jules had just put the tin lid on a dreadful day.

My breakdown inevitably arrived later that evening in the comfort of Solomon's home as I ranted and raved against the injustices of the world, my speech patterns growing every quicker. I didn't stop talking until 5am, oblivious to the discomfort of my host.

Solomon was unused to being around mental illness and my presence left him, unsurprisingly, on edge as I spoke gibberish, many of my sentences without rhyme or reason. He did not understand my illness, but few people did.

This chapter started with an apology and ends with one too. I'm so sorry Solomon saw that side of me and I'm also sorry for the distress I caused him in his own home.

He drove me into London later that morning on the back of his motorbike, but a distance was put on our friendship and we lost contact for almost 20 years.

Louis would be proud of his son as Solomon has gone on in those two decades to build an even more formidable career and now represents a string of world class talents, including Take That, Jessie J and Lady Gaga.

Early in 2017 we re-connected again via social media, much to my delight. We've shared a couple of messages and there was genuine warmth from Solomon for my welfare and the success of this book.

Time is a healer and I hope to see him again one day for a coffee, because I miss his warm and genuine presence. I might even turn up in a Burberry suit, just to see the look on his face.

18

To this day, I remain adamant that Javier believes I stiffed him out of a significant five figure sum in a record deal involving Cafe Mambo, but he couldn't be more wrong.

It was only two-and-a-half grand.

But let's not get ahead of ourselves – as I was contemplating another mental health decline in the summer of 1994, sectioned for that first stint at Ward 30 in Stirling Royal Infirmary, Mambo had opened its doors and was suffering its own episode of schizophrenia.

Even on a limited budget the place looked great although its feature decks, which now take pride of place in the window at the front, were tucked down by the bottom of the bar, next to the toilets.

Its personality was as split as its clientele, Spaniards who wanted to sit and nurse a drink and a British and European customer base who were looking for something a little more lively. It served food, deciding in the end to focus on fajitas, chilli, enchiladas and burritos.

Wilson, on a trip back home to Stirling, was taken by the food on offer at Archie's, the local Mexican, and basically copied their menu. My cousins Roddy and Irene ran the kitchen and Roddy still laughs and claims it was his secret ingredient in the chilli, a spoonful of cocoa powder, that set Mambo on its way.

Roddy was present at the turning point, however, in the summer of 1994 when a flustered PR arrived at Mambo shortly before midday as my cousin was prepping for lunch. The PR worked for Kiss FM, the hip London radio station, and they were in a panic.

They broadcast from the island every summer but the venue they had originally booked to host their live session that evening had fallen through. Could Mambo help?

Roddy asked for an hour and roused Javier, who understandably slept late, to come over for a chat. He readily agreed to host them and, at a stroke, put his bar on the road to becoming the best and most successful in island history.

Kiss FM was really trendy and credible to a London dance audience and, by association, Mambo quickly became the hippest hangout in San Antonio.

One of the biggest gigs on the island at the time, a real golden ticket, was hosted by Space, called 'We Love Space', and it started at the bizarre time of 7am on a Sunday morning. Suddenly, pre and post clubbers took to hanging out at Mambo.

It was terrible for Roddy and Irene's kitchen. Mambo served next to no food on a Sunday and Monday as all the punters were out of their faces on recreational substances, but their presence certainly helped build the reputation of the bar.

Three years may have passed but Javier and I never lost touch, despite the challenges around the opening of Mambo and my subsequent breakdown. We still spoke regularly on the phone and he called with another life-changing offer early in 1997.

He was planning to open a new bar that summer, called Savannah, and wanted me to be part of his team. It was a fabulous site, only a couple of hundred metres from Mambo on the promenade that was fast becoming known as the Sunset Strip.

Better still, it gave Javier and Wilson bars that bookended the whole block, with Mambo and Mint at one end and Savannah at the other. The job offer was more than generous – £150-a-week, plus accommodation in my own flat, for two hours work every afternoon acting as PR frontman and mein host for the venture.

The bar, really, was a spanker. Mambo had been opened on a budget and, in the early days at least, that was reflected in the fixtures and fittings, including plastic seating and tables in its outdoor area. No expense was spared on Savannah, however, which was top of the range inside and out, cool blues and whites and a hip but minimalist nineties design.

I accepted Javier's job offer in little more than a blink of the eye, not least because I enjoyed working with my pal, despite the strains of Mambo, and spending time in his company.

Furthermore, I missed the White Isle and what could have been so taxing about working a couple of hours every afternoon at such a new and relevant hang out doing what I did best, talking with people?

Admittedly, there was also some commercial self-interest at play. I'd had tentative discussions with my pal Andy Thompson, head of dance at Virgin Records, about a Cafe Mambo CD.

He was dead keen and over a few months we bounced a few ideas off each other, wondering if we could capture the atmosphere on compact disc that had come to define the holiday experience for so many British tourists.

At Andy's behest, I approached Javier with the proposal and he immediately saw the promotional possibilities. He gave me the go ahead to pull it all together with Virgin on his behalf. It was staggeringly, surprisingly casual – a nod of the head from Javier, almost a 'just get on with it and let me know how you get on.'

As a record company executive, never mind a friend, Andy was very dependable and creative, as were Virgin, who boasted a stable of artists the envy of most.

We pulled together a three CD collection – we could have easily have filled six – and 'Cafe Mambo – Cultura Ibiza' was a collection of 42 mellow tracks and sun drenched mixes of Balearic mood music that featured an 'A' list of talent including The Source and Candi Staton, Inner City, Underworld, Electra, DJ Quicksilver and William Orbit.

It established the series of Cafe Mambo CDs that continues to this day. Andy was also a marketing whizz and spent a small fortune on promotion – he sent 500 Cafe Mambo beach bags to Ibiza, as well as 500 sarongs.

Yours truly was strolling around San Antonio with a swathe of silk around my waist a full 12 months before David Beckham was caught on camera wearing the same before the World Cup in France. We probably looked equally as ridiculous.

The CD was released to rave reviews and decent sales and Andy even paid tribute to me on the sleeve notes, which acknowledged my role in its production as well as my wanderlust. The dedication read simply, 'To Scooby, wherever he is on the island.'

The CD made me swell with pride, not just because I'd helped in its creation but also because I featured on it too, as part of Beautiful Imbalance. It was a musical collective I had pulled together the previous year to work on 'The First Picture Of You', my favourite ever summer track, by Liverpool band The Lotus Eaters.

Beautiful Imbalance consisted of me, my old DJ pal Dave 'CL' Young, producers Andy Haldane and Calum MacLean, a pal from Stirling named Neil Innes and a lovely English girl, Lorraine Darwin, who was the girlfriend of Neil's mate, Jim Carney.

Dave re-wrote the lyrics and one of the appeals of Lorraine was her fabulously posh accent, which we recorded in a bathroom in a Victorian house in Stirling because it had high ceilings which created a killer sound of exceptional clarity as she stated: "The first picture of you, the first picture of summer".

A chum who was a music industry lawyer, Sue McAuley, loved the track and set up a deal with Slate Records, who had some solid connections in the industry. Financially, the deal was nothing to write home about – Neil still thinks to this day I pocketed £1 million.

In truth, it was a £500 advance and the record label also received £250 from Virgin for allowing the track to be used on the Mambo CD, of which we received nothing.

Really, the money wasn't anywhere near as important as the professional contacts Slate brought to the table. Jem Kelly, one half of the Lotus Eaters, even sat in on one of the sessions in the Apollo studios and gave our work his blessing, which was a thrill.

Ultimately, Slate wanted more mixes so we sent Calum back into the studio with a fistful of joints and a fish supper and we pulled together a package of tracks that soon attracted the attention of some of the industry's big boys.

It was listed in Paul Oakenfold's top five for the summer of 1996, for example. It also opened Danny Rampling's 'Love Groove Dance Party' and played on his popular Radio One show for four weeks in a row.

The track won music industry respect but, sadly, enjoyed little commercial success. At the 23rd Precinct record store in Glasgow customers frequently came in with scraps of paper on which were scribbled that week's top 20 as recommended by leading DJs such as Oakenfold or Frankie Knuckles.

They would try and look nonchalant, as if they were picking their vinyl at random, all the while sneaking a look at their lists. One kid asked Colin Tevendale behind the counter for Beautiful Imbalance and was told: "Actually, my mate made that – he lives in Stirling."

The boy threw him a look of horror, as if anything so relevant could ever be made in Scotland, and handed the record he'd been offered straight back. It was his loss, but maybe commercially we were too far over the heads of most.

We followed up 'The First Picture Of You' with a remix of the brilliant Blue Nile track 'Tinseltown In The Rain'. The popular River City soap actor Tom Urie joined Dave 'CL' Young on vocals, but it bombed.

Andy at Virgin Records may have been a mate, but I don't believe he put Beautiful Imbalance on the Mambo CD as a favour because it caught the vibe of the times perfectly and found a natural home with those other laid back tracks.

Javier was happy to let me deal with the negotiations around the CD because he knew little about the music industry then, although you can bet he has learned since.

The bottom line is Virgin handed me a modest advance of £5,000 for helping pull the Mambo deal together and, by rights, Javier should have received half. He has never, ever raised it as an issue but as the summer progressed and he saw the lifestyle I was living, he could have been forgiven for thinking I was given 10 times that amount.

On the memory of dear Mac and Alex, Doobie the dog and Groovy too, I swear I didn't fiddle you out of nearly as much as you might have been tempted to think, old pal.

Anyway, you owed me for all those records you 'acquired' from me a few years previously when I was almost nicked at Ibiza airport, as well as all the overtime I ended up working at Savannah and which wasn't part of the original deal. Let's call it quits!

Savannah was a cool space, the ground floor of an old hotel that housed Club 18-30 tourists although, surprisingly, it didn't attract them. Maybe it was a little too cool for the kids looking for cheap beer and an easy lay, but it was never pretentious.

The DJ booth, like that at Mambo, looked out on the sun setting across the bay and it had a funky dance room in the back in addition to its greatest asset, a magnificent terrace that was at least twice the size of its near neighbour's.

There's no way I could only have worked there for two hours a day – and Javier knew that fine well. In the first fortnight I easily put in at least 60 hours a week to make sure the project got off to a flying start.

My pal was not holding me on a leash, I was having the time of my life. Javier and Caroline were as good as gold with the accommodation, but the flat immediately above Mambo? It was too much, even for a party animal like me.

In addition to a couple of hours of meet and greet, I was also stepping behind the DJ booth for several hours at a time and Javier had given me a licence to play anything I wanted, from hip hop to trance to pop.

He trusted me enough to allow me to stamp a musical identity on Savannah – and Christian even came along on a few occasions to play some tracks to a growing and appreciative audience.

At Cafe Mambo, the chic and sophisticated set were listening to cool beach grooves while, along at Savannah, I was playing an eclectic mix that included Hanson's 'MMMBop', that summer's big smash hit, and even 'Never Forget' by Take That.

In addition, I was playing more credible sounds for my audience, including Nuyorkin Soul's 'Masters at Work' and Ultra Nate's 'Free'. Ever astute, Javier didn't mind in the slightest. He was doing all right from both ends of the market, thank you very much.

The inconvenience of the accommodation should have had me fretting but the five grand advance from Virgin Records cleared in my account early in the summer as my good fortune took another couple of outrageous swings north.

I knew the flat above Mambo wasn't a suitable long term option and drove around the island in a hired Jeep, trying to scout a suitable replacement apartment. I headed to Cala Salada and, to this day, don't know why I pulled over to a fairly imposing house on the left hand side, a couple of kilometres further up the winding road.

There was no sign to suggest it was a hotel, but as I looked around it became clear I'd stumbled into a boutique joint called Casa Datscha and, next to Pikes, was considered by many to be the best place to stay on the island at that time.

I met a friendly German, Horst Muller, who was the owner of the joint and must have caught him on an especially good day. It cost around £100 per person, per night for a room at Casa Datscha and he asked how long I wanted to stay.

I told him the entire summer and he offered me a bed for £400-a-month. Pennies! I dug out £1,200 from my wallet – Javier's two-and-a-half grand was fast being spent – and thrust it into his grateful hand. My digs amounted to a mini apartment under the swimming pool, but it was spacious and had everything I needed.

Casa Datscha hosted a string of German VIPs that summer, including executives from the Mercedes Formula One team and other leading business figures from Berlin and beyond.

I enjoyed my jester's role, which only endeared me still further to Horst and his pals. I'd frequently reach for my guitar around the pool at night and lead a community sing song for the incredibly well to do, who were all taken with their new Scottish pal.

One industry bigwig even flew in on his private jet with his mistress and asked me to look after her for a week while he returned home. She was an absolute stunner and I had her on my arm for seven days, taking her for dinner, coffees and drinks.

I was so loved up with Fiona I didn't even make a pass – I stayed faithful to my girlfriend in Scotland all summer, a sad boast but a first for me – and, anyway, why shit where you eat? Her boyfriend returned the following week and, bizarrely but wonderfully, arrived off his jet with a guy playing bagpipes, a gesture of gratitude to the kind Scot who had looked after his girl.

I was pulling together deals like Arfur Daley at his peak. Come off it, Casa Datscha for £100-a-week? That was the equivalent of two balloons and a penny whistle.

It may have been more remote than most digs, but even that became a non-issue when I was put in touch with an English lad who had driven his Jaguar to the island, then hit a run of bad luck and couldn't afford to keep it on the road. I offered him £100-a-month to hire it and he almost bit my hand off.

It's little wonder Javier thought I was living high on the hog on the back of his earnings from the CD, with a billet in Casa Datscha and a Jag to drive.

He wasn't the only one. Later in the summer, as I prepared to depart for home, I dropped into one of my usual haunts and broke the news to the barman I was leaving the island.

There are two types of people on Ibiza – tourists and workers. The tourists are, for the most part, blissfully unaware of the underlying politics that make island life run smoothly on all levels, but the workers know the score.

My barman acquaintance looked at me distraught and told me I couldn't go. I asked why not and he replied: "You're the main drug dealer on the island. What are we going to do now?"

He genuinely believed, on the back of my laid back style, dress sense, car and accommodation that I was a figure of some underworld substance. He couldn't, of course, have been further from the truth.

The sarong apart, my usual get up that summer was a cowboy hat and shorts and a V-neck tartan tank top with a bandana. I rarely shaved and when I wasn't smoking good hash, I was on Cohiba cigars.

Life had never been so good, although I made sure it was all balanced out by my daily intake of Lithium. It's little wonder Barry Fraser's calls from Edinburgh about that interest from Pete Tong and Warner Brothers in 'Yeah Oh' were going unanswered or were being largely ignored. The absence of Fiona apart, my existence had never been as sweet.

As the summer continued, my work at Savannah opened doors for me on the rest of the island. I was approached about a residency at the bull ring, situated between San Antonio and Ibiza's old town.

Admittedly, it was the graveyard shift, a warm up slot between 7-8pm for DJs Brandon Block and his sidekick, Alex P. Block became notorious in 2000 when he stormed the stage at the Brit Awards, full of bevvy, and confronted presenter Ronnie Wood.

The raves in the bull ring attracted thousands every week, but there were only ever a few hundred through the door when I stepped behind the decks. However, it was all good experience – and at £400 per show, it wasn't exactly chickenfeed.

I was still funding a hash addiction, although cocaine was less a part of my life at that stage and I rarely touched ecstasy. On the rooftop above Savannah and the Club 18-30 hotel there was an apartment known as the 'Attico' which was rented out for the summer to a fine couple from Argentina, Juan Blanco and his wife, Mercedes.

They spent their days at the yachting club in San Antonio teaching kids how to sail – and at night they absolutely caned drink and drugs in their flat, even though they were both in their seventies.

They had an Old English sheepdog, who wore a bandana, and I formed an immediate friendship with them after they stopped to chat while walking along the promenade and I discovered their old faithful mutt was named Groovy.

Pretty soon, we were as thick as thieves. I spent the whole summer with them and while Mambo and Savannah rightly raved about the quality of the sunsets from their terraces, it was nothing compared to the view from the Attico 100 feet above.

Juan Blanco and Mercedes built a huge barbecue on their terrace and every night we sourced thick slabs of Argentine steaks and sides of salted beef, all washed down with buckets of red wine and hash.

They were ferocious party animals. As sailors, I gifted them a bottle of Johnnie Walker Swing, decent whisky shaped in a bottle with an irregular base that allowed for movement at sea. It barely made it out the box, never mind the harbour, as they tanned it in a couple of hours.

I wasn't much of a drinker, but the joints they rolled were fatter than the cattle who had sacrificed themselves in South America for our lavish nightly feeds. Drunk and stoned, we took Groovy for a walk along the strip every night and he was treated like a celebrity by every holidaymaker we met.

The fun times couldn't last. Sadly, they never do. Savannah established itself that summer and I'd like to think I played a part in its success and, despite everything, Javier, Wilson and I remained good friends.

As Radio One moved in for the first of its Mambo residencies that summer, following the path set by Kiss FM, I knew my old friends were on the brink of the big time their efforts deserved.

Me? By September 1997 my mental health was still holding strong, but the release of 'Sunchyme' by Dario G had pissed me off as I finally lifted my head to the realities Barry had tried to explain in countless phone calls over the previous three months.

I had to get back to Britain and fight Warner Brothers for what was legally mine, I decided.

In my absence, I had handed the keys to my flat in Plean to Barry and my old pal Jok, but didn't bother to tell them I was on my way home.

I walked unannounced through the door one midweek night to find Jok and 13 of his mates sitting in the living room, all out their nuts on hash. I told them all to fuck off, Jok included. He immediately made for Nick Tahoo's place in Falkirk, where he found a home from home for another few years with PK1 and PK2, surrounded by those gaudy yellow walls.

Unfortunately, my own outlook was soon to turn battleship grey.

19

I called The Samaritans and they hung up the phone.

It sounds like the punchline to an old gag but as the Millennium approached, I wasn't laughing. Those heady days of Ibiza in the summer of 1997 already seemed a long time in the past as my bi-polar really began to bite.

For my part, a failure to take meds when released from the psychiatric units in Stirling and Falkirk started to take its toll. It's a classic scenario, played out time and again by those who suffer mental illness.

A sectioned spell inside a locked ward cured all, didn't it? There was no need to continue with the meds after psychiatrists had spent months re-connecting all the wires under the bonnet of a damaged brain, right?

Wrong. So wrong.

It's a lesson it took me years to learn and my wellness since 2009 owes much to an acknowledgment on my part that medication will be a central part of my life forever.

Admittedly, my health wasn't helped by a consistent failure of the authorities to prescribe the correct levels of Droperidol, an anti-psychotic. They regularly over dosed me to the point I would sit beyond shaking, in a zombified state, knowing everything was far from well with their prescription process.

I was urged to sue the local health board, even going as far as retaining a firm of local lawyers. In the end, I settled for an apology from the head of the Forth Valley health board.

My medical records tell the brutal tale of those dark, harrowing times. In 1999, the year I called the Samaritans, I spent 31 days sectioned, a virtual long weekend in comparison to the periods that followed.

In the year 2000 I spent 216 days in hospital, 257 days in 2001 and 111 days in 2002. I was sectioned for little more than four weeks in 2003 but 12 months later I was back under lock and key for a further 126 days, dropping to 125 days in 2005 before the graph headed north again, 149 days in 2006.

My call to The Samaritans was made at the height of one of my increasingly frequent episodes of mania, at 2am when my mind was racing and, pretty soon, so was my voice.

It was always an indicator of my ill health as words spilled out at breakneck speed, very often with little rhyme or reason. I harboured those Richard Branson fantasies and spoke to the counsellor on the other end of the line of a million and one business ideas that had been racing around my head in the days previously.

I spit balled proposals solidly for at least half an hour without a single break in my speech pattern, most of it drivel and delusions of grandeur. I outlined plans beyond the belief of most men.

The counsellor could possibly have handled the call better, but what more could he do when he couldn't get a word in edgeways than eventually tell me gently: "I need to hang up now, mate."

The previous year, towards the end of the summer in 1998, I had also attempted suicide for the first time in my life but even that was accompanied by elements of dark farce.

I pondered for two months on the easiest way to end it all and decided a hose from the exhaust pipe of my car through the driver's window would be least painful. There was one slight problem. I didn't know where to source a hose wide enough to fit around my exhaust pipe, nor a jubilee clip to hold it in place to ensure the fateful deed was completed successfully.

I was struck by a eureka moment one day passing a hoover repair shop in the centre of town and paid a couple of pounds for my materials of doom.

The owners, John Haxton and Billy Hulston, were close buddies of my old pal Jim Ford and called him immediately to reveal my purchases, suspecting the last thing on my mind was a repair job on a Bosch or Whirlpool.

Jim called Fraser Hotchkiss, my dearest friend, and by the end of the week he was leading me into the hospital for another spell under the lock and key of a section order.

Before Fraser tracked me down, however, I went as far as setting up my suicide scene. I drove to Cock-a-Bendy Castle on the outskirts of Plean and attached the hose to the exhaust and fed it through my window.

I stared at the key in my ignition for what seemed like an eternity, urging myself to give it a decisive turn to its right. Did more than an hour pass? Possibly, but time meant little as I sat there, scared out of my wits.

My mind was empty, but deep inside my soul a spark of life refused to allow itself to be extinguished. In the end I opened the car door, unclipped the hose from the exhaust pipe and drove straight home to my parents' house.

I sat with them that evening and had a meal of egg and chips, never daring to tell them of the calamity that had almost befallen. Anyone on the outside looking in would have seen a picture of familial bliss. If only they knew.

I was motivated to take my own life in the aftermath of my break up with Fiona. Depressingly, as always, I had absolutely no-one to blame but myself for our split. We had been going steady for two years and to that point she was the only partner in life to whom I had been faithful, even throughout the rampant hedonism of Ibiza 97.

We shared everything of ourselves and, even now, the details of the end of our relationship are still painful to recall. I must stress, it was all on me – Fiona was absolutely blameless.

She was working the sinful Thursday evening when my ego and arrogance took control and I had a one night stand with a girl about whom I remember little beyond her blonde hair and big boobs, my pathetic weaknesses.

Fiona found out and, understandably, there was no way back from my dreadful breach of trust, despite my long and increasingly desperate pleas.

Why did I find it hard to be so faithful? An easy explanation is to say that when you were running a club or in control of the DJ booth the offer of sex was always there, available on a plate when you wanted.

I didn't have liaisons with a million girls, but I knew the type I liked and if a fling was offered, inevitably I would consent because I found it hard to say no. Greedy? Yes. Shallow? Undoubtedly. Conceited? Definitely.

Fiona was nothing like my usual type but she was all I ever wanted and then I fucked it up. Why do we retain such capacity to destroy the things we truly love most? More than two decades on and I still don't know the answer.

I used to howl primitively in the middle of the night at my flat in Plean over the loss of our relationship, bawling my eyes out so loudly my pal Alex McDonald would frequently come through from the flat next door and offer comfort.

Understandably, Fiona cut all ties. In the months afterwards I met her just once, on the stairs in Rainbow Rocks of all places. RUN-DMC were pounding through the speakers in the background, 'It's Like That'.

She looked absolutely amazing and shot me a glance. It meant everything to me as I looked in her eyes for the sun, the moon and the stars. I yearned for hope and found nothing but indifference. RUN-DMC's lyrics cut deep: "And that's the way it is."

I sought sanctuary in Hong Kong. It was the idea of a pal, Ian McChord, who was known as The Badger for his capacity to sniff out opportunities and adventures. The Badger had been a great confidante and advisor in my ultimately fruitless battle with Warner Brothers over the provenance of 'Sunchyme' and our friendship had gone from strength to strength towards the end of 1997.

He built amazing sound systems for businesses and night clubs and landed a contract in the far east. I borrowed a grand from my mum to fund the trip and was further emboldened by the offer of work from a record company out there, who were looking for a remix of the Men Without Hats track 'Safety Dance'.

I managed to hold myself together when I was out there – just – but a full breakdown was looming. Ever the entrepreneur, I returned from Hong Kong with 500 Ralph Lauren polo shirts of questionable authenticity I had sourced in Stanley Market, but they were destined never to leave their cardboard boxes.

The Badger did his best to offer comfort and support but Fiona was constantly in my thoughts and my mind was as cluttered as the street stalls I'd raked for stock to punt in Stirling.

I was still smoking a bit of hash, maybe not as much as before, but the swings in my mood suggested my bi polar no longer needed the catalyst of consistent consumption of good blow. I'd created a monster and now it was roaming free in my head without the need to be prodded from its slumbers by marijuana and cocaine.

I'd been back in the UK barely a couple of weeks when Fraser was guiding me back to Ward 30 at Stirling Royal to be sectioned again. As a frequent visitor to my flat, he knew the signs of my mental distress better than most.

In time I would spend longer periods in hospital but that spell, in early 1998, was the worst I ever felt. I developed a pathological fear of opening letters, for example, so not only did rent go unpaid, benefit cheques also went uncashed. I was fucked, really fucked.

The extremities between my mental highs and lows were best illustrated in my relationship with music. I gathered a group of my closest friends together at a bar in Glasgow – Colin Tevendale, Andy Haldane, Calum MacLean and Barry Fraser – and pulled out the last four grand I owned.

I laid it on the table, convinced we could work as a production collective and create a clutch of tracks that would rocket all of us to superstardom. It was another bold and brash idea but my friends looked at each other and knowing the mental depths to which I was descending, gently convinced me the money would be better banked for a rainy day as they tenderly returned it to my pockets.

Unconvinced, shortly afterwards I put the entire wad in a single envelope with a first class stamp and sent it to Barry at his record store in Edinburgh and encouraged him to use it to start his own label.

I forced the package, which resembled a half brick, through the post box, the seal on the flimsy envelope barely sticking. Amazingly, it arrived at Barry's shop 24 hours later untouched, even though it was obviously stuffed with cash.

His eyes almost popped out his head. He drove through to see me later that day and returned the cash to my not so safe keeping.

A few weeks later I decided to end my relationship with music all together. It still breaks my heart that I sold my entire collection of records, thousands and thousands of discs, to a dealer in Stirling for just £500.

The collection was packed with white labels, limited editions and rarities and must easily have made him at least 100 times the sum he paid. He knew the delicate state of my mental health and it rankles me still that he took advantage, but he pulled his business hat on and left his morals at the door.

Ever so canny, he put his newly acquired stock out in dribs and drabs over the subsequent months and drew a greater customer base as a result, all keen to get their hands on the soundtracks of my life.

My records were easily distinguished from the rest because I had placed a sticker in the top right hand corner of every cover noting the beats per minute of each particular track.

My last fling with music for a long time – I can tell you next to nothing about the subject from 1998-2012 – came when I joined forces with a new pal from Fife called Rab Donaldson, who ran a very successful company with links to the construction industry.

We'd been introduced through a mutual friend, who had mental health difficulties she was battling to overcome, and that should have been warning enough about Rab's own fragile state.

We spoke about establishing a record label together and he certainly had the money to co-fund such a venture, but it soon became apparent he was losing his mind. I was on a rare but short cycle of wellness when we took a trip to Amsterdam and his extravagant gestures of generosity, including buying drinks for everyone when we visited a bar, were signs of bi-polar that had yet to be diagnosed.

It hit home when we went on holiday to Florida and he disappeared to have a tattoo inked. He returned a couple of hours later, his skin unblemished, but clutching the tattooist's artbook, which he wanted to study more closely before deciding on his final design.

Unfortunately, he declined to mention to the tattooist that he was taking his signature book from the studio, which was effectively his calling card, his entire life's work.

We returned to the studio the following day when Rab had a clearer vision of the tattoo he wanted on his arm, but it cut no ice with the furious tattooist. He pulled out a gun before we barely had time to drop the book on the table and were chased from the studio, running for our lives while he brandished the weapon in the air behind us.

Our fortunes didn't improve a few days later when we drove to Miami and arrived at our pre-booked apartment. Within 48 hours Rab was inviting strangers into our 'home' and it became clear he was trying to sell the apartment when we had only rented it for a week.

We kept in touch on our return to the UK, but it was a fraught relationship from which even I knew I had to negotiate a delicate exit.

My bi-polar was always present, obviously, but it made its excessive public appearances when it was least expected and always when prescribed medication had been ignored, which inevitably led to another spell in hospital.

Some of the interventions of the police in my life, for example, were downright bizarre. One morning I met a mate in a bar in Stirling and ordered a glass of milk, for which I was charged a hefty £2.50.

The milk barely amounted to a half pint and, as I looked at my receipt, I noted there was a charge of VAT also included. I began to rail against the audacity of the government slapping a tax on a drink that, I argued loudly and to no-one in particular, was a life staple.

I began to shout and yell, frightening bar staff who immediately dialled 999. The law arrived shortly afterwards and quickly recognised this was no ordinary breach of the peace. Another section beckoned.

There was black comedy, about which I can only now raise a smile. I once popped into the Abbey Inn at Cambuskenneth and found myself rattling on about the masons, an organisation of which many of my family were members.

I told anyone who would listen that, in masonic code, if you asked someone the price of an old slipper their reply informed you of the lodge number to which their membership was linked. I still don't know the accuracy of that statement, but it provoked a discussion that left me so deep in thought I wandered into Stirling town centre the following day and bought a new pair of slippers.

Predictably, I was sectioned within 24 hours and spent the next three months under lock and key, only to be discharged and forced to face the madness all over again.

Time always stood still when I returned to my flat as it remained untouched during my spells in hospital. I opened the fridge door and there, on the top shelf, sat my new slippers. In my unbalanced mental state, the night before I was sectioned I clearly decided the topic was too hot for me to handle so put the symbols of confusion in the fridge to cool down.

I once walked past the Post Office in Stirling in the build up to Christmas and decided on the spur of the moment to pop inside and apply for a £4,000 loan. I had no recent employment history and yet, to my utter amazement, I received a letter a few days later to tell me of the success of my request.

The purpose of the loan? On the application form I scribbled a desire to write a book, even if it wasn't exactly my motivation. I returned to the Post Office and withdrew the entire sum in £100 notes to fulfil my original plan of giving local pensioners a festive season to remember.

I wandered around Bannockburn sliding the big red notes through the letterbox of every OAP I knew, without even a card to explain their unexpected windfall.

My psychiatrist found out a week later and, furious, wrote an angry letter to the Bank of Ireland, who had issued the loan through the Post Office in the first place. She castigated them for their wilful disregard of vulnerable people and explained in no uncertain terms the impossibility of me paying back the money over the terms outlined in the agreement.

She really went to town with the moneymen and received a reply, almost by return of post. The Bank of Ireland apologised profusely, accepted their checks and balances had fallen well short of what should have been expected and promised to update their policies to prevent future repeats. Finally, they told her, it went without saying the loan would be written off. I didn't have to pay back a bean.

In 2012, approximately three years into my wellness, I pulled an old and rarely worn winter coat from the back of my wardrobe and went for a walk on a chilly November afternoon. I stuck my hands in the pockets – and found, to my delight, a wad of £100 notes I'd long forgotten about from the original loan.

I counted out more than a grand. Let's just say I didn't rush to the Post Office to tell of my discovery.

In my short periods of wellness before 2009 I fought desperately hard for acceptance in a world that was increasingly turning its back, mostly out of embarrassment at the shell of the man I had become.

Many of the people who had played such an integral role in my life previously were suddenly afraid of me. They had no idea how to deal with my illness. I was never violent, but I was angry.

A fellow patient at Stirling and Falkirk, an older woman named Maggie, worked hard to soothe my soul with a balm of kindness and alternative thought. In my periods of poor health, she visited me virtually every day in hospital with my mum, Mac.

Maggie took a more holistic and spiritual approach to her wellness and often refused medication for her own health issues, preferring instead to rely on non traditional methods. She willingly roped me in to assist her in laughter therapy, for example.

A small group dressed as clowns and toured old folks' homes, kids' wards and the likes, introducing slapstick humour to raise smiles and giggles, which it most often did, not least because Maggie had the best and richest laugh I've ever heard, before or since.

I never put on make up or wore a red curly wig, but I contributed to the band of colourful characters with some ropey chords from my faithful old guitar.

The loneliness and isolation were a killer and poor mental health can be brutally de-humanising. Fraser and Kate Hotchkiss were wonderful sources of friendship, comfort and support, along with John and Alison Crozier, but it wasn't always easy to view the terrain around the deep hole into which I had plummeted.

In the year 2000 I spent more than 200 days in hospital, but they weren't consecutive and when you're in and out of locked wards every few months it constantly chips away at your self-esteem.

John visited me at Ward 19 in Falkirk Royal and brought me a beef and tomato Pot Noodle, into which staff added warm water so I could enjoy my snack. In a catatonic state I dropped it at my feet and then followed it to the floor, slumping on my hands and knees and eating it like a dog, going so far as licking the carpet while one of my dearest friends looked on, heartbroken and distraught.

It could be an unintentionally degrading environment as an initial 28 day section could turn into a period of incarceration that lasted for months on end.

I sought solace in popular religion, but to no avail. As a baby I was christened in the Church of Scotland at Bannockburn and, in a rare period of wellness in 2006, I was also baptised in Stirling Baptist Church.

Ultimately, however, I found the congregation cold and unwelcoming, too middle class and cliquey, and left its arms. I went so far as hosting prayer groups in my flat and three or four of us would gather on a weekly basis, but they quickly fizzled out.

It was a pity as I feel much of Christianity involves fellowship and the gatherings were an antidote to sitting at home alone, which I did with increasing regularity.

I even turned to the local evangelical church and kindly members of the congregation frequently came to see me in hospital. After one discharge I signed up for 'Cool Water', a counselling service offered by Christians in Falkirk and it helped maintain my wellness.

In the meantime, I was also playing bass guitar in the evangelical church band. My happiness was short lived when the pastor approached and asked about the counselling service I was accessing in the next town. He hit me with a bombshell – I couldn't play in the band if I continued to see my counsellors.

Disgusted, my reply to him could never be found in the bible. I quit his mission there and then and, in time, turned my back on Christianity for good.

My discomfort and awkwardness manifested itself openly and one of the most challenging and emotionally draining aspects for anyone who suffers from poor mental health is having to justify our wellness to everyone we meet.

When I bumped into acquaintances in the street the conversation always, always, took the same form. They started by asking: "How are you Scooby?" and I then felt I had to spend the next five minutes outlining my most recent medical history when, really, it was none of their business.

I defined myself completely and utterly on how long it had been since I had last been sectioned. I would always reply: "How am I? I'm fine. I've not been in hospital for the last five months and my psychiatrist is really pleased with how well I'm progressing. I'm heading in the right direction."

They would smile sweetly, patronise me unintentionally with a couple of general comments, and then move on. It was really exhausting.

Nowadays? I don't feel the need to justify myself or my mental health to anyone I meet. If I need to speak about intimate emotional issues then, like most people, I have a tight circle of family and friends with whom I can share my thoughts, as well as some wonderful healthcare professionals.

It has taken me a long time to reach the point where I can finally look the world in the eye again and greet it on my terms. At the height of my mental distress I drove around the streets in my car, uttering flights of fancy and random thoughts into a dictaphone, none of it making any particular sense or relating any kind of narrative order, but it did at least give me a comfort.

Pretty soon, even that simple yet eccentric pleasure was denied me because every period spent in a mental health facility was followed by three months in which I was forbidden to drive by DVLA.

In fact, they put a restriction on my licence and forced me to re-apply for it every three years. Even in the time of my wellness I've been forced to write three times for permission to drive my car, which is a lifeline.

I hated walking, not least because I could see from the side of my eyes people I once knew well crossing the road to avoid being in my presence. Then, on the occasions we did collide, I would launch into those heavy and defensive conversations about how well my mental health was holding up when ordinarily we'd have spoken about sport, music, or the escapades of mutual friends.

I moved into the centre of Stirling at the turn of the new century and lived in a flat that threatened to induce the type of trips even a sackful of magic mushrooms could never have provoked.

The wallpaper was paisley patterned, the sofa was lurid green and the curtains were striped like a convict's fancy dress costume. It's little wonder I tried never to sit around too long indoors, but even that threw up issues for my battered self-confidence.

The flat was only a couple of doors from the salon of one of my closest pals, hairdresser Ross Waddell, but I couldn't bare to look in his window when I passed, never mind cross the threshold for a chat or a cup of tea while he waited on his next client.

Call it shame, but every time I passed Taguchi I kept my head down for fear of catching the eye of Ross, scared of seeing pity in his glances at the shadow of the man I used to be.

20

My fightback to wellness began the day and minute Claire Campbell ordered me out of her car and back into Falkirk Royal Infirmary with an order to not be so bloody stupid.

She has always liked to call a spade a spade.

It was towards the end of March 2009 and 10 minutes earlier my psychiatrist, with whom I had a love-hate relationship – we'll call him The Man – had shot me a knowing glance as I prepared to end my 23rd section in 16 years across 36 different hospital wards.

As always, I was handed my meds on departure but casually dismissed the offer of Risperidone, the anti-psychotic, because I told The Man I didn't need it. I'd manage fine without it, I assured him. The Lithium and sodium valporate, both mood stabilisers, would be enough.

His withering look spoke five solemn and truthful words: "See you again soon, sucker."

I recounted the incident outside to Claire, who had become one of my dearest friends (and still is) and she went through me. She told me it was time I accepted my illness and recognised the devastating effects it would continue to have on my life if I didn't take the prescribed medication that would keep my brain chemically balanced.

She scolded me like a schoolboy and sent me back through the front door with my tail between my legs. To this day I still don't know why I followed her instruction, but it was the moment my life began to get better again. I've never missed a tablet since.

Claire and I met at a party in the late nineties, thrown by the aunt of one of my closest pals, Gerry D'Ambrosio. Gerry is a trained classical guitarist, a wonderful musician, and we used to meet daily at a cafe in Stirling called La Ciociara, which we nicknamed the Ding Dong.

Gerry provided me with much needed structure and support in my life at a difficult time and I'll forever be grateful. We used to sit and put the world to rights, drinking thick, black coffee and smoking cigarettes like laboratory beagles at a time when the law allowed customers to puff to their hearts' discontent inside Scottish licensed premises.

There was one slight problem with the party invite. I had been sectioned once more and was re-acquainting myself with Ward 30 at Stirling Royal. Unlike Ward 19 the doors weren't bolted shut but, nevertheless, patients were hardly free to come and go as they pleased.

They allowed us 15 minutes a day to witness the outside world but Gerry's Aunt Connie made pasta for a living so I was up for more than sampling fresh air. I met straight-talking Claire and her husband, Dean, at the party and we got on like a house on fire. Almost in the blink of an eye, 15 minutes became three hours.

Like an errant teenager I phoned Ward 30 and told them I was having a ball, could they give me another hour on a curfew I'd admittedly long since blown?

They asked for the location of the party and within 20 minutes a police car pulled up and two officers appeared to gently escort me back to the hospital. Thankfully, the party continued in full swing.

The noughties were, for the most part, a hugely distressing period and there were times I didn't know if I had been sectioned with a view to making a full recovery, or to serve a penance.

Ward 19 was akin to a pressure cooker, all the time simmering and waiting to boil over. I've never been violent, but I grew increasingly angry at a lot of aspects of the mental health system under the heading of Care in the Community.

I spent three months at Bellsdyke Hospital in my very first admission and emerged to enjoy three years of good mental health. I pushed back against the merry-go-round of Care in the Community and its revolving door policy, which is perhaps why it took me so long to accept my illness and stick to my medication.

Since 2009 I have been blessed with the best CPN – Community Psychiatric Nurse – in the business. Danny visits every fortnight and we have forged a relationship of respect and understanding but it took me a long, long time to learn to build trust.

Danny is a hugely professional operator who considers it a privilege and not just a job to be invited into my home to discuss the most intimate aspects of my life.

I've known some very kindly CPNs but also some dreadful individuals, who have taken such invites for granted and approached vulnerable patients in a brusque and high-handed manner. Some patients even had to check in every morning to the local day hospital where they would be patronised and made to participate in a 'current affairs group', for example, which amounted to someone reading them a newspaper.

Care in the Community wasn't always beneficial to nurses either and I know of at least two who were held at knifepoint on home visits to some seriously damaged individuals.

Over 16 years I came into contact with dozens of nurses, but there were only ever five with whom I could relate, including a fabulous man I knew from our days in the Tamdhu, Norrie Ritchie. I never did know the surnames of Carol-Marie or Hugh but, like Stewart McNeill and Linda Stronach, they also took an approach to nursing that put the patient at the centre of their care always.

They were warm and compassionate but too often, in Ward 19 especially, the nursing staff were heavy-handed bullies in their dealings with the men and women under their care.

Ward 19 was an ICPU – Intensive Care Psychiatric Unit – and it was a locked ward, with 12 additional locked bedrooms for a dozen patients of both sexes, with six nurses to oversee it all.

Patients would gather in the opium den of a smoking room, across from the staff office where we were watched like hawks. They thought nothing of piling in for even the most minor misdemeanour, often exacerbating an already charged situation with a thuggish approach to patient well being.

Staff would regularly drag a patient to their room where two or three would hold them down while another administered an injection to knock them senseless for the next 24 hours.

238

Sadly, too many staff seemed to revel in the confrontation and humiliation. There were some bullies inside a locked ward you knew wouldn't dare look twice in your direction if they saw you in the street.

I understand it was a locked ward and I get why I was in there, but it wasn't a good place and nurses knew only one way to act when it all kicked off.

I once shared the ward with a patient who was the meekest and most timid individual I'd ever come across, but one night he cracked and went berserk. Tables and chairs went up in the air while the staff steamed in and carried him unceremoniously to his bedroom to render him unconscious with the knockout jab.

Ward 19 had six small, two-seater couches for 12 patients and they were impossible to lie across. When the place went up we simply got to our feet, stood back and watched it all unfold.

We couldn't return to our own bedrooms because they were locked so those of us who weren't involved simply kept our backs to the wall until the storm had passed, like casualties of war waiting for a truce.

It was brutally inhumane and degrading and every stay at Ward 19 chipped away at your soul until you feared being left with no emotions at all.

Once I was well I took up a volunteer post at the radio station of the new hospital that now houses mental health services, Forth Valley Royal. I frequently passed nurses in the corridor who once looked after me and although they often caught my eye, Linda and Stewart apart they would never acknowledge my presence.

I understand the ethical code and boundaries to be observed, but did I sense a little arrogance in their manner? Possibly. Was there also a little shame about how they had treated patients like me? Most definitely.

Ward 19 shook every patient who ever passed through its doors to their very core. It's little wonder we scrutinised staff so carefully whenever they approached the exit and jabbed the four digit code with their fingers and headed off into freedom.

They knew all the tricks and always positioned their bodies between the door and our stares so they gave nothing away and, for additional security, the code was changed every couple of weeks. No-one ever did escape. In quieter, unguarded moments, a few of us find ourselves pulled back to that wretched environment in our minds still.

I've tried hard to recall moments of light heartedness around Ward 19, but they were few and far between. There was a camaraderie of sorts in the smoking room as we plotted and schemed but with a group of patients suffering personality disorders, schizophrenia, clinical depression, bi-polar and suicidal tendencies the mix was always volatile.

We were on tenterhooks anyway given our mental health conditions. The animosity felt towards many of the nursing staff, who always had those numbing injections at the ready, only made matters worse.

We tried our hardest to form a community and watch the backs of each other. I was still close to Andy Thompson, head of dance at Virgin Records, and we were in discussions at the time over a couple of projects that might have led to another record deal.

I gave him my new phone number, but little did he know it was the direct line to the patients' payphone at Ward 19. The patients were well rehearsed if anyone with an English accent called and I was lying under sedation in my room, out of it completely. They'd say: "I'm sorry, Mr Cochrane isn't available at the moment. Can I take a message?" I still don't know if Andy ever grew suspicious at the number of PAs apparently on my payroll.

Across in Ward 30 at Stirling Royal, the mental health facility was less intimidating. Ward 19 was hardcore and barbaric but at Ward 30 the underlying disciplinary code amounted to, 'You better behave yourself – or else'.

It reflected their different purposes. Ward 19 was an ICPU, but Ward 30 was an Acute Assessment Unit For Mental Health. The staff ratio at the Falkirk facility was one to two but in Stirling it was one to six – four nurses for 24 patients.

Furthermore, at Ward 30 approximately half of admissions were for men or women suffering one-off periods of mental trauma, usually associated with the death of a loved one, a relationship breakdown or another unexpected life event such as redundancy or job loss.

Many were also admitted to treat problems around alcohol and drugs dependency and they didn't always develop to become chronic mental health issues that would necessitate a transfer to Ward 19.

At Ward 30 they used to give us tai chi in the morning to help re-duce stress and there were beauty groups for women to teach them make-up and hairdressing.

Men were much more difficult to please and didn't necessarily respond positively to the offer of group therapy, but we were al-ways up for the countless mini-bus runs to local garden centres and coffee shops, as well as tourist towns such as Callander and Aberfoyle. I'd gone from doing drugs to overdosing on Douwe Egberts in Dobbies.

Seriously, my drugs intake was on the wane. I stopped taking cocaine entirely around 1998, mostly for reasons of affordability, and found I didn't really miss it. Throughout these lost years I still smoked an occasional joint, mostly when I met up with my buddy Jok, but my cannabis consumption eventually trailed off to zero shortly before I finally understood to take a firm grip on the ownership of my illness for the first time in 2009.

The loneliness was hell and I was lost completely for a while in 2003 when a relationship I treasured dearly ended for reasons I didn't dis-cover until undertaking research for this book.

After Fiona I feared I would never find a partner again, particu-larly with a growing list of psychiatric admissions, but love really is a wonderful thing.

For several months after my aborted suicide attempt my self-confi-dence was in the gutter and one night in 1998 I turned up at Nick Tahoo's new place in Stirling – my yellow walls in Falkirk must have got to him in the end – and was met by a pretty face, vaguely familiar.

Her name was Shaz and she recognised me too from a night out we'd enjoyed five years previously, when she had admitted to being smitten by my blue gingham shirt and long hair.

Five years down the line the roles were reversed and it was me who was hooked on this confident, outgoing woman. My joie de vivre, on the other hand, had shrunk considerably.

Nick was a hairdresser and was cutting her locks and she had even turned up with her dinner on a plate as he preened over her with scis-sors and comb, preparing her for a big night out.

I was desperate to ask for her phone number, but my confidence was shot. Eventually, after several weeks of accidentally-on-purpose meetings around Stirling, I plucked up the courage to ask her to the cinema. To my astonishment, she said yes.

Shaz worked for the Post Office and gave me everything, unconditionally. She was a brilliant firebrand, a real campaigner for justice, and she became a wonderful thorn in the side of the healthcare authorities.

She constantly asked: "What medication is Stuart on? What's the dosage? What's his care plan?" Every single question she asked was for my benefit. They didn't like her. I quickly fell in love with her, also because she didn't take any of my garbage.

She embraced my illness, understood it even, but she gave me short shrift if I was ever anything other than honest and straight talking during my periods of wellness.

I moved into her place in Alloa after a year and another 12 months later, in August 2000, I asked her to marry me. She said yes, even agreeing to the venue – at The Borestone, where the statue of Robert the Bruce stands in the field at Bannockburn.

I paid a £50 deposit to the registrar and we came up with the music. I opted to walk down the aisle to a fabulous dance track by American electro musician BT called 'Remember'. I encouraged her to pick the song for walking back up the aisle and what else could she have chosen but the number one track at the time by Ronan Keating, 'Life Is A Rollercoaster'?

The wedding never did go ahead. I was sectioned again when we were in the middle of planning it all and the opportunity was lost, never to return. Shaz, ever canny, chased the council for the deposit, supposedly non-refundable, and in the circumstances they showed generosity of sorts by sending her a cheque for £37.50.

Shaz put up with hell, but never once complained. She accepted my mental illness as part of me, the man she loved, and yearned for more of the happy days we enjoyed, such as the time we took her elderly Aunt Katy and both our mums out for Mother's Day.

We ended up at the bingo via Duck Bay Marina at Loch Lomond, then rounded it off with drinks at the Boulevard Hotel in Clydebank, where the young and trendy pre-clubbing crowd spoiled them rotten with round upon round of cocktails and spirits.

I was performing a mental health Hokey Cokey – in and out, in and out. I carted more white sacks over my shoulder than Santa Claus at Christmas. Every time you were released back into the community you gathered all your clothes, toiletries, shoes, books and magazines in a thick, white plastic bin bag, marked for patients' use only. I went through so many of them they would have been cheaper gifting me a set of Louis Vuitton suitcases.

It's no proud boast, but there were few patients who were such an integral part of the Forth Valley mental health sector at that time than yours truly. The only good thing was that after each spell in Ward 19 or Ward 30 you invariably went home to a cheque from the social security for several hundred pounds – if you remembered to cash it, which I didn't always.

I lived in Alloa but my natural homes had become the district's mental health wards and not once did Shaz flinch at the responsibility.

As a postie, she was up at 4.45am and worked until 2pm and shortly after 3pm she'd come to see me. If I was in Ward 19, my conversations wouldn't have made much sense but she stayed every time until 5pm then returned two hours later before the wards were finally closed to visitors at 8pm.

She did this on hundreds of occasions and never once complained. That was love. She was super strong, but it must have taken its toll.

We eventually parted in 2003 and, typically, she refused to cut me loose completely and ensured I was safe in that new flat in Stirling first, even if its decor was so garish.

I tried to keep in touch, probably made a nuisance of myself to her and her family if truth be told. I knew she had bought a new black Volkswagen Golf and for months my eyes scanned every model in that colour I saw in the hope I would catch a glimpse of her inside.

After a long while she moved on, as we all must do, but it still didn't prevent me feeling devastated when I called her home one night over a year later and her new partner answered the phone.

Early in 2017 I met Shaz for coffee as part of research for the book and plucked up the courage to ask why she had left. I long suspected my mental health issues had worn her down, but her reply left me dumbstruck.

"It was your dad, Stuart," she said gently. "He asked to meet me one day and said: 'Let it be, Sharon. Go your own way now and live your own life. We don't think Stuart is ever going to get better.'" Her admission cut deep at first, not least my father's role in it, but I could see even then how he was moving to protect her – and maybe even me too.

The Mystic Law of Buddhism works in mysterious ways. Meeting Shaz and Jake, in particular, after so many years and talking through our issues of the past has given me the comfort of closure in relationships whose memories I will always cherish dearly.

They say certain people come into your life at certain times for certain reasons – a reason, a season, forever as the old adage goes. Claire and Dean Campbell certainly fall into that category, as does Pauline Brown, who was introduced to me by Gerry.

Her sister Natalie has also been really kind. Pauline has been an exceptional friend through thick and thin, even taking the time to invite my old mum Mac and me to her place for Christmas dinner on several occasions.

As an airline attendant, Pauline was also a valuable source of duty free fags, not to say colourful t-shirts from her trips to exotic locations around the globe.

Another close friend, whose support I've cherished, is Rick Ritchie. He lives in Bannockburn and has never been afraid to tell me home truths I've occasionally needed to hear. He is caring and compassionate and his door is always open for a cup of tea and a chocolate digestive.

I've never had kids – it has been hard enough looking after myself – but I consider Leon Moodie the son I never had, not least for the love, support and unstinting friendship he has shown throughout the years.

I first met Leon in 1995 when he was learning to DJ at the skilful hands of Fraser Hotchkiss and not only did he go on to become a trusted confidante, he also became my saviour during those lost and lonely years when I was at my lowest ebb.

I struggled to live in my own silence and my life during my periods of wellness had little shape at all. I was a loose cannon, with only the structure of my mum's for dinner, the Ding Dong for coffee with Gerry and visits to Leon's record shop to keep me on the right track.

I roamed the world from 9am to 10pm, leaving my flat first thing before knocking on the doors of friends and acquaintances, all the time trying hard not to make a nuisance of myself.

I know I especially tested the patience of John and Alison Crozier and Fraser and Kate Hotchkiss although typically they only ever responded with love and kindness and an open door policy. I'd stay for a coffee or two, all the while trying desperately hard not to overstay my welcome – and I didn't always succeed.

My mind was a hamster wheel, constantly whirring, but with Leon I found peace and contentment. He opened a record store in the centre of Stirling called Soundscape and had a limitless supply of coffee.

On nicer days we'd stand outside and smoke cigarettes, while inside we'd play backgammon and turn up the volume on whatever music from the shop took our fancy. He has always had my back and was a frequent visitor whenever I went unwell. He has become one of my closest friends in the world.

I tried hard to make a contribution to society during my periods of wellness, although I now know cynical nursing staff were taking bets on how long I would last after I was appointed a peer support worker for a mental health programme known as the Intensive Home Treatment Team.

It was Scottish government funded in 2008 and 24 of us around the country were chosen to participate. It was the brainchild of the Health Secretary and an expert was flown in from a renowned recovery centre in the States to lead the education programme for the new staff, all of whom had been affected by mental health issues themselves.

There were two jobs in my area, one in the wards and one in the community and as I had a car I was contracted for 16 hours to deliver services in a huge geographical expanse from Crianlarich in the north to Bo'ness in the south.

I was a mentor for those who were facing mental health challenges in their early stages, and initially it was enjoying and fulfilling. However, my colleague who had been given the job of peer support worker in the local mental health wards quit her post after only six weeks and I was asked to take over her responsibilities as well.

As a patient I had yearned for the four digit passcode for Ward 19 and now I had it, it was the last thing I wanted. Not only was I expected to cover a huge geographical swathe of the country in my car, but in the same 16 hours I was also expected to offer ward support.

I was given no assistance whatsoever by the authorities, while the nurses resented my presence on their beat when I had only recently been under their care. I was told to be positive in my note writing on patients, for example, but staff were dismissive of my upbeat comments.

I clung to small victories, however. One patient in Ward 18, where less acute mental health issues were treated, painted flowers every day on canvas and when I visited him the background of his composition was dark brown.

With the consent of senior staff, I took him for coffee and we opened up about our experiences in the system. The following week I returned and his daffodil was painted against a backdrop of bright yellow. He gave me both pictures, which I treasure still.

The stress of it all led to another relapse, but I was taxed hard for my short-lived spell of employment, just seven months. As a result of working within Ward 19 and Ward 30 I could not be treated there as a patient so was sent 35 miles to St John's Hospital in Livingston.

It was winter time too and as people struggled to make the trip it only increased my isolation from a world that still wasn't making much sense.

Still, at least I was spared further run-ins with The Man, the psychiatrist Claire would later demand I return and visit with a red-faced request for my fully prescribed medicines.

I really liked him at the start too. He was younger than me, well dressed, seemed interested in some of the nonsense I spouted, especially around business – if Dragons' Den had been on the BBC at the time they'd have given me a season ticket to pitch my ideas.

He was a good listener. I was attracted to him. He was charismatic and not staid or overly formal like the other doctors, although there were still boundaries to be respected.

The nature of our relationship changed when he told me I was the worst patient he'd ever treated, which I thought unfair. How could that ever give anyone any hope for making a full recovery?

He made the remark at one of our weekly Kardex sessions, where patients would get together and discuss their action plans for the week and also what they'd done well the week before. The Kardex included notes from the nursing staff, the highs and lows of the previous seven days, and were absolutely crucial in securing a release after a 28 day section.

A good Kardex and you could be sent out again to rejoin polite society. Dubious reports sealed your fate in the unit for at least another seven days.

The Man had clearly watched me closely over the course of a few sections and, seeing how often I'd been treated, he might even have been at a loss to explain my condition. In the end, he settled for a declaration I suffered from schizoaffective disorder which I took as psychiatric shorthand for he didn't really know.

In reality, he started to get harder with me and was unwilling to play the game any more. He was probably quite right, too. In hindsight, I was cocky and often belligerent. I refused to accept my illness and the off-handed way I chose to address doctors by their first names was another sign of my arrogance.

No-one had as many mental health admissions as me in the area. No-one. It's not something to be proud of, but The Man had clearly had enough of my antics, caught up in the revolving door of mental health.

That day I took unwell in the centre of Stirling the police took me to Ward 30 in the back of their van to be assessed. The Man opened the back door on its arrival, took one look at me and declared: "Ward 19 in Falkirk." No assessment. Nothing.

One of my closest pals hosted a party for his 40th birthday and I turned up at his home to be greeted with a beautiful sea of old, familiar faces – and The Man in a pair of jeans and a green t-shirt.

I thought it best to keep out his way so headed into the kitchen and started a conversation with a warm, sociable woman. She had a great sense of humour and a range of interesting things to discuss. Turned out it was his wife. I called it an early night and made a sharp exit.

Seven years into my wellness, and five years after I started volunteering at hospital radio in Forth Valley Royal, I picked up the keys for the studio from the security office one day, near the corridor for the mental health unit. I turned to walk away and bumped straight into The Man.

In the ward, he had the power to do anything but now, with the fading of time and my confidence growing from my own period of wellness, I could see him as the man he really was, which wasn't a bad guy after all.

We spoke amicably for 10 minutes and I told him I hadn't missed a tablet since the day Claire had forced me to return to see him. I explained I was in a long term relationship with a woman I loved, was undertaking voluntary work in local schools and that I was practising Buddhism and had taken responsibility for my illness.

I felt our conversation had brought some kind of closure. However, I was still unprepared for the phone call I received the following week from my old Ward 19 mucker Abie Bennett, the patient who had once offered me that four grand from his safe for the nightclub dating game after my smoking room pitch.

He was back in the locked ward and said, matter-of-factly: "I've been sectioned again Scoobs and I've just been talking to The Man. He said I should be using you as a positive example of how to get well again and stay well."

In Buddhism, we refer to such transformations as turning poison into medicine. I've had my fill of the former, but I know I'll never be free of the latter. For the sake of my ongoing positive mental health, it's a deal I'm happy to make.

21

And then a wonderful thing happened.

In 1999 I had met a Japanese Cockney buddhist named John Koyanagi, a student at Stirling University and a flatmate and friend of Leon's. He was a 'fortune baby', which meant he was the offspring of parents who both practised Nichiren Buddhism.

It's a school of Japanese Buddhism from the 13th century and one of its three essential aspects is the chanting of 'Nam Myoho Renge Kyo'. It's a mantra, representing devotion to the mystic law of life, and like many who practice Nichiren Buddhism it soon helped tune me into the rhythms of the earth.

I think of it as a pin number for greater self awareness and understanding for the limitless potential of our existence.

There has always been something special about John. I've met a lot of people but he remains, by far, the most balanced and self-aware individual I've come across.

Unlike those mind-bending cult leaders from that awful Paddington hotel, John has always carried himself with an aura of self-knowledge and contentment, based around a principle of kindness and living as you wish, so long as it's the best life possible.

He has never asked me for anything, demanded of me financially or emotionally, but has given unconditionally of his time and wisdom over the last two decades whenever it has been needed.

In 2012, more than a decade after we first met, I called and told him I'd had enough of the formal, Christian church and had been thinking more and more about Buddhism. "Brilliant," he replied. "Once a day, for 100 days, chant 'Nam Myoho Renge Kyo' and meditate on something you really want and you'll get it. It's known as 'actual proof'. We'll speak about it more fully after 100 days."

All I wanted was a girl.

My swagger around the opposite sex had long since been replaced by an awkward shuffle. Once upon a time I could click my fingers, a la The Fonz, and women would appear at my side. Shallow? Absolutely, but now I was way out of my depth in the relationship game, my confidence having long since disappeared.

It didn't stop me trying, with often darkly humorous results. I signed up for a dating agency, eharmony, which required members to provide in-depth details about their life so they could find the most suitable partners. I did – and they teamed me up with a psychiatric nurse from Falkirk.

I joined Match.com and met a casino worker from Glasgow for coffee and a couple of dates. Finally plucking up the courage, I invited her back to my flat – and she literally turned on her heels when we pulled up outside my council-owned property, the prospect of entering it clearly abhorrent to the social snob.

I didn't drink, but dated a girl on a couple of occasions who would down a bottle of wine then phone her ex, in my presence, to tell the man she'd never got over: "George, I'm in Stirling with him now, George."

Here's the brutal truth – I hadn't had a women in my life since Sharon in 2003 and was crippled with loneliness. I had female pals, for sure, but no-one to love and hold me close which, at heart, is all we ever want and need.

I focused on chanting 'Nam Myoho Renge Kyo' every day as I dipped my toes into Buddhism, wary of the apparent formality of the gohonzon, the Chinese and sanskrit scripts in the altar to which I chanted making me uneasy initially.

I worried I was honouring a false God until I became aware I was actually looking at a reflection of my own life. The chanting was helping me polish the mirror so I could see my own world staring back at me with ever greater clarity.

My second Buddhist meeting was held at a hall in Stirling's Raploch district and I was captivated by a woman who offered me, of all things, a packet of cheese and onion crisps. The simplicity and kindness of the gesture chimed, as did her playful eyes.

Her name was Veronica, I discovered, and she also hosted meetings at her home in Plean. I plucked up the courage to find the date of the next one and couldn't help but feel crushed when I attended and a guy, who clearly lived in the house, came through the front door and headed upstairs, giving space to those of us gathered in the living room.

I made an excuse to strike up a conversation when he re-appeared 10 minutes later in the kitchen to make a cup of tea. "How do you put up with your wife hosting the meetings?" I asked him, doing everything but taking out a fishing rod in my feeble attempts to assess the nature of their relationship.

He almost spat out his tea: "That's not my wife – it's my maw." It was Sean, Veronica's son. Love really is blind.

My spirits soared and on August 14 2012 Veronica Spellman agreed to go on a date with me to Delivino, a fabulous restaurant in Crieff. I blurted out absolutely everything about myself, real heart on the sleeve stuff, and she remembered John Koyanagi coming to visit me in hospital on the frequent occasions I had been unwell.

She also told me about her boys, Sean and Brian, and that she was originally from Glasgow and had been on her own for 10 years. She had moved to Stirling when her boys were young, so knew absolutely nothing about my colourful past and it was maybe just as well.

It was only two weeks after I'd first started chanting and the delivery of the 'actual proof' as John had termed it, made me realise there might be something in this Buddhism after all.

Veronica and I quickly became an item and she immediately accepted everything about my past, unconditionally. I took her to see my mum, Mac, and those two strong Glaswegian women got on like a house on fire. My mum was in her late seventies and took great comfort in knowing I was finally settling down with such a woman of substance, my soulmate.

Veronica takes the mickey constantly, calling me darling in a false home counties accent that could not be further from the truth of where we were both raised. She cracks me up. She has the heart of a lion and, besides her beauty, there's an honesty in her soul that's captivating.

She always tries to see the best in people, but doesn't suffer fools. She's a straight talker who can't be taken in and her work in homelessness is a vocation more than a job as she does her very best for her clients always, many of whom are vulnerable.

She's generous and funny and after years when my self esteem felt crushed and battered, just being in her presence makes me a better and more confident man.

She took me for who I am and I can't imagine my life without her. We're like a pair of old slippers and the warmth and strength of our love is something I could never have imagined at this stage of my life.

She even taught me cooking. Once I didn't do anything for myself in the kitchen, but now I'm never more happy than when I'm making her a meal. She's a shining star. Those days of infidelity are long, long in my past. There's happiness and contentment in my life and 'contentment' wasn't a word much in my vocabulary before.

As a younger man I was never satisfied. I always needed new clothes, a new car, new decks. Now? I'm really happy. The things I once coveted in life I've already enjoyed so I'm in no rush to have them all over again.

It's fitting Veronica and I went for our first date on August 14 as it's the same day as my mother and father's wedding anniversary. We got engaged on June 21 2013, her birthday. I'm never likely to forget those days.

The support of Veronica has allowed me to deal best with the slings and arrows of life's rotten fates, not least the death of my beloved mum on October 3 2015 at the age of 83. I had been tortured, since my first relapse in 1997, by the thought of a failure to hold up emotionally and mentally when she passed away.

I genuinely believed I wouldn't make the funeral and that, if I'd been enjoying good mental health at the time, I would have suffered a catastrophic breakdown. Mac contracted cancer earlier that year and I had already confided my fears to Veronica.

We chanted daily for strength and courage. Mac's terminal diagnosis was also put into perspective by another friend, who offered a new slant on such devastating news by pointing out it gave us time together to leave nothing unsaid, a gift not many are given.

We talked and talked in the months leading up to her death, our love secured forever. Mac died peacefully on a Saturday night, not long after scolding me for coming to see her without first having had a shave.

Without a word of contradiction, her funeral was a joyful occasion. I was proud of the way I got through the day and the courage I found, through my chanting and with Veronica at my side, to stand with a genuine smile on my face and shake hands, with confidence, of everyone who attended.

I always was a mummy's boy. She went out to her favourite, 'When Will I See You Again?' by the Three Degrees. I held it together and afterwards family and friends laughed and joked and shared our warm collective and individual memories of a wonderful woman. A week later the Three Degrees came on the wireless and I immediately burst into tears. The dangers of listening to Radio Two.

Mac died nine years after her beloved Alex, taken also by cancer at the age of 79. He spent his final weeks in Strathcarron Hospice, where I was a regular visitor.

I was only three weeks out of hospital after another section but, with the ever loyal Gerry D'Ambrosio doing the driving, I helped organise his funeral. Dad had already told me exactly what he wanted after he passed away, including the order of service, hymns and prayers and his funeral at our Allan Church, like my mum's, was packed and almost £2,000 was raised for charity.

I made my peace with dad at the end. He said he was proud of me, which wasn't something he said very often. To hear it once was enough.

A couple of weeks after the funeral I was going through his personal papers and came across articles and mementos from my career in the music industry. He'd even kept my Queen's Badge from the Boys' Brigade. The tears sprang and ran as fast as our beloved Bannock Burn.

Death casts its shadow and, in addition to mum and dad, there are several people in the book no longer with us. Those great Dundee pals, including Jimmy Mackenzie, DJ Ned Jordan, Mark Goldinger and Willie The Pig have all passed away and the death of friends such as Anne Louden and Seonaid McIntosh also cut deep.

DJ pals including Dave Calikas and Dave 'CL' Young have also gone, as well as that brilliant nurse Norrie Ritchie, but it's Vinny Doyle I miss most.

He was the first person I employed at Rainbow Rocks, he was my sidekick at Littlejohn's, Fat Sam's and Woody's Bar although, sadly, there was a period of estrangement after it plunged into the red.

We made up after several years, thankfully, but I couldn't attend his funeral. I had been at a dozen funerals of family and close friends in a period of 12 months and my psychiatrists warned it was in danger of doing me serious damage.

It broke my heart to tell Vinny's brother, Derek, I couldn't carry the coffin. Derek understood. Thank you, Derek. On the morning of Vinny's funeral I went for a run in my car – to where, I still couldn't tell you – and thought of nothing but the good times we'd enjoyed.

Life has been simpler in recent years and my confidence is slowly returning again, although I know with certainty I can never take my wellness for granted.

I've accepted my illness and I've taken responsibility for it. I know its triggers, which include a yearning for tobacco and less than six hours sleep a night. I steer clear of cigarettes and make sure I'm in bed every night at a reasonable time. I'm still vulnerable, but I've come to accept that self-knowledge as a strength and not a weakness.

I'm a success story, enjoying a strong relationship for almost a decade with my CPN Danny and my psychiatrist, Dr Morag Macleod.

I get up every morning at 7am and, after making a cuppa, chant in front of my gohonzon for at least 20 minutes for six basic principles in life: worldwide peace, happiness, for my prayers to be answered, to change my karma, to change myself through human revolution and, finally, for Buddhahood and to see Buddhahood in everything else.

The discipline of chanting sets me up well for my day and gives it purpose and structure. In addition to chanting and my formal NHS medication I also attend the Rapha Centre in Braco once a year for additional nutrients, via a hair test.

The Rapha Centre owner, Rosalie Dickinson, is a practitioner in nutritional health and helps keep me balanced with additional minerals that ensure there's no greyness in my pallor, for example.

Where once I knocked golf balls at Cambuskenneth, I now visit holistic practitioner Caroline Bell, a saviour who also helps me with a range of therapies and in the practice of kinesiology.

Slowly but surely I'm emerging from a shell of self-doubt that encased me for so many years. I worked with a local charity, Street Sense, on my drugs past and from that my cousin Liz Brown, community police officer at Wallace High School in Stirling, asked me to talk to pupils about my experiences.

I now speak regularly at schools, youth groups and even to the police across the central belt of Scotland about my life and the lessons to be learned, in particular, from too much cannabis consumption.

I don't spare the details. It's hard hitting but it resonates. I'll always maintain cannabis is a gateway drug. The brain doesn't fully formulate until the age of 24. Start smoking weed extensively as a teenager and you run the risk of doing it a lot of damage.

Coke is also so widespread across society these days, not just among teenagers. Let's have open discussions about the issues facing young people and give them the best information to allow them to make the wisest and most informed choices.

Recently, I've also began to fully re-connect with many of my oldest friends, such as Fraser Hotchkiss and Steven Croal, on equal terms. I've helped organised a couple of successful club nights for charity, host a show on Stirling City Radio with Leon every Saturday afternoon and I'm even making music again with Barry Fraser and Andy Haldane.

Our new group, Leap of Faith, even have an album due for release and this time, if Warner Brothers pick up the phone, their calls won't be ignored.

As for Ibiza? Well, I've been back a couple of times in recent years, most recently in April 2018 when I travelled with film maker David Street of Journey Pictures and my co-author of this book, Gary Ralston, to shoot for a planned documentary on my life.

We interviewed, among others, DJ Alfredo in his home town of Jesus, Tony Sonrisas at his fabulous family restaurant in the village of Santa Agnes (it really is worth a visit), Horst Muller (still lord of his fabulous Casa Datscha), as well as the Anadon boys, Christian and Alan, now making a wonderful mark in the music business as the Mambo Brothers.

The time of year suited me to make the visit. It was the calm before the storm of a new season and devoid at that stage of the hedonism and glorious madness on which I used to thrive.

Fraser and Kate kindly invited me to join them on their holiday there a few weeks later, a generous offer from two fabulous friends, but I know my weaknesses. I'll continue to visit the White Isle, but only off season.

255

And then, of course, there was Javier and Caroline. Still generous to a fault, they put us all up in their amazing apartments on the strip, with the best sunset views, and treated us like kings for five days.

They were as generous with their time as they were with the praise for my role in Mambo's history.

I reflect with pride on the successful business of top bars, restaurants and hotels they have built, with Mambo still the beating heart of their thriving empire. There's no envy, just satisfaction and admiration for all they have achieved.

We're all a little older, definitely a little bit greyer, but they still radiate with the same warmth they did when we rolled off those flights as kids laden with black pudding, sausages and Irn Bru from home.

They say I'm the man who could have had it all. They tell me I was within touching distance of greatness – of wealth, fame and fortune, before it all crumbled to dust before my very eyes. They hint but never quite say it was all my own self-inflicted fault. It's true, of course.

I once gave a talk at Wallace High School and a particularly sparky 14-year-old asked if I would change anything about my life then looked surprised when I told him, with total honesty, I'd run the same race again.

Where would I be had I answered those calls about my Dream Academy re-mix? Where would I be had I stayed on at The Tunnel and Fat Sam's and not been so loose with my knowledge around the establishment of the rave scene at 'Love'?

Where would I be had I invested my money (and my dad's!) in bloody Premium Bonds and not the damned BCCI? Where would I be today if I hadn't gone unwell in those months leading up to Mambo's opening? Where would I be had I stood at the right hand of Javier and Caroline and helped them build their new business to great heights?

Everything considered, across everything I've done, I'd be wealthier, for sure, but I'd probably be on my third marriage, with a serious cocaine addiction. I know my personality.

It has taken years of self-discovery, but I can finally say I understand myself and my weaknesses. I'd have attracted hangers-on I would believe were close friends and have the external trappings of success – the phone, the watch, the car – in an ultimately meaningless existence, never quite understanding why my soul remained so empty.

Most importantly, I'd never have Veronica.

In Buddhism, the adage holds that to find enlightenment you first have to suffer. I've suffered enough, I reckon. Now it's time to get back to the glorious ride of living my life again.

APPENDIX

SCOOBY'S MUSICAL LEGACY

Access to Scooby's music legacy can be found at Soundcloud.com/ StuartScoobyCochrane. He has produced the following tracks under the following names:

1.	1992	Area 51	Let It Move You
2.	1992	The Reef	What A Feeling
3.	1992	The Reef	What A Feeling Remix
4.	1992	Skonk	Banjo'd
5.	1993	La Rue	Cathedral Song
6.	1994	DJ Sueno	Tribute Para Es Paradis
7.	1994	DJ Sueno	Cerang Vol 1
8.	1994	True Blue	Coop
9.	1994/1996	Espirit-Rozalla	Sueno Ibiza
10.	1996	Ramirez feat Pizarro	Habalando
11.	1996	U2 (edit)	Bad Hip Hop
12.	1996	Beautiful Imbalance	First Picture Of You
13.	1996	Beautiful Imbalance	First Picture Of You Remix
14.	1996	FK15	Knockin' On Heaven's Door
15.	1997	Various Artists	Cafe Mambo Vol 1
16.	1997	Dos Piratas	Sonrisas
17.	1997	DJ Sueno	Ibiza Cultura

18.	1997	DJ Sueno	Yeah Oh
19.	1997	Fool Boona	Popped
20.	2007	Moroder/Oakey (edit)	Together In Electric Dreams
21.	2008	East Side Beat (edit)	Ride Like The Wind
22.	2008	Simple Minds (edit)	Alive And Kicking
23.	2008	The Cult (edit)	She Sells Sanctuary
24.	2009	DJ Sueno	Angelic Madness
25.	2013	Kyo Bros	Tinseltown In The Rain
26.	2014	Kyo Bros	Going Back to My Roots
27.	2014	Kyo Bros	Nam Myoho Renge Kyo
28.	2014	Kyo Bros	We Are Free
29.	2014	Kyo Bros	We Are Free Remix
30.	2015	Kyo Bros	That Loving Feeling
31.	2015	Kyo Bros	That Loving Feeling Remix
32.	2015	Leap of Faith	38.98
33.	2015	Leap of Faith	The Sound of Ku
34.	2015	Kyo Bros	Crazy Man
35.	2015	Kyo Bros	An Unguarded Mission
36.	2015	Leap of Faith	Always And Forever
37.	2015	Alan Rankine	Sandman

SCOOBY'S MUSICAL ODYSSEY

As Gary and I embarked on the writing of the book we quickly realised there was a stream of musical consciousness winding its way through the story. As a result, we decided to track list the music relevant to me at those stages of my life, through all the different chapters. It was a struggle to restrict the choices to around only 20 tracks per chapter as music has played such a beautiful part of my life, but I hope you like them and maybe even find inspiration in them.

Chapter 1 (1993)

Elton John – Rocket Man, John Lennon – Imagine, Aretha Franklin – I Say A Little Prayer, Buffalo Springfield – For What It's Worth, Gipsy Kings – Bamboleo, Blue Pearl – Naked In The Rain, Felix – Don't You Want Me, Arrested Development – Mr Wendal, Sunscreem – Perfect Motion,

Robin S – Show Me Love, Jaydee – Plastic Dreams, Quench – Dreams, D'Ream – Ur The Best Thing, David Morales – Gimme Luv, Mariah Carey – Dream Lover, Gabrielle – Dreams, Jam + Spoon – Follow Me/ Right In The Night, Urban Cookie Collective – The Key The Secret, South Street Players – Who Keeps Changing Your Mind, Bizarre Inc – Playing With Knives

Chapter 2 (1976 – 1980)

Evelyn 'Champagne' King – Shame, SOS Band – Take Your Time Do It Right, Sugarhill Gang – Rappers Delight, Jackie Moore – This Time Baby, Jimmy Bo Horne – Spank, Machine – There But For The Grace Of God Go I, Fleetwood Mac – Never Goin' Back Again, Joy Division – Love Will Tear Us Apart, Sex Pistols – Pretty Vacant, Bob Marley – Is This Love, Lou Reed – Walk On The Wild Side, Talking Heads – Psycho Killer, Peter Gabriel – Solsbury Hill, Blue Oyster Cult – Don't Fear The Reaper, The Undertones – Teenage Kicks/ Jimmy Jimmy, David Bowie – Heroes/Sound And Vision, Gino Soccio – Dancer, Japan – Quiet Life, Sheila B Devotion – Spacer, Chic Sister Sledge – Le Freak/Lost In Music

Chapter 3 (1968 – 1976)

Steve Harley + Cockney Rebel – Make Me Smile (Come Up And See Me), The Rolling Stones – (I Can't Get No) Satisfaction/The Last Time, The Eagles – Hotel California, Gilbert O'Sullivan – Get Down, Sweet – Blockbuster, Sparks – This Town Ain't Big Enough For The Both Of Us, Electric Light Orchestra – Mr Blue Sky, Queen – Bohemian Rhapsody, The Crystals – Da Do Ron Ron, The Monkees – I'm A Believer, Thin Lizzy – The Boys Are Back in Town, David Bowie – Jean Genie/ Sorrow, The Byrds – Mr Tambourine Man, T-Rex – Ride a White Swan/ Get It On, Slade – Cum On Feel The Noise/Mamma All Crazee Now, Simon and Garfunkel – Cecilia, Jerry Lee Lewis – Whole Lotta Shakin' Goin' On, Black Sabbath – Paranoid, Boston – More Than A Feeling, Bay City Rollers – Shang A Lang/Saturday Night

Chapter 4 (1980-1982)

Sylvester – Do You Wanna Funk, Bohannon – Let's Start to Dance Again, Indeep – Last Night A DJ Saved My Life, Blondie – Rapture,

Richie Havens – Goin' Back to My Roots, The Human League – Don't You Want Me, Grandmaster Flash – The Message, U2 – I Will Follow, Duran Duran – Planet Earth/Girls On Film, Spandau Ballet – To Cut A Long Story/Instinction, David Bowie – Ashes to Ashes / Fashion, Depeche Mode – Just Can't Get Enough, The Church – An Unguarded Moment, The Rolling Stones – Start Me Up, Grace Jones – Pull Up To The Bumper, Soft Cell – Tainted Love, New Order – Ceremony/Blue Monday, Martha and The Muffins – Echo Beach, OMD – Messages/ Enola Gay, Split Enz – I Got You

Chapter 5 (1982 – 1983)

Michael Jackson – Beat It/Billie Jean, Toto – Africa, Julio De Piscopo – Stop Bajon, Prince – Little Red Corvette, U2 – New Year's Day, Haircut 100 – Fantastic Day, Simple Minds – The American, David Bowie – Let's Dance, Captain Sensible – Glad It's All Over, ABC – Poison Arrow/ Look of Love, The Associates – Party Fears Two, Divine – Native Love, Yazoo – Don't Go/Situation, This Mortal Coil – Song to the Siren, Echo And The Bunnymen – The Cutter, Carly Simon – Why, Lotus Eaters – First Picture of You, Aztec Camera – Oblivious, Cock Robin – The Promise You Made, Jon and Vangelis – I'll Find My Way Home

Chapter 6 (1984)

TalkTalk – It's My Life/Dum Dum Girl, Prince – When Doves Cry/ Purple Rain, U2 – Pride, Eurythmics – Here Comes The Rain Again, Don Henley – The Boys Of Summer, Frankie Goes To Hollywood – Relax, Bryan Adams – Run To You, Pointer Sisters – Automatic, Womack and Womack – Love Wars, Cocteau Twins – Pearly Dew Drops, Van Halen – Jump, Alarm – 68 Guns, The Human League – The Lebanon, Matt Bianco – Matt's Mood, Wang Chung – Dance Hall Days, Talking Heads – Slippery People, Bronski Beat – Small Town Boy, Simple Minds – Don't You Forget About Me, Fox the Fox – Precious Little Diamond, George Kranz – Din Daa Daa

Chapter 7 (1985 – 1986)

Off – Electrica Salsa, A-ha – Take On Me, Simple Minds – Alive and Kicking, Phil Collins and Philip Bailey – Easy Lover, Frankie Goes To Hollywood – Two Tribes, Chaka Khan – I Feel For You, Killing

Joke – Love Like Blood, Prince – Raspberry Beret/Kiss, Farley Jack Master Funk – Love Can't Turn Around, The Cult – She Sells Sanctuary, Hipsway – Ask the Lord/Tinder, Adriano Celantano – The Language Of Love, Dead or Alive – You Spin Me Round (Like A Record), Jesus and Mary Chain – Never Understand, Dizzi Heights – Would I Find Love, Kate Bush – Running Up That Hill, Colonel Abrams – Trapped, Dream Academy – Life In A Northern Town, James Brown – Living In America, INXS – This Time

Chapter 8 (1986 – 1987)

Fleetwood Mac – Everywhere, U2 – Where The Streets Have No Name, Prince – Sign o' The Times, Steve Silk Hurley – Jack Your Body, Yazz – The Only Way Is Up, Marrs – Pump Up the Volume, Suzanne Vega – Luka, Chaka Khan – Ain't Nobody (Frankie Knuckles Hallucinogenic Mix), Nitro Deluxe – Let's Get Brutal, Jackson Sisters – I Believe In Miracles, Iggy Pop – Real Wild Child, Joyce Simms – All In All, Rhythim is Rhythim – Strings of Life, The Fatback Band – Yum Yum/Bus Stop, Johnny Wakelin – In Zaire, Danny Wilson – Mary's Prayer, Chris Rea – On The Beach, Sterling Void – It's Alright, Joe Smooth – Promised Land, Ce Ce Rogers – Someday

Chapter 9 (1988 – 1989)

Rozalla – Everybody's Free, S'Express – Theme From S'Express, KLF – What Time is Love, Black Box – Ride On Time, Soul 2 Soul – Back To Life, Raze – Break For Love, Tyree Cooper – Turn Up The Bass, The Primitives – Crash, Happy Mondays – WFL, 808 State – Pacific State, Sueno Latino – Sueno Latino, A Guy Called Gerald – Voodoo Ray, Jungle Brothers – I'll House You, Electribe 101 – Talking With Myself, Texas – I Don't Want A Lover, The Beloved – The Sun Rising, Kraze – The Party, Inner City – Big Fun/Good Life, Starlight – Numero Uno, Raven Maize – Forever Together

Chapter 10 (1989 – 1990)

Zoe – Sunshine On A Rainy Day, KLF – The White Album, Soul 2 Soul – Keep on Movin', Deee-Lite – Groove is in The Heart, C+C Music Factory – Pride, Two In A Room – Somebody In The House Say Yeah, Wood Allen – Airport 89, Lil Louis – French Kiss, Awesome

Three – Hard Up, Candi Staton And The Source – You Got The Love, Primal Scream – Loaded, Happy Mondays – Step On, The Stone Roses – Fools Gold, Sister Sledge – Thinking of You, Together – Hardcore Uproar, Adamski – Killer, The 49ers – Touch Me, Last Rhythm – Last Rhythm, BBG – Snappiness, Bocca Juniors – Raise

Chapter 11 (1991 – 1992)

Nirvana – Smells Like Teen Spirit, Massive Attack – Unfinished Sympathy, Glam – Hell's Party, Toxic Two – Rave Generator, Njoi – Anthem, Black Box – I Don't Know Anybody Else, Bassheads – Is There Anybody Out There, Gat Décor – Passion, Moby – Go, Enigma – Sadness Part 1, The KLF – 3am Eternal, Brothers In Rhythm – Such A Good Feeling, The Stereo MCs – Creation Slam Remix, The Shamen – Progen, Sound of Blackness – The Pressure Part 1, Seal – Crazy, East Side Beat – Ride Like The Wind, Dina Carroll – Ain't No Man (Brothers in Rhythm Remix), Jinny – Keep Warm, Inner City – Pennies From Heaven

Chapter 12 (1992-1993)

The Cure – Friday I'm In Love, U2 – One, Reel to Real – I Like To Move It, Praga Khan – Injected With Poison, Transformer 2 – Pacific Symphony, Ramirez – Habalando, Corona – Rhythm Of The Night, Liquid – Sweet Harmony, SL2 – On A Ragga Tip, USURA – Open Your Mind, Stone Roses – I Am The Resurrection, House Of Pain – Jump Around, Leftfield – Not Forgotten, Golden Girls – Kinetic, KWS – Please Don't Go, New Atlantic – I Know, Stereo MC's – Step It Up, Aly US – Follow Me, Hyper Go Go – High, Lemon Interrupt – Big Mouth

Chapter 13 (1993)

Talizman – Only You, Inner City – Hallelujah, M People – Someday (Sasha Remix), Jam and Spoon – Stella, The Good Men – Give It Up, Helicopter – On Yer Way, Everything But The Girl – Missing, U2 – Even Better Than The Real Thing, Bedrock – For What You Dream Of, Bjork – Big Time Sensuality, Leftfield and Lydon – Open Up, Energy 52 – Café Del Mar, Freak Power – Turn On Tune In Cop Out, Sub Sub – Ain't No Love, X Press 2 – Muzik Express, Gipsy – I Trance You (Paradiso Mix), Harri – Skelph, La Rue – Cathedral Song, Atlantic Ocean – Waterfall, Led Zepplin – Stairway To Heaven

Chapter 14 (1994)

Oasis – Live Forever, JX – Son Of A Gun, Tom Wilson – Techno Cat/ Perplexer Remix, U2 – Lemon, Livin' Joy – Dreamer, Strike – You Sure Do, Warren G – Regulate, Mory Kante – Ye Ke Ye Ke, The Original – I Luv You Baby, Tony Di Bart – The Real Thing, Billie Ray Martin – Your Lovin' Arms, The Bucketheads – The Bomb, Blast – Crayzy Man, Alison Limerick – Love Come Down, OT Quartet – Hold That Sucker Down, John Paul Young – Love Is In The Air 12" Remix, DJ Sueno – Kerang Vol 1, Happy Clappers – I Believe, M People – Movin' On Up, Seal – New Born Friend

Chapter 15 (1995 – 1996)

George Michael – Fast Love, Chicane – Off Shore, Jamiroquai – Space Cowboy, Robert Miles – Children, Sky Plus – Nylon Moon, BBE – Seven Days in One Week, Rozalla – Everybody's Free 96, Tall Paul – Rok Da House, Faithless – Salva Mia, Grace – Not Over Yet/Down To Earth Ascension Mix, The Night Crawlers – Push the Feelin' (MK Remix), Farley and Heller – Ultra Flava, Y Traxx – Mystery Land, Underworld – Born Slippy, Pauline Taylor – Constantly Waiting (Epic Remix), Blue Boy – Remember Me, Garbage – Stupid Girl, Hysteric Ego – Want Love, PJ – Happy Days, Daphne – Change

Chapter 16

Robert Miles – Children

Chapter 17

Dream Academy – Life In A Northern Town

Chapter 18 (1997)

Run DMC With Jason Nevins – It's Like That, The Verve – Bittersweet Symphony, Hanson – MmmBop, BT – Remember, Ultra Nate – Free, Nalin and Kane – Beach Ball, Olive – You're Not Alone, Da Hool – Meet Me At The Love Parade, Tori Amos – Professional Widow (Armand Van Helden Remix), Bjork – Hyperballad, Todd Terry – Something Going On, Faithless – Insomnia, Daft Punk – Da Funk, The Beach Boys – Wouldn't It Be Nice, Disco Citizens – Footprints, Dos Piratas – Sonrisas, Kirsten W – The Land Of The Living (Dekkard

Remix), Blue Amazon – And Then The Rain Falls (Angel Moraes Garage Dub Mix), Bodie and Doyle – Scary Bizcuits, Sunscreem – Looking At You (Gomez Remix)

Chapter 19 and Chapter 20

In 2008, as I slowly began to fight my way back to recovery, I turned to a form of musical therapy to chart my path to wellness, which didn't really begin in earnest until the following year. I produced five CDs under the title of 'Beautiful Imbalance' and I can reflect now and see they were really a form of musical motivation, a conversation with myself, from 'Patience' by Take That to 'Movin' On Up' by M People. There was hope and optimism within the track listings I pray I'll never lose.

Volume One

Patience – Take That, It's Alright – Sterling Void, Peace – Sabrina Johnston, Get It Right Next Time – Gerry Rafferty, Take It Easy – The Eagles, You're In My Heart – Rod Stewart, I Wanna Be Your Lover – Prince, The 59th Bridge Street Song – Simon and Garfunkel, Let Your Love Flow – The Bellamy Brothers, It's Alright – The Eurythmics, Love and Affection – Joan Armatrading, Down To Earth – Grace, Take Your Time – SOS Band, Everlasting Love – The Love Affair, Changes – David Bowie, God Is A DJ – Faithless.

Volume Two

Music – John Miles, Sometimes You Can't Make It On Your Own – U2, Fine Day – Opus 3, All You Need Is Love – The Beatles, Open Your Heart – Human League, Unchained Melody – George Benson, Let Me Show You – The Jacksons, Free Again – Pure Love, Alive and Kicking – Simple Minds, You're My Best Friend – Queen, I'm Your Man – Wham, Movin' On Up – M People.

Volume Three

Still Haven't Found What I'm Looking For – U2, Son Of My Father – Chicory Tip, be Thankful – William De Vaughn, Connected – Stereo MCs, Get The Balance Right – Depeche Mode, I Am The Resurrection – Stone Roses, Relight My Fire – Take That, reward – Teardrop Explodes, You Gave Me Love – Crown Heights

Affair, Something Going On – Todd Terry, You Got The Love – The Source featuring Candi Staton, Somewhere Over The Rainbow – Israel Kamakawiwoʻole, Long And Winding Road – The Beatles, What Can I Say? – Boz Scaggs.

Volume Four

Solsbury Hill – Peter Gabriel, Ya Mo Be There – Michael McDonald, Masterplan – Diana Brown and Barrie K Sharpe, Constantly Waiting – Pauline Taylor, Fingers Crossed – Angelique Bianca, Love Changes Everything – Climie Fisher, Easy – Commodores, Magic Fly – Space, Never Forget – Take That, True – Spandau Ballet, Sexual Healing – Marvin Gaye, With God On Our Side – Bob Dylan.

Volume Five

Now Is the Time – Jimmy James, Shine – Take That, Live Your Life – Belinda Carlisle, Going Back To My Roots – Richie Havens, Paradise – Sade, Ray Of Light – Madonna, Relax – Frankie Goes To Hollywood, The Key The Secret – Urban Cookie Collective, Young At Heart – The Bluebells, Diamonds On The Soles Of her Shoes – Paul Simon, Skin Deep – The Stranglers, Dignity – Deacon Blue, I'm Free – Soup Dragons, Remember Me – Blue Boy, Precious Little Diamond – Fox The Fox.

Chapter 21

Izzy Bizu – Talking To You, Taylor Swift – Shake It Off, Kolsch – Left Eye Left, Kylie Minogue – Stop Me From Falling, Arcade Fire – Everything Now, Roy McLaren – Out Of The Darkness, David Guetta and Sia – Titanium, Sigrid – Strangers, Justin Timberlake – Can't Stop The Feeling, Portugal, The Man – Feel It Still, Lorde – Green Light, Fatboy Slim – Where U Iz (12" mix), George Ezra – Shotgun, Leap of Faith – The Glory Of The Ride, Sigala and Paloma Faith – Lullaby, Adrian Hour – IWANNA (Original Mix), Bicep – Aura (12" mix), Bicep – Opal (Four Tet Remix), Eric Prydz – Opus; Jasper James – Listen To My Buttons.

I met Scooby Cochrane's reputation before I met the man himself because he was forever the talk of the town – 'Scooby did this, Scooby did that. Scooby says this, Scooby says that.' Imagine my shock when I clapped eyes on him for the first time. Surely that couldn't be him? He was way too young. He was sitting on a wall outside Ronnie's Bar in Stirling, smoking a joint and holding court. There was such an air of devilish confidence about him, not to mention a certain resemblance to a young Sylvester Stallone. We later moved in the same circles, around Rainbow Rocks, and I could see only a bright future opening up for him, full of success, wealth and fame.

He was enormously generous with his time and emotional energy. One year in the eighties everyone, including my parents, forgot my birthday. I mentioned it to a pal who organised an impromptu get together without my knowledge. Coaxed to go for a drink to cheer me up I walked into a hastily arranged party, with Scooby already holding centre stage with his guitar, leading a singalong for me. I got way too intoxicated for a school night, but the songs and laughter and the memories of watching the sun rise above Stirling Castle with my friends will stay with me forever.

As the years moved on I was given updates of Scooby's Ibiza trips and growing fame. I was proud to know him and still believed he would be a household name. Sadly, stories also began to emerge about too many drugs, money problems, mental breakdowns and hospital sections in locked wards. I felt it was such a waste of talent and enthusiasm, promise and charisma.

We lost touch for a few years until I was invited to a friend's barbecue and saw a vaguely familiar face standing in the corner. Did I know him? A pal told me his name. 'What do you mean, that's Scooby?' I asked, genuinely shocked. His looks had gone, along with his teeth. He had gained weight and he shook from head to foot. Apart from the extreme physical differences there was no sparkle, no confidence, no anything. I was so overwhelmingly sorry for his awkwardness and desperate state. I didn't know what to say, found it all quite embarrassing and, I'm ashamed to say, I kept my distance.

He hit many lows and must have thought he'd never find contentment ever again but he did, despite the odds. He is now happy and settled with his fiancée Veronica. They are a great team. He works with Police Scotland to present his story to schoolkids so they can hear first hand the damage drugs can inflict. I know his words reach many of them and if that saves one life, one mother's tears, then it is all worthwhile.

Fate rekindled my friendship with Scooby in 2015, following my marriage break-up, when I moved to become a close neighbour in Bannockburn. He spoke of a desire to write a book about his life, researching his past the old fashioned way by conducting interviews with dozens of old friends, recorded on C90 cassettes. There was only one problem. Those shaking hands, the result of his medication, made it impossible for him to type or write for prolonged periods. Looking to fill my diary with something to do, I enthusiastically accepted the job as transcriber. A system developed and we catalogued all those memories from tapes into journals, which we then wrote and re-wrote into a chronological order of his life.

At that stage we really had no idea how these recollections would evolve into a book and were not working to any deadline. There were occasions we were sidelined and spoke about our beliefs and philosophies on life. I knew Scooby and Veronica practised Buddhism and I was curious, so questioned them at length and converted to Buddhism myself. It was a turning point in my own life and one of the best decisions I've ever made.

Once Gary joined the crew our boat had a captain and a rudder and the pace ramped up. When I read the first chapter, even the first sentence, I was blown away. I am proud to have been part of this project. We have cried some, laughed a lot and worn away countless pencils, but I wouldn't have missed the opportunity for the world.

Janice Wilson
June 2018

"No one can better bask in summer's balm than those who have endured winter's bite. Similarly, it is those who have suffered through life's darkest hours who are able to truly savour the bright dawn of happiness. The person who has transformed the worst of fate into the best of fortune is life's champion." Diasaku Ikeda

I went for a hair trim one Saturday morning in Stirling and ended up being cut in on a friendship for life. It was February 2015 and one of my best pals, Susan Dodds McEwan, was running late as usual for work at her salon (love you, Soo!). I nipped into the cafe next door, where Nancy Dennehy made a mean bacon roll, and sat at the counter along the window enjoying a coffee and that morning's edition of the Daily Record.

I glanced to my right and clocked a guy reading my restaurant review in the Saturday magazine – I penned a weekly column in addition to my sportswriting brief – and couldn't help but notice, apart from his remarkably good taste in reading, a slight tremor in his hands as he turned the pages. Shamefully, I put it down to a heavy Friday night on the tiles but struck up a conversation nonetheless and if the guy was shaking off a heavy one I couldn't help but notice there was still a spark of energy in his eyes.

Our chat went like this:

Me: "Do you like that guy's restaurant reviews then?" (Scandalously, I was on the lookout for the words of affirmation all journalists crave).

Him: "Aye, they're very good." Pause. "But the guy who did them before him, Tam Cowan? His were funnier."

I laughed and called him a cheeky bastard, although I knew he was right as big Tam's easy one liners always made me chuckle more than my own forced efforts at humour in print. I told him I wrote the review he was reading and after a couple of minutes of 'naw, reallys?' we settled into a chat about the local restaurant scene, about which he was well versed and knowledgeable. That would have been that until a few days later when a good pal, Steve Shaddick, called and asked if he could give my number to Scooby, who had been in touch (Scooby and I discovered Shads was a mutual pal when we were chatting in the cafe). Apparently, the guy fancied coming out on a restaurant review with me.

Puzzled, I asked Shads: "Who's Scooby?"

Now it was his turn to laugh, until he remembered I came from Glasgow and had only moved to Stirling as a teenager to study and wasn't on first name terms with many of the local characters from the town. "He says he met you on Saturday morning waiting for your haircut at Susan's," he replied. "Gary, everybody knows Scooby. Do yourself a favour. Take him for dinner. Journalists like good stories. Scooby's is a cracker."

Shads has never let me down in 25 years of friendship and wasn't about to start. Scooby gave me a call, we headed to the Bridge Street Kitchen in Dollar (a 26 out of 30, if I remember) and his story slowly unfolded after an apology he didn't need to make about that tremor in his hands. Turns out it wasn't drink after all, but a side effect of the heavy medication he has taken for many years for his chronic bi-polar, about which he has always been devastatingly honest.

We chatted, joked, laughed, shared a few experiences and the seeds of a friendship were formed I knew would last long beyond the cheese-cake dessert. He had a yearning to tell his story and, as the weeks and months passed and I learned more about his upbringing, adventures and diligent research into his own troubled history, I also developed a passion to help him reveal his truths.

Scooby detests the word 'journey' so we have always smiled and referred to his crazy existence – it has been like the Paris-Dakar rally on pharmaceuticals – as his 'voyage'. We've crossed the seven seas and more these past couple of years old pal – I'm currently writing this in a hotel in Lima – but I wouldn't have changed anything for the world.

Thanks for your honesty, candour, good humour, insight, time and patience.

More than that, thanks ever so much, Scooby, for a friendship I've come to cherish.

Gary Ralston
2018

Acknowledgements

"Life is a daring adventure... or nothing"

One definition of an adventure is a journey of unknown outcome. I hate using the word 'journey', but I have certainly been on a trip and now I feel like Indiana Jones.

This book has been two-and-a-half years in the making, compiling a series of my life's high and low points. It has managed to clarify a lot of things and given me closure in areas where I wasn't even aware I needed it.

Anyway, enough of the slush. Big thanks to everyone who helped on the project.

Respect is due to Vee – simply the best, my mum and dad who I know would be proud. Gary and Janice because it wouldn't have been possible without you, Shads for making it happen, Fraser, Kate, John, Alison, Alex and Lyndsey for putting up with me all those years, Uncle Billy and Auntie Elsie for everything, Dean and Claire for Fridays and scones, Dick, Margaret and the rest of the Cochrane family, Lorna, Maggie and Kenny, Henrietta, Mandy, John Koyanagi (The Geezer), Leon Moodie, Danny and Dr Macleod, Vinny Doyle – miss you, champ – Rick, Ger, Roddy, Irene and Alison who keep me well with conversation and coffee during the week.

David Cruickshanks and Gordon Bell for photography and design, David and JD Street for filming, Jim Mc, CJ The DJ and Costa for playlists. Moira Newlands for proof reading, Dev and Roy McLaren for compiling the music legacy, Willie McKenzie for T-Shirt design, Andy

McLean for photos, Ben Speck and Lauren McQuade for transcribing, Linda Stronach for her knowledge of the ward, Sean G, and to The Ibiza Crew of Javier, Caroline, Christian and Alan – The Mambo family, Tony Sonrisas, Horst and Alfredo. Closer to home, big thanks and love to Bridge of Allan's Jam Jar gang, especially Rachel Bruce - our loss is Oz's gain. Big hugs to Adrian and Kaye Bechelli and the team at the Allan Water Cafe for the best bacon rolls and constant support.

Also, thanks to everyone who allowed me into their home with a tape recorder, C90 tape and a polaroid camera. You are Andy Haldane – without you I wouldn't have had a music career – Baz, Colin Barr, Davy T, DCL Young – gone too soon – Franny, Fordy, Francine, Gaz, Jake, Jamie, Jokmaster, Killy, Linda Masterson, Paddy, Roddy and Mags, Ronnie and Max, Ross and Moally, Sean Le Bon, Shaz, and Tony Cochrane.

I've put a lot of credits into the jukebox of life – I'm still due a few more spins.

If anyone who reads the book finds themselves in need of support for mental health issues then please, please reach out. Access your local GP practice as well as organisations (if you're based in Scotland) such as the Scottish Association of Mental Health (www.samh.org.uk), Scottish Recovery Network (www.scottishrecovery.net), as well as Heads Together (www.headstogether.org.uk) and, yes, The Samaritans on 116 123 (they won't hang up on you, promise). If anyone is interested in Nichiren Buddhism, check out www.sgi-uk.org – and Gary can be contacted on gary907@btinternet.com.

Nam Myoho Renge Kyo
Stuart (Scooby) Cochrane

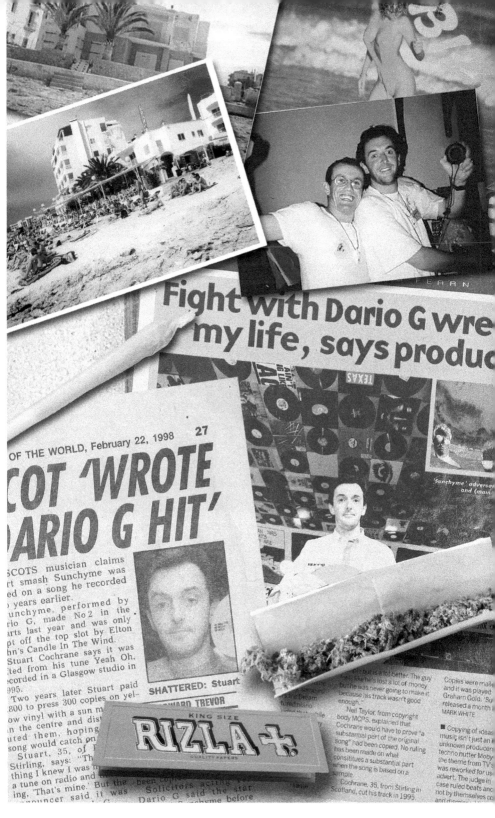

Fight with Dario G wre
my life, says produc

'Sunchyme' adversar
and (main

NEWS OF THE WORLD, February 22, 1998   27

COT 'WROTE
ARIO G HIT'

SCOTS musician claims
rt smash Sunchyme was
ed on a song he recorded
years earlier.

unchyme, performed by
rio G, made No 2 in the
arts last year and was only
pt off the top slot by Elton
hn's Candle In The Wind.
Stuart Cochrane says it was
ted from his tune Yeah Oh,
corded in a Glasgow studio in
995.

Two years later Stuart paid
800 to press 300 copies on yel-
ow vinyl with a sun m
n the centre and dist
uted them, hoping
song would catch on

Stuart, 35, of
Stirling, says: "Th
thing I knew I was
a tune on radio and
ing, 'That's mine.' But the
announcer said it was

SHATTERED: Stuart

EDWARD TREVOR

but is a lot better. The guy
he's lost a lot of money,
but he was never going to make it
because his track wasn't good
enough."

Neil Taylor, from copyright
body MCPS, explained that
Cochrane would have to prove "a
substantial part of the original
song" had been copied. No ruling
has been made on what
constitutes a substantial part
when the song is based on a
sample.

Cochrane, 35, from Stirling in
Scotland, cut his track in 1995

Copies were mail
and it was played
Graham Gold. 'Su
released a month
MARK WHITE

■ Copying of ideas
music isn't just an i
unknown producers
techno nutter Moby
the theme from TV-
was reworked for us
advert. The judge in
case ruled beats and
not by themselves co
and dismiss

been cop
Solicitors acting
Dario G said the star
Sunchyme before

RIZLA+
KING SIZE
QUALITY PAPERS